To all the therapists in the world, present and future, doing sacred work

Contents

Acknowledgments

Many thanks to my editor at Norton, Deborah Malmud, who first approached me with this idea about a book to help advance the cause of helping men become better men. She and Kristen Holt-Browning, as well as Andrea Costella and Kevin Olsen, helped shape this work. It has been a pleasure to work with this team again!

I would also like to thank my many mentors along this path of believing in men and helping them. Some of these mentors I know personally, others I know only through their work. Some of them are no longer with us, but their voices and vision are everywhere in this book: Don Dutton, Matt Englar-Carson, John Gottman, Amy Holtzworth-Munroe, Jackson Katz, Ron Levant, Don Meichenbaum, Bill O'Hanlon, Bill Pollack, Terry Real, John Sanford, Sandy Shapiro, David Shephard, Steven Sosny, and Holly Sweet. All good ideas stand on the shoulders of ideas of others. It takes a village.

And, always, my deepest appreciation to the most important people in my life: my daughter Juliana, my son Joe, and my wife Connie.

Preface

Therapy has always seemed to me like a very feminine activity. The qualities that usually come easier to and are usually better developed in women than in men come in very handy in managing the complexity of intimate relationships. Helping men develop these qualities in themselves is a noble path.

But in the postfeminist turmoil of relationship landscapes, men have been struggling to find a way to relate intelligently, parent sensitively, and manage their emotional needs with more consciousness and depth. It's just that many men haven't exactly figured out a way to do all these things and still really feel like a man, or at least feel like they are integrating these higher-level qualities in a way that suits men.

Men often enter the world of counseling or therapy because someone else has insisted that they do so. Typically, when I ask men who come in for an initial therapy session my standard question, "What are you doing here?" the answer I hear most often is, "My wife told me I needed to be here." Other times it may their boss or their grandmother or even a probation officer.

Think of what we typically ask men to do in, let's say, couples counseling. We ask them to recognize that something is wrong, admit that they need help, openly discuss and express emotions, get vulnerable, and depend on someone else to help them. Unfortunately, these tasks don't typically fit with the Guy Code.

Part of what makes it even more challenging to treat men is that male psychic pain is not always broadcast as articulately as is that of women. Author William Pollack describes men's anger as their "way of weeping." And men also weep by drinking, withdrawing, getting irritable, developing somatic complaints, acting competitive, and philandering.

It has taken a while for the values and methods of all forms of psychotherapy (individual, couples, group, cognitive–behavioral, psychodynamic, etc.) to become more user-friendly for men. Still, plenty of models are alienating for men or insist on training men in ways that feel more threatening than welcoming.

That's what inspired me to write this book: to pass on a deeply compassionate understanding of men and strategies for reaching men that are most likely to succeed. Contemporary theory and research tell us that men can benefit from therapy and counseling approaches that are profoundly respectful of male vulnerabilities and capitalize specifically on male strengths.

In our field, we are left with two choices: We can try to shove men into a process that has traditionally been more user-friendly for females. Or we can do everything within our power to reshape what we do and how we present it to increase the likelihood of reaching our male audience.

I vote for the second option, and that's what this book is all about. Here's hoping that all of you who already work well with men will work with them even better—and that you will keep in mind that our message to men is that we are trying to help them become better men, not to be more like women. Not that there's anything wrong with that.

MEN IN THERAPY

Chapter 1

The Myth of Masculinity

This book is about how to do therapy with men better than we have done it before.

But before we design interventions and strategies for helping to bring out the best qualities in men, we have to put 21st-century men in perspective. Understanding 21st-century men, of course, also means getting a historical perspective on what it has been like to be male in the 20th century and for many centuries prior. This perspective must be in the background—and often the foreground—of anything we say or anything we do in a therapeutic context.

Masculine Gender Role Stress

Masculine gender role stress (MGRS) is completely dependent on the ways in which men assign meaning to specific situations in their lives, particularly the meaning of a situation as it relates to their identity or competence as a man (Eisler & Skidmore, 1987; Saurer & Eisler, 1990). The MGRS experience is directly related to a man's attachment to traditional masculine gender roles. If a man judges himself as failing at the task of "being a man," based on the definition of manhood that he has integrated throughout his socialization process as a male, then he will experience MGRS.

MGRS research indicates that men will experience stress when they judge themselves unable to cope with the demands of being truly male or when a situation is viewed as requiring "unmanly" or feminine behavior. Several years ago, I was on a family trip in Paris. My wife and I were sitting on a bench at a plaza in central Paris. She wanted to relocate to a spot across the plaza; since she was carrying a few shopping bags, she asked me to grab her purse and carry it over to our new spot. I couldn't do it. I knew I was being stupid, but I couldn't do it. The 15 seconds that would expose me to possible humiliation for carrying a purse were beyond my capacities as a card-carrying male. My wife looked at me like I was nuts and shook her head disgustedly. I consider myself to be quite comfortable with my masculinity and certainly quite experienced with challenging antiquated notions of masculinity. And I couldn't do it.

My son is, at the time of this writing, 17 years old. One of the true joys in my life used to be watching the delight he experienced with his male friends. He loved them. He lit up when he saw them and even when he was telling stories about them. He would come home and relate a goofy story or joke from one of his pals and he would get a dreamy look in his eyes, as if this friend was just the coolest guy in the whole world. I watched and listened with envy, knowing how hard it is for boys and men to express so much delight with anyone except a lover. Until he hit puberty—and suddenly his responses to his friends were muted, characterized by consciously lowering his voice and grunting noncommittally. To express more would be a violation of the code. It would be too vulnerable. It would be girlish or even (the worst male code violation of all!) "gay."

And here's a recent story from *Esquire* magazine (Jacobs, 2008) parodying the pain of living with traditional MGRS:

My Masculinity, 39, Dies

My masculinity, the gender to which I have belonged since birth, died Tuesday in my living room in New York. It was thirty-nine. The cause was the ninety-three minutes I spent wearing my wife's polka-dotted breast-feeding pillow strapped around my waist in an attempt to feed a bottle of soy-based formula to my infant son.

The Myth of Masculinity

My masculinity led a vigorous life that included discussions of hot news anchors, two white-water-rafting trips, semifrequent uses of the word bro, and the occasional fist pump. It had, however, been ailing for some time. In 2003, it suffered a near-fatal blow during a shopping trip with my wife that involved several hours of looking at sconces. But the maternity pillow—whose brand name is My Breast Friend—was the official cause of death. It is survived by my marriage. (www.esquire.com/features/this-way-out/obits-0308?click-main-sr)

Any social historian would have to be foolish to deny the enormous privilege that men have experienced throughout human history—and particularly (in the Western world) men of the majority white culture. The feminist movement that exploded into cultural consciousness in the 1960s and 1970s critiqued this privilege and ushered in a wave of changes in gender roles and gender politics that may have had a greater impact on our world than two world wars and a worldwide economic depression combined.

Among other things, the feminist analysis of gender politics successfully challenged male entitlement and exposed the privileges that men enjoyed over women across many areas of social, economic, and sexual life. Now, several decades later, in the early years of the 21st century, we are identifying another piece to this puzzle much more clearly than ever before: despite this social privilege, it's not all that easy being a man, either! It has become especially complicated in this postfeminist era. The traditional roles that men have typically followed have become muddled and radically stripped of their traditional status.

Despite the fact that, even today, men continue to wield more political, social, and economic power than women, we are uncovering an epidemic of men who do not experience themselves as powerful. And, perhaps even more important, men who do not experience themselves as being "connected." This cocktail's ingredients include the masculine social pressures to achieve, to be strong, to be tough. Combine these with the psychological experiences of early loss, shame, and separation that many boys have experienced and covered up. Stir in a healthy dose of testosterone. Add the element of stoicism that lies at the core of many traditional masculine values, inhibiting men from consciously experiencing, properly labeling, and appropriately expressing their emotional experiences. The results of this mixed cocktail? Compared to women, higher rates of alcoholism and drug addiction. Vastly higher rates of violence and aggression. Higher rates of successful suicide. Earlier mean ages of death. An epidemic of vague, difficult-to-articulate depression and life dissatisfaction in interpersonal relationships as well as in the arenas of achievement.

It makes sense to think of these patterns and symptoms as a representation of the male tendency to externalize psychological distress through action, distraction, and compulsive acting out (Cochran & Rabinowitz, 2000).

Psychologist and social researcher Ron Levant (2007) describes the conflicts that men experience:

> To many men, the question of what it means to be a man today is one of the most persistent unresolved issues in their lives. Raised to be like their fathers, they were mandated to become the good provider for their families, and to be strong and silent. They were discouraged from expressing both vulnerable and caring emotions, and required to put a sharp edge around their masculinity by avoiding anything that hinted of femininity. Unlike their sisters, they received little, if any, training in nurturing others, and in being sensitive to their needs and empathic with their voice. On the other hand, they received lots of training in logical thinking, problem-solving, staying calm in the face of danger, risk-taking, and assertion and aggression. Finally, they were required at an early age to renounce their dependence on their mothers and accept the pale substitute of their psychologically, if not physically, absent fathers (www.drrolandlevant.com/whystudy.html).

The scales measuring MGRS focus on five areas of potential stress: physical inadequacy, emotional inexpressiveness, subordination to women, intellectual inferiority, and performance failure. Men who are most affected by MGRS seem to be excessively preoccupied with issues like being outperformed at work by a woman, appearing less athletic than a friend, or not making enough money. Studies indicate that high-MGRS men may be especially stressed by a female partner's behavior that they construe as threatening their masculinity ideology and by situations that they construes as gender-relevant (Eisler & Skidmore, 1987).

The ultimate fear that these models of masculinity issues illuminate is the fear of femininity. The fear of femininity consists of strong, negative emotions associated with stereotypic feminine values, attitudes, and behaviors. Men's gender role socialization and the masculinity ideology and norms are shown as conceptually related to this fear. The overattachment to masculinity ideology and norms can tragically define, restrict, and negatively affect boys' and men's lives.

That's why I couldn't carry my wife's purse across that plaza in Paris. That's why my son had to lower his voice and mute his enthusiasm.

Gender Role Conflict

Gender role conflict (GRC) constructs are similar to MGRS and have been pivotal in making sense of masculinity traps. GRC identifies four masculinity constructs that keep men "in the box" (O'Neil, Good, & Holmes, 1995).

Restrictive emotionality (RE) is defined as having restrictions and fears about expressing one's feelings as well as restrictions in finding words to express basic emotions: *I have difficulty expressing my tender feelings.* The second factor, restrictive affectionate behavior between men (RABBM), represents restrictions in expressing one's feelings and thoughts with other men and difficulty touching other men (see my son, above): *Affection with other men makes me tense.* The third factor, success/power/competition (SPC), describes personal attitudes about success pursued through competition and power: *I worry about failing and how it affects my doing well as a man.* Finally, conflict between work and family relations (CBWFR) reflects experiencing restrictions in balancing work, school, and family relations, resulting in health problems, overwork, stress, and a lack of leisure and relaxation: *My work or school often disrupts other parts of my life such as home, health, or leisure.*

These patterns of elevated GRC levels are directly related to relationship dysfunction. Restrictive emotionality, in particular, has been consistently associated with lower marital or relationship happiness. Several studies have found that each of the GRC patterns negatively correlates with marital satisfaction (Campbell & Snow, 1992; Sharpe, Heppner, & Dixon, 1995). Mahalik (2000) found that SPC significantly predicted rigid and dominant interpersonal behavior and that RE and RABBM were significantly related to hostile and rigid interpersonal exchanges. Other studies indicate that RE has been significantly associated with problems with sociability and intimacy (Sharpe et al., 1995), a lack of interpersonal competence/closeness, and less intimate self-disclosure (Berko, 1994; Bruch, Berko, & Haase, 1998). In addition, college men's RE, RABBM, and CBWFR have been significantly correlated with family conflict, avoidance, and enmeshment/disengagement as well as decreased cohesion with both parents (Scott, 2001).

Furthermore (and this should not come as any big surprise), at least four studies have shown that men's elevated GRC levels relate to *women's* depression, anxiety, and marital satisfaction in relationships with these men (Breiding, 2004; Rochlen &Mahalik, 2004).

Again no big surprise: when men's RE is increased, fathering self-efficacy and fathering satisfaction are decreased.

So, if you are male, and if your GRC levels are elevated, you are more likely to be unhappy in your intimate family relationships, your wife or partner is more likely to be unhappy, and you are less likely to be an effective father or to reap the pleasures of parenting. This is an argument in favor of sociocultural changes, psychotherapy, men's therapy groups, lots of drum-beating in the wilderness, or all of the above.

The "Boy Code"
Ever since childhood, boys have been exposed to what William Pollack

refers to as the "Boy Code" (Pollack, 1998a). This code, written nowhere but understood everywhere, insists that boys be stoic, stable, independent. They should be bold, adventurous, and risk-taking. They should achieve status, dominance, and power. They must be tough on the playground, keep their vulnerable emotions in check, restrict impulses toward expressing affection, and laugh or keep quiet when another boy is being victimized. They must act as if everything is under control, and, perhaps most crippling, they must not reveal feelings or express themselves in such a way as to appear "feminine."

Violations of any of the central precepts of the Boy Code often lead to ridicule and the experience of shame. And, once shamed, boys are extremely unlikely to venture into the dangerous territory again. Most boys will incorporate these values not only as social and psychological survival mechanisms, but as truths about the way the world is and should be for other men and for their own sons a generation later. Being shaped by the Boy Code, with its early restriction on emotion and self-expression, contributes to adult men abiding by the adult version: the Guy Code. And, although there are many wonderful and socially desirable qualities associated with being male and acting masculine, emotional life and interpersonal life are often—to one degree or another—crippled by the excessively restrictive indoctrination that men have received.

Understanding the Boy Code (a.k.a. the Guy Code) helps us understand how male behavior seems to be guided by socially constructed rules that demand for men to be competent, strong, successful, and in charge. The codes set a standard for men to maintain these roles in their relationships, at work, and in their roles as fathers and husbands. And it is often difficult for men to shift gears and enact different roles in their other world of relationships—where cooperation, patience, compromise, setting aside one's own needs, and interdependence come in a lot handier. If men have no context in which to place the attitudes and behaviors that are more relationship-friendly and emotion-friendly, then they have no viable alternative beyond frustration and failure.

It all depends on the story that men tell themselves, and those of us who treat men are in the business of helping men develop alternative and more flexible stories.

David and Brannon (1976) originally identified their version of the four central components of what it means to be a "real man" in our culture (and in many other cultures as well), which was later developed further and popularized by Pollack as the "Boy Code" (Pollack, 1998a):

1. *The big wheel*: The value of being a "big wheel" is embodied in the importance of being successful, important, powerful, and in charge. This is a shame-based pressure; boys, and the men they grow up to be, are perpetually scrambling to avoid being in any situation that might cause them to experience shame. And they are perpetually trying to build a structure in their lives and interpersonal world that eliminates any likelihood of this experience. The success–status norm is reflected in the expectation that men succeed in their professional careers, which is often measured by income (e.g., "Success in his work has to be a man's central goal in this life").

2. *The sturdy oak*: The importance of being a "sturdy oak" is portrayed in the masculine ideals of being tough, self-reliant, and confident. Toughness includes physical, mental, and emotional toughness (e.g., "A man must stand on his own two feet and never depend on other people to help him do things"). Men are expected to be physically strong and masculine, highly competent and knowledgeable, and able to solve their own emotional difficulties and avoid showing vulnerability.

3. *Give 'em hell*: "Give 'em hell" means being aggressive, competitive, and powerful both on the playing field and off. Boys learn that they are supposed to be daredevils—or else. A client of mine had a teenage son who was falling apart and had even gone through several months of residential treatment to help him bail out from his depression, school failure, lying and stealing, and increasing substance abuse. When he came back home, the boy went to a party where he got drunk and passed out. He told his father that he woke up the next morning lying on a pool table. His father shook his head, but grinned and said, "That's my boy!" This father, so worried about his son's destructive behavior, couldn't restrain himself from communicating pride about his son's hard-drinking manly ways.

4. *No sissy stuff*: "No sissy stuff" requires restraining from showing affection, emotion, or any behavior that might be construed as feminine. This is the most central factor of all. The male ideal, or at least the caricature of masculinity that is embodied in the Boy Code, is a fundamental rejection of anything that smacks of what Arnold Schwarzenegger would refer to as "girly man" behavior. Think of the most shameful playground put-downs in boy world: "You throw like a girl" or "you act like a girl" or "you look like a girl" or "you sound like a girl." The antifemininity norm is the belief that men should avoid stereotypically female activities, behaviors, or occupations (e.g., "It bothers me when a man does something I consider 'feminine'").

This is, of course, never more evident than in the power of the ultimate insult in the world of boys: "faggot." Queer, gay, sissy. And nastier names, more and more graphic, to heap ultimate humiliation on boys who are perceived to be violators of the Boy Code.

The damage of these taunts to boys and young men who happen to actually be gay is obvious. Not so obvious is the damage to all the boys who are straight as well. The terror of being perceived as gay restricts boys to only engage in behaviors that are absolutely, positively guaranteed to prove that they do not have a gay bone in their body: walking with a swagger, restricting emotional expression and vulnerability, maintaining certifiably male interests, "scoring" with girls and women, and so on. As male educator Paul Kivel said: "These kinds of taunts make it unsafe for all of us" (Kivel, 1999).

Boys are never to show any weakness: *This is nothing to cry over*. I once said this to my son when he was whining about some now-long-forgotten situation that I thought was ridiculous. He withdrew from me–and from his emotions—and muttered: *Thanks a lot*. He was sarcastically rebuking me for invoking the Boy Code and dismissing his feelings. And I am grateful that he busted me on this.

If boys express any tender feelings, they run the risk of committing the cardinal sin of acting like a girl. My son was on a Little League team and the manager told the boys (9 years old) that they had to wear

"Minnie Mouse pins" on their cap if they ever let a called third strike go by. Mickey Mouse wasn't humiliating enough—it had to be Minnie! Paul Kivel, in his work with the Oakland Men's Project, describes this as the pressure of staying "in the box" (Kivel, 1999). If a boy conforms to the rules of how boys or men are supposed to be, what they are supposed to do, how they are supposed to act, what they are not supposed to do or display—then he is one of the rare boys who feels safe. He may be rigid, he may feel pressured to maintain this posture, and he may lack the emotional intelligence required to sustain a meaningful intimate relationship, but at least he feels safe. However, if he (like almost all boys and men at some time or another) fails to completely measure up, if he steps outside the box in any way, then he runs the risk of ridicule and the following litany of labels: weak, sissy, wuss, girl, pussy. And the crown prince of "no sissy stuff" labels: gay.

Nelson Mandela (1994) describes in his autobiography the intense pressure that he and all boys in his tribe experienced at puberty during the excruciatingly painful rite of circumcision. This is the rite that catapults a boy into true manhood, and it requires enormous powers of pain tolerance and suppression of the truest and most vulnerable emotions. The naked boy is expected to shout out the African cry of "*Ndiyindoda!*" at the moment that the knife is wielded. A "boy" would whimper and cry—but a "man" can shout out the word! Mandela hesitated several seconds before shouting "*Ndiyindoda!*" Those few seconds of hesitation were enough to shame him and to cause him—and, he suspected, the other men observing him—to doubt his readiness for manhood. There is very little room for error or opportunity to step outside the box of the Boy Code.

This is the code that generates the scene from *Good Will Hunting* (Bender & Van Sant, 1997) in which Will Hunting (Matt Damon) and his best buddy, Chuckie (Ben Affleck) talk about what has just happened in Will's life. In casual conversation, Chuckie asks Will about how things are going with "your lady." Will tells him, affectless, that she's gone. Neither man shows any display of emotion. After a few grunts and monosyllabic responses, Chuckie uncovers the information that Skylar has taken off to medical school in California. A week ago!

Chuckie sips from his can of beer, raises his eyebrows a little, and responds: "That sucks."

The empty spaces in this guy conversation are deafening. Will is emotionally handicapped. He suffers from the restrictions of the Boy Code. Not only is he ill equipped to properly put a label on what he is feeling, but he is also deathly allergic to acknowledging how much he cares, how much he needs her, and how deeply his heart is broken. He is grieving deeply, but the Boy Code has ingrained in him the prohibition against acknowledging this. It would look too damn weak and needy.

MGRS and Psychological Distress

The more that men endorse higher levels of MGRS, the more likely it is that they will suffer from a wide range of symptoms of psychological distress. They are more likely to be depressed (Good & Mintz,, 1990; Good & Wood, 1995). They are more likely to experience relationship distress and have problems with intimacy(Ludlow & Mahalik, 2001). They are more likely to think and act like abusive and aggressive men (Finn, 1986; Franchina, Eisler, & Moore, 2001; Vass & Gold, 1995). And they are more likely to avoid—like the plague—seeking out any kind of counseling or other interventions for their distress (Good, Dell, & Mintz, 1989).

So, a man who endorses high levels of MGRS items and is thus excessively attached to traditional definitions of masculinity—what I often refer to as a caricature of true masculinity—is more likely to be suffering from what I think of as a "triple whammy."

First of all, he is unhappy. Depressed, restless, unsatisfied with his life. More resentful of others. Second, his intimate relationships are less rewarding, both for him and his partner. The tremendous sustenance that is available through the closest relationship bonds is something that he is much less likely to take advantage of. And, third, he is the least likely candidate of all men out there to get some help.

This is the worst combination of all: the very men whose lives are suffering the most (and whose attitudes and behavior are more likely to generate suffering for those around them) and who are most in need of help are the ones least likely to seek it.

One of the ways to make sense of this level of distress is by understanding what "discrepancy strain" (O'Neil, 2008) means to men. This emotional distress occurs when men have difficulty living up to the masculine standards they have internalized. This strain is completely governed by perspective and perceptions: the "story" that this particular man is telling himself about the situation in front of him. The strain occurs when a man feels that he has acted "unmanly." Most men feel pressured to act "masculine," based on the particular definition of masculinity that they have integrated over their years of training in being a man. The more attached a man is to traditional masculine qualities, the more vulnerable he is to the possibility of falling short of these standards: the discrepancy strain.

For some men, this may center around traditional masculine qualities such as physical strength. For others, the capacity to be powerful, dominant, and successful in business or relationships may be paramount, or they may feel an intense internal pressure to be—at all times—decisive, self-assured, rational, and competent. Other men may be horrified by the possibility of their own show of (self-perceived) weakness or sexual failure of any kind. And, especially in the 21st century, a man may experience discrepancy strain even if he feels like he is not communicating well with his wife or spending enough time with his kids—if he has integrated these values as being essential to his masculine identity.

Another form of MGRS strain that contributes to psychological distress is known as "dysfunction strain" (O'Neil, 2008). This simply describes the emotional and interpersonal limitations that often develop from fulfilling the requirements of the traditional male role. Although this is an enormous generalization and all of us could identify many exceptions, in general men are socialized to compete and to value winning at the expense of intimacy, whereas women are socialized more to value intimate relationships and seek harmony and intimacy. Men are more socialized to withhold (or, in many cases, not even to be aware of) a range of emotions. This is especially true for any emotional states that reek of vulnerability or seem in any way to represent "nonmasculinity."

12

MGRS dysfunction strain also helps us make sense of men's reluctance to seek help for both physical and emotional distress. In general, men have less fully developed social support networks than women (Antonucci & Akiyama, 1987; Burda, Vaux, & Schill, 1984; Wohlgemuth & Betz, 1991), and they have more reluctance to seek help from the social networks that they do have (Husaini, Moore, & Cain, 1994; Oliver, Reed, Katz, & Haugh, 1999). A man who relies on others and seeks help may identify himself and be identified by others as violating the "sturdy oak" component of the Boy Code. This just does not conform to the expectations of traditional masculine ideology.

In making sense of these perspectives, it behooves us to never forget that women have their own problems, and men have plenty of coping strengths. But our understanding of classic masculinity issues also informs us that many men appraise situations using the schema of what is an acceptable masculine response rather than what is (by some more objective standard) the genuinely best response.

Normative Male Alexithymia and Emotional Intelligence

Alexithymia literally means "lacking the words for emotions." The term has Greek origins: *lexis* means "word" and *thymos* means "emotion." Combined with the prefix *a-*, meaning "not" or "without," the term *alexithymia* has emerged. In severe clinical cases of alexithymia, the individual is crippled by this handicap; he or she is unable to consciously know, and certainly unable to communicate, anything about his or her internal states.

The most central theme of the alexithymia condition involves problems identifying, describing, and making sense of one's own feelings. True alexithymics cannot empathize. They are hopelessly confused by physical sensations often associated with emotions, their imagination is severely limited, and they highly overemploy concrete, realistic, and logical thinking. It's all they know. Alexithymics also show a limited ability to experience positive emotions, leading some researchers to describe these individuals as anhedonic (Krystal, 1988; Sifneos, 1987).

The ability to identify internal experiences is an essential component of being human. Without it, we lack something that makes us quintessentially human, and we are limited in our ability to relate to others.

True clinically diagnosed alexithymics just seem different; they come across like Spock-like aliens living on a different social planet from others.

Normative Male Alexithymia

Ron Levant coined the term *normative male alexithymia* to describe a widespread phenomenon in our culture (Levant & Pollack, 1998). The word "normative" does not imply that it is problem-free and thus "normal"; it simply indicates that the incidence of these patterns is so widespread as to be to considered statistically "normal." Men experiencing such gender-linked, normative, mild to moderate alexithymia do not demonstrate the severe classic symptoms associated with clinical alexithymia: wooden facial expression, inability to identify even traces of physiological sensations associated with emotions, and a concrete, conventional cognitive style that is void of any capacity for introspection or attention to inner experience.

However, although it may not reach the level of clinically significant proportions like bona fide alexithymia, normative male alexithymia still represents a "condition" that plagues many men, to varying degrees, in their emotional lives and in their relationships. The term describes mildly (or sometimes more severely) emotionally shut down (and often depressed) men who struggle to identify their inner states. We don't yet have any solid data on exactly how many men meet the threshold for this description, but at this point it is helpful simply to think of this as a descriptive term that identifies some of the emotional intelligence issues that many men experience.

Normative male alexithymia thus refers to the emotional patterns of boys who grow up to become men who are unaware of their emotions and even of their own bodily sensations. They rely only on their cognitive descriptions, analyses, and opinions. Because of this gap in self-awareness, many men are limited in utilizing the simplest and most effective method for dealing with complex feelings and difficult moods: that is, identifying, thinking about, and expressing feelings. These skills are essential aspects of emotional intelligence that usually (not always) are more highly developed in women than men. For the most part, women simply do better. Many women who are in relationships with men complain that they just can't get through to the man, and this may help explain it. He may simply not be reading her cues or speaking her language. It may seem like he is actively lying, avoiding, or denying, but this is not necessarily the case: often he just doesn't understand what she is talking about or how she wants him to respond.

When a man lacks an adequate ability to identify his truest feelings, he is often left with a limited range of responses because he only identifies a limited range of internal states. Author Adam Cox has identified the term *dyslexithymia*, a made-up diagnostic label (Cox, 2006). If we think of the reversal component of dyslexia and integrate this with the emotional cluelessness component of normative male alexithymia, we find a man who responds in a way that is emotionally opposite to the appropriate response.

For example, a man's wife is suffering from a long and lingering illness that is not responding to treatment. How does this man feel? Helpless, powerless, frustrated, worried, sad. However, since these emotions are unfamiliar and not easily or comfortably identified because of normative male alexithymia, the husband responds only to the vague sense of unrest and unhappiness as if it is a familiar emotion: anger. The behavior that emerges? Instead of compassion or simple, straightforward expressions of sadness or helplessness, he blames his wife for bringing this on herself or not following through properly on her treatment. He has reversed (in dyselxic fashion) the emotional state, and this has led to a reversed, inappropriate, and destructive interpersonal response. This is tragic. This man could be identified as cold or narcissistic—or we could activate the narrative that he is just plain old "dyslexithymic." The second label offers us all more hope because it is a more treatable condition than pure coldness or pure narcissism.

One male client of mine accidentally stepped on his wife's toe and she squealed in pain. His first reaction? "Hurry up and move!" And when she told him later that she wanted him to comfort her a little bit instead of blaming her, he got defensive. This was a classic "dyslexithymia" reaction. Seeing her in pain, because of him, made him feel bad. Unable to tolerate this, he felt extremely threatened and reacted defensively. He blamed her. Later he told her that he was embarrassed about being perceived as "soft" if he had acted soothing or tender toward her.

Modern family structures call for men to take on new roles (Levant & Pollack, 1995) and the handicap of normative male alexithymia has become even more significant for men trying to "measure up" in these roles. More and more, 21st-century men need the ability to listen actively, express emotional empathy, and discuss their own feelings. They are expected to take on a greater share of nurturing activities with their children. Their wives and partners expect more in terms of open, honest, and deeper levels of communication. Many men are not well prepared for these roles because the male socialization process has limited their development of putting words to one's emotions (Levant & Pollack, 1998).

Men with high MGRS levels, who are the most plagued by the masculinity traps we are identifying here, are also often the most plagued by normative male alexithymia.

Levant, Good, Cook, O'Neil, Smalley, Owen, et al. (2006) have developed a questionnaire called *The Normative Male Alexithymia Scale (NMAS)*, which assesses what they describe as the frequency, intensity, and awareness of affect. The questionnaire asked people to respond to statements like this:

> I am often confused about what emotion I am feeling.
> I don't think I am upset but then I get a headache, upset stomach, or stiff neck and then I realize that I have been upset.
> When I am upset, I don't know if I am sad, frightened, or angry.
> If someone asks how I am feeling, I typically say what I am not feeling (e.g., "not too bad").
> I am comfortable talking with a friend who is upset.

These sample items help form a portrait of the normative male alexithymia pattern: The man who endorses these items clearly has difficulty identifying internal and emotional states. Even when he notices some feelings, the sensations are vague, undifferentiated, and unqualified. He doesn't know quite what to do with them. And he gets critical feedback from others in his life, frustrated by their inability to "get" this man or connect with him. People want him to explain or articulate more.

We don't know for sure how much of these patterns in men that show up differently in women are attributable to gender-specific brain characteristics. We might think of this as an emotional learning disability. One theory posits a disconnection between two of the most important brain centers: the neocortex and the limbic system (Sifneos, 1991). The feeling centers operating in the limbic system are firing, but they are not sending the signals to the neocortex in an intelligible way. It is also possible that the signals are getting through, but that the verbal coding centers in the neocortex fail to function optimally.

Research studies and clinical observations have given us an increasingly clear portrait of how boys learn early on that the male role involves keeping feelings inside and "sucking it up." Studies indicate that, even at the age of two, girls refer to feelings more frequently than boys do. Throughout the different stages of child development, boys and girls receive subtle and not so subtle messages that shape gender identity and the role of emotional expression. Mothers use more words about emotions when they speak to their young daughters than they do with their sons (Dunn, 1987). Fathers, too, use a wider range of language that expresses emotions with their daughters than with their sons—and their teasing is more aggressive with their sons than with their daughters (Gleason, 1983). Facial expressiveness diverges as boys and girls grow up: boys show less expression on their faces as they grow older, and their mothers find it more difficult to read the feeling behind the face (Buck, 1977). And if your own mother can't even read your emotional state, something is not right.

After about age four or five, boys are held less than girls. The expression of vulnerable emotions (such as fear and sadness) in boys are more likely to be discouraged (and sometimes punished) by parents—in contrast to the response to the emotional expression of girls (Dunn, Bretherton, & Munn,1987; Fivush, 1989). Studies also show that both parents tend to talk more about emotions with their daughters than with their sons. Fivush (1989) found that mothers were much more likely to speak about the *experience* of emotions with girls, in contrast to the *causes* and *consequences* of emotions with their boys. This is not a conscious process, but its unconsciousness and its subtlety does not make it any less significant in shaping boys.

Boys who are attached to their mothers are treated with a certain disapproval in a way that girls attached to their fathers are not. And girls, with their superior verbal abilities in childhood, talk and talk and talk about their feelings with their cohorts.

Levant and Pollack (1998) summarized this developmental process for boys:

> Normative alexithymia is a predictable result of the male gender socialization process. Specifically, it is a result of boys being socialized to restrict the expression of their vulnerable and caring/connection emotions and to be emotionally stoic. This socialization process includes both the creation of skill deficits (by not teaching boys emotional skills nor allowing them to have experiences that would facilitate their learning these skills) and trauma (including prohibitions against boys' natural emotional expressivity, and punishment, often in the form of making the boy feel deeply ashamed of himself for violating these prohibitions). (pp. 41–42)

Levant and Pollack referred to the male socialization process as "trauma that is so normative that we do not think of it as trauma at all" (1998, p. 37). Many boys are left with no alternative but to shut down emotionally, implode with internal pressure, act out, or escape. Grown men may feel that, because of this hard-wiring and ingrained socialization, they have no alternative. As clinicians, we need to be profoundly respectful of this belief that men carry. However, men do in fact have the ability to transcend this cultural, psychological, and neurochemical programming.

The social context that helps maintain normative male alexithymia beyond boyhood, into adolescence, and beyond has everything to do with MGRS. Boys who deviate from expectations for emotional reserve often experience harsh punishment by their peers (Pollack, 1998). Based on these research findings and clinical observations, Levant theorized that mild to moderate forms of alexithymia occur more frequently among men who were especially socialized as boys to conform to the requirements of traditional masculine norms, and thus were required to restrict emotional expression (Levant, Hirsch, Celentanos, & Cozza, 1992; Levant & Pollack, 1995, 1998). As men, they often have great difficulty finding words to describe their emotions, even when they are in obvious distress. Many lack an immediate bodily felt experience of their emotions; thus, they tend to rely on cognition to logically deduce what they are feeling. Some tend to transform their vulnerable emotions into aggression and to respond with aggression when hurt.

It would be a mistake to think that men who fall into this "normative male alexithymia" category don't really feel anything. The dysfunction lies in the connections between feelings and everything else: cognition, judgment, expression, behavioral choices, empathy. They lack the skills to know what their feelings are, and they are especially unable to put their feelings into words. At severe clinical levels, this describes an emotionally and interpersonally paralyzing clinical condition. At mild to moderate levels, it describes most men. Most importantly for our understanding of male psychology and the health of male relationships, it specifically inhibits the ability of many men to properly label the distress, emptiness, anxiety, and pessimism that they are experiencing. Further, such men have often missed out on developing the emotional skills that might be applied to self-understanding, self-care, emotional empathy, and richer interactions with others because of their lack of awareness of emotions.

So what does a man do if he feels depressed (or "hurt" or "frustrated" or "worried" or powerless")? He can't really call it those things if he is not skilled, trained, or hard-wired to form the connections.

Emotional Intelligence and Relationship Skills
Emotional intelligence describes an ability to perceive, assess, and manage the emotions of oneself and of others, and to make positive behavioral decisions in interpersonal situations. The first published

attempt toward a definition was made by Salovey and Mayer (1990) who defined emotional intelligence as "the ability to monitor one's own and others' feelings and emotions, to discriminate among them and to use this information to guide one's thinking and actions." It wasn't until the publication of Daniel Goleman's book *Emotional Intelligence* (1995) that the term and concept entered the popular consciousness. Although emotional intelligence is defined somewhat differently by different researchers and theorists, Goleman's model (Goleman, 1998) and others' (Stock, 2007) typically outline four main emotional intelligence constructs:

1. Emotional self-awareness—the ability to read one's emotions and to be aware of one's feelings, and to recognize their impact on arousal levels, attitudes, and behaviors.

2. Emotional self-management—controlling one's emotions and impulses and adapting to changing circumstances, plus having the skill to influence the emotions one wants to experience, rather than being the victim of whatever emotions occur; the ability to use emotions to take positive action even in the face of emotional distress.

3. Social awareness/empathy—the ability to sense, understand, and react to others' emotions (the ability to listen effectively and accurately enough to put yourself in the other person's shoes) while making sense of the social transactions and interpersonal needs that are taking place.

4. Relationship management—the ability to deal with others effectively based on this awareness, to activate empathy, and to inspire, influence, and develop others while managing conflict; setting a positive tone of cooperation no matter how difficult the situation or conversation and having others' best interests in mind while focusing on achieving resolution.

In other words, if someone knows his emotional self, can use this self-knowledge to make intelligent behavioral decisions, can read and empathize with the emotional states of others reasonably accurately, and can apply this knowledge to manage his relationships successfully, then he quaifies as being emotionally intelligent and he is much more likely to be more successful in his relationships.

Unfortunately, a vast array of research indicates that many of the central aspects of MGRS and normative male alexithymia are inversely correlated with levels of emotional intelligence (Parker, Taylor, & Bagby, 2001). Study after study indicate that men, on the whole, tend to be more deficient in relationship skills, and the relationship between conformity to masculine gender role norms and emotional intelligence shows up consistently in measures of relationship intimacy.

Tannen's (1990) studies showed that men are more comfortable with language that emphasizes status and independence, as opposed to language that emphasizes connection and intimacy. Men often engage in conversation that communicates their knowledge and skill (status factors) rather than a display of similarities or matching of experiences. She describes this as a preference for "report talk" rather than "rapport talk."

The greater a man experiences high levels of gender role conflict and MGRS, the lower the levels of his relationship intimacy and relationship satisfaction (Campbell & Snow, 1992; Cournoyer & Mahalik, 1995; Ludlow & Mahalik, 2001; Rochlen & Mahalik, 2004; Sharpe & Heppner, 1991; Sharpe et al., 1995). Both men and women report that their relationship satisfaction is increased when they and their partners are willing to self-disclose personal information, thoughts, and feelings (Boyd, 1994; Jones, 1991; Siavelis & Lamke, 1992), but research indicates that (in general) men are less emotionally expressive and self-disclose significantly less than women do (Brody & Hall, 1993).

It's not just emotional expressiveness that is a factor here. Women are (in general) better listeners than men (Miller, Berg, & Archer, 1983), and they are much more likely to offer social support (Cutrona, 1996). Farrell's (1987) commentaries on male communication patterns identified a pattern of men "self-listening"; they pay attention to a conversation looking more for opportunities to jump in and discuss their own experiences, rather than genuinely appreciating or connecting with what the other person is saying.

In marital relationships, women are more likely to confront marital problems (for better or worse) and men are more likely to stonewall and become defensive (Gottman, 1994). Relationship satisfaction is also linked to the degree to which one's partner (male or female) has traditionally feminine traits, such as nurturance and being kind, gentle, affectionate, and other centered (Antill, 1983; Ickes, 1985; Kurdek & Schmitt, 1986; Lamke, 1989; McGraw, 2001). Plenty of men, of course, are kind, gentle, affectionate, and other centered, but these levels in men are inversely correlated with the GRC and MGRS issues.

Pleck, Sonenstein, and Ku (1993) found that men with traditional masculine attitudes had more sexual partners, had less intimate relationships with women, and were more likely to view relationships between men and women as adversarial. It is especially telling that *both* men and women report that their relationships with women are higher in intimacy, enjoyment, and nurturance (Sapadin, 1988).

The Development of Masculinity

How do boys become boys and men become men? The development of a gendered self occurs, subtly but extensively, through the closest of interpersonal relationships. This is first with the mother and father, and later with anyone else who is meaningful to the developing child—and this development always interacts reciprocally with the values of the society and culture at large. These deeply personal, unique, and emotionally charged relationships provide the basis for the development of the boy's conception of what it means to be a boy and later inform his notions of what it means to be a man (Rabinowitz & Cochron, 2002). Each of these significant people and each of these significant social systems communicates some of their own constructs and messages about the meaning of being a boy and how to be a boy.

Tyranny of Separation and Autonomy for Boys

In recent years, psychologists and social researchers have identified—and challenged—the tendency for little boys to be pushed from connection to their mothers at an early age. We know that Western culture values autonomy as an essential aspect of masculinity and that dependency is stigmatized because it exposes neediness and vulnerability. Neediness and vulnerability do not conform to our cultural expectations of masculinity, and mothers who unconsciously and automatically suppress these traits in boys may be acting in conformity with our cultural values related to masculine independence.

Pollack's research on male development suggests that little boys may experience this push away from maternal caretaking as a profound loss: a loss without words or even the most remote social or cultural validation for this experience. This early and often premature separation may cause a "trauma" that predisposes boys and men to deny needs for emotional connection—and defensively identify this capacity for denial as positive. This serves as "an impingement in boy's development—a normative life-cycle loss—that may, later in life, leave many adult men at risk for fears of intimate connection. This traumatic experience of abandonment occurs so early in the life course that the shameful memory of the loss is likely to be deeply repressed" (1995, p. 41).

According to this perspective, we see the evolution of classic patterns of masculinity interfacing with the processing of emotions and with interpersonal relations. This results in a tendency to develop patterns of defensiveness and emotional maintenance that resemble narcissism (Cochran & Rabinowitz, 1996; Pollack, 2001). Boys (and later the men who have emerged from these boys) become emotionally self-protective. They develop firm defenses against the experiences of loss, grief, and emotional pain. They often become defended against the possibility of vulnerability in relationships, either by avoiding relationships, inhibiting genuine intimacy, or defensively responding to perceived threats to their self or threats of abandonment. Pollack called this "defensive autonomy." This early activation of psychological defenses emerges from "a normative male, gender-linked loss, a trauma of abandonment for boys which may show itself, later, as an adult through symptomatic behavior, characterological defense, and vulnerability to depression" (Pollack, 1998b, p.154).

When men develop a defensive, self-protective pattern of dissociation and a dismissive attachment style, they tend to lose out on the psychological growth that emerges from healthy grieving and mourning. The emotional resiliency that is supposed to develop from these "necessary losses" (Viorst, 1986) is retarded, impairing the normal pattern of making and breaking of intimate emotional attachments to others throughout the life span. Self-protective defenses and more primitive emotional reactions emerge instead: anger, shame, coldness, control. Furthermore, many men whose emotional development has been derailed through this development desperately seek to avoid the impact of uncomfortable and particularly "unmanly" emotions. This perspective helps us understand why so many men turn to escapist, denial, and suppressive behaviors like drug and alcohol use and why so many men tend to either avoid or act out many of their emotions—often in destructive fashion.

Dependency becomes associated with disapproval and shame becomes associated with the presence and enactment of needs and vulnerability. This excessive reliance on the self—at the expense of interdependency and relatedness—results in a boy or man who must "stand on his own two feet" and not ask for help or support, ever. While personal autonomy is in many ways a tremendous asset, we also see that boys and men have a tendency to prefer autonomy to relatedness and a deep-seated, if not unconscious, discomfort in response to demands for interpersonal connection.

Culture and Socialization
Of course, another crucial factor in the development and construction of masculinity is through culture and socialization. Gender role socialization affects both males and females. The first thing we notice about other individuals is whether they are male or female—and if, for some reason, we are not sure, then we get confused. A culture's influence on how boys and girls are raised affects practically every-thing: clothes, speech patterns, choice in movies, ways of touching, and what kinds of emotional expression are allowed. And when it comes to the patterns of emotional expression and interpersonal rela-tions, it is obvious that our culture has encouraged women to be more

relationship-oriented and men to be more self-reliant (Rabinowitz & Cochran, 1994).

All boys are exposed to a multiplicity of messages about what it means to be a boy or man. Many of these messages are direct ("take it like a man!"); many are subtle (handshakes instead of hugs).

I spoke to a pediatrician colleague who described how clearly he observed this phenomenon in his office. He said that when little 5-year-old girls come in to his office to get a shot, they cry and resist. And the response for their parents is most typically something like, "That's okay, honey, it's going to be all right, I'll be right here with you."

Yet the typical response he observes when a 5-year-old boy starts crying before his shots is usually something like this: "Come on, now, don't cry, be a big boy. You can take this."

The message: It's okay for girls to express their feelings and we will help them, as part of an interpersonal connection, cope with this stressful experience. In contrast, boys need to find a way to tough it out and deal with it themselves.

The reality here? Both of these strategies for coping are actually of value to all of us. But boys get the clear message that the interpersonal coping strategy, relying on the connection with an "other" to get them through, is less of an option and actually associated with weakness and shame.

The little boy is like the little girl: dependent on early caretakers for feeding, holding, and shelter as well as love and support. This is a universal human developmental experience, yet in our American culture (and many others), boys get the message early on that they are not allowed the same breadth of emotional expression and the same access to depend on others as girls are. That would not be considered masculine.

Attitudes about relational dependence are really the core issues at play here. Often, the longing and gratification that the little boy experiences are culturally devalued as he grows into manhood. Furthermore, as boys grow into men they experience a constriction of social roles and emotional options based on these constructions of masculinity. Why do men who earn less than their wives elicit social stigma? Why do the guys who appear more at school functions or at weekday playgrounds have lower status and make everyone (including the women in their lives) uncomfortable? Even among "enlightened" men and women, these simply do not feel natural.

There is a great scene from the movie *Smoke Signals* (Eyre, 1998) that illustrates these cultural expectations. Two Native American young men discuss the image they must portray to the world. One coaches the other in the best presentation for Native American masculinity:

VICTOR: . . . I mean, how many times have you seen *Dances with Wolves*? A hundred, two hundred times?

Embarrassed, Thomas ducks his head.

VICTOR (cont'd): Oh, jeez, you have seen it that many times, haven't you? Man, do you think that shit is real? God. Don't you even know how to be a real Indian?

THOMAS (whispering): I guess not.

Victor is disgusted.

VICTOR: Well, shit, no wonder. Jeez, I guess I'll have to teach you then.

Thomas nods eagerly.

VICTOR: First of all, quit grinning like an idiot. Indians ain't supposed to smile like that. Get stoic. You got to look mean or people won't respect you. White people will run all over you if you don't look mean. You got to look like a warrior. You got to look like you just got back from killing a buffalo.

THOMAS: But our tribe never hunted buffalo. We were fishermen.

VICTOR: What? You want to look like you just came back from catching a fish? It ain't *Dances with Salmon*, you know? Man, you think a fisherman is tough? Thomas, you got to look like a warrior.

Goldberg (1976) was one of the first to describe the "impossible binds" that our culture imposes upon men. These include the expectations to be strong and in control but to also be sensitive and responsive (the gender bind), to be physical and active but also savvy and in command of oneself (the kinetic bind), and to take risks and challenge oneself but also to care for and nurture oneself (the hero bind). Such messages often conflict with boys' and men's inner experiences of emotional need and desire. But, by the time boys develop and have been shaped by masculinity messages, their emotional expression of sadness, anguish, fear, and tenderness have all been toned down—like my son talking to his friends.

The men who eventually make it into our offices for counseling (whether they come on their own, or because their wife has demanded it, or because the court has ordered them to) are often products of these conflicting messages and these restricted options. When men experience the normal range of human emotions and needs, but have been trained to deny, ignore, or rechannel them, we end up with men who retreat from relationships, experience unnamed depressions, become excessively attached to achievement, and act out.

Honoring Masculinity Traits

In our zeal to identify the ways in which the cultural definitions of masculinity and male cultural training hinder men's development, it behooves us to remember one thing: There are many aspects of masculinity that are great. The goal of this gender-based understanding of men's psychological and interpersonal issues is not to turn men into women. It is to turn them into better men.

Don McPherson, former All-America quarterback for Syracuse University and NFL quarterback, is a bold, dynamic African-American male who has (after his retirement from his football career) committed himself to speaking out to men about the pressures of being male. He joined the staff of Northeastern University's Center for the Study of Sport in Society, before becoming the first executive director of the Sports Leadership Institute at Adelphi University. He regularly speaks at college campuses as a critic of gender roles, stating that the standard constructions of masculinity and femininity both limit men's emotions and overall well-being and contribute to gendered violence such as domestic violence, stalking, and rape (McPherson, 2005).

Don and I both presented at a conference on men's issues in 2005. After his presentation, a member of the audience began a question by stating what seemed to be obvious: Men's insistence on enduring pain without speaking out has been a tragic and debilitating force in men's lives and in the lives of the people around them.

Don interrupted the audience member: "We all know that this is true in lots of ways. But not always. It's important to honor what's so *right* about masculinity. I learned from playing football that, when I was out there in a big game, I wanted men around me who would not complain about being physically banged up or enduring tough weather. I didn't want to hear about their self-doubts or their anxieties. I just wanted them to suck it up and come through. There's a time and a place."

Men who are able to put their feelings aside and perform heroic tasks—in war, pulling bodies out of burning buildings, risking jail for their beliefs, or performing on the football field—are worth keeping around. And the masculine traits that contribute to performing these tasks are worth preserving. Many of the classic male gender roles have served men—and societies throughout humankind's evolutionary history—extremely well.

Men are determined and focused on getting things done. They are often quite successful at the "compartmentalization" of suffering and emotional distress—which can be a problem in relationships but often comes in very handy. They are traditionally able to transcend fears and emotional misgivings to take risks and to seek out new lands. And, throughout history, they have not been too shabby at hunting for food or making a living for their families. Men are often extremely loyal, both to their families and to their buddies.

So, while we call upon men to take on new roles and cultivate their emotional intelligence, let us always keep in mind the valuable qualities of masculinity. And let us also have a propound respect for the fact that we are often calling upon men to violate traditional male codes that have evolved for millennia. We are also asking them to develop skills that they usually have not been well trained to do, such as revealing weakness, expressing their most intimate feelings, and nurturing children. When they worry that they will not be successful at what 21st-century values are calling upon them to do, they often withdraw or disavow the value of these skills. For all of us men out there, it may take awhile but we are getting there. The more that those of us who are trying to draw out the best qualities of men really understand this struggle, the better off all of us—men, women, and children—are likely to be.

Chapter 2
Broken Mirrors and Broken Narratives

In the field of self psychology, the term *selfobject* refers to something outside oneself (an "object") that is experienced primarily in terms of its relationship to the self. A selfobject does not exist as an independent being or entity. It only exists as a psychological construct and emotional experience as part of a relationship between the self and some "other." In fact, using the word *selfobject* as a noun does not really convey its meaning. It makes more sense as an adjective, as in *selfobject experience* or *selfobject function* (Shapiro, 1995).The most primary and meaningful self-objects are typically interpersonal, but a job, a church, a photograph, a bank account, a football team, and a thousand other possibilities can all provide the material for a selfobject relationship. It all depends on the meaning attached by the individual.

In *How Does Analysis Cure?* Kohut describes the core experience of feeling unity, strength, and integration if, at each stage of life, the self receives the appropriate responses from the selfobject environment. The selfobject (or, more appropriately, the selfobject relationship) is like the oxygen that is necessary for life. Kohut describes the selfobject (when the selfobject is based on a person) as "that dimension of our experience of another person that relates to the person's functions in shoring up our self" (1984, pp. 49–50). The selfobject is always an intrapsychic experience, one that is based on an interpersonal event or some other "other." When an individual has been blessed with a good enough wealth of selfobject resources, as a result of fortunate parenting, fortunate constitution, or fortunate therapy, a bad day or broken relationship can be coped with more successfully by calling upon these resources.

Self psychology outlines multiple types of selfobjects, such as the idealized selfobject, the kinship (or twinship or alter ego) selfobject, the adversarial selfobject, the efficacy selfobject, and so on. They serve different functions and take on different dimensions, but they are unified in their role in enhancing integration: bolstering the structure of the self.

The Mirroring Selfobject

No selfobject, however, is more primary that that of the *mirroring* selfobject. The self psychology theory of normal child development (Shapiro, 1995) highlights the normal developmental process in which all children need validation and acknowledgment from parental figures. The content of the needs is different at different developmental stages, but the process is the same: the parental figures serve as the mirroring selfobjects. Over time, if the child experiences a primary pattern of these positive interactions, the child develops the capacity to feel noticed, valuable, and worthy. He develops a structure for taking realistic pride and pleasure in his accomplishments. Most importantly, he is more likely to genuinely believe that his "self" is valuable.

This represents a fundamental process that takes place for all of us in any meaningful relationship in our lives. We look to the response from the other person and observe his or her reaction. Does he smile when he sees me? Does she look interested? Did they laugh at my joke? Did he even notice I was here? Is the class paying attention to what I am saying? If we read the response as essentially positive, then a positive mirroring experience has taken place. This mirror reflects back a picture to the individual that he is noticed, valued, or confirmed.

Good-enough levels of mirroring selfobject experiences enhance the development of *self-cohesion*: feeling solid, together, whole, confident, integrated. This need for self-cohesion is primary and when self-cohesion disintegrates, the individual experiences a state known as *fragmen-*

tation. Its origins lie in the original needs between the young child and the most central attachment figure, usually the mother. The child has a compelling need to look into the face of his mother and see, reflected back to him, eyes that say "You are wonderful" and a smile that says "You make me happy."

When a child looks into these eyes, he sees reflected back to him a loving and approving mirror. His basic sense of himself is deeply validated. He feels alive and worthy. Similarly, when an adult looks into the eyes of his or her partner and sees reflected back a look of love and delight and profound respect, he or she likewise feels alive and worthy.

This is the magic mirror: the mirroring selfobject.

This process is, of course, not fundamentally any different for women than it is for men. It's just that men are typically less aware of how powerful these needs are and more likely to withdraw or act out when the needs are not met. And men ascribe a special power to the women in their lives to validate their self-worth.

Broken Mirrors

Often, children are deprived of these essential mirroring responses. They are not recognized by the key figures in their lives, they are abused by them, or they are simply ignored or abandoned by them. Often, children are subjected to criticism and ridicule for their efforts to achieve or simply for their existence. This leads to a developmental arrest in confidence, competence, self-worth, and trust of the interpersonal environment.

A child's mirroring figures, as we all know rather too well, may be quite fragmented or overwhelmed themselves and have little capacity to offer the loving and confidence-enhancing reflection that the child desperately requires. Or, in some cases, there is a mismatch between child and mirror-figure such that the child eternally feels a lack of understanding, a dearth of genuine appreciation, and a fundamental gap in attunement.

Even in the best of situations, the mirroring can be experienced as incomplete. The child thus develops gaps in his sense of self. He mistrusts and disrespects his own internal signals and states, and he doubts his own self-worth and competence. He desperately turns elsewhere for validation and he becomes excessively sensitized to signals that might suggest that he is unappreciated, unneeded, or unsuccessful.

What does this lead to in adulthood? All adults seek validation and mirroring; this is a basic human longing. But the adults who, as children, experienced more significant mirroring deficits are always looking to some outside source of approval or recognition or validation. The adult psychological crisis is that no mother, no father, no teacher, no coach, and no therapist ever provides the perfect mirror. Not even a lover can do it.

Some disappointment like this is inevitable in the course of human relationships and the recognition of limits. The problem with a man who does not handle this experience successfully in his relationships is that he has mistaken the flood of good feelings that comes from a close relationship with a promise that the good mirror will always reflect back to him what he needs to see. So, in his eyes, the mirror breaks, his sense of self shatters, and he blames the mirror. Stosny (Stosny, 1995) describes these men as "attachment abusers." When they see reflected back to them an image that makes them feel unlovable or inadequate, they feel ashamed. They blame the mirror for the reflection. And, depending on their personal history, social training, and individual constitution, they act out: some by direct aggression, others by passive-aggressive behavior, some by intense withdrawal, and others by abusing alcohol or drugs, or seeking love elsewhere. Some just slowly shut down and seal themselves up.

Why would a man blame his partner because he feels bad? *Because she promised. She promised to fill up the empty spaces inside me till death do us part. It says so in our marriage contract somewhere!*

White and Weiner (1986) offer a valuable description from the self-psychological perspective of the experience of the abusive parent. They identify the narcissistic rage that stems from the parent's inability to make the child react as if the child were part of the parent's self and this absolutely knew what was wanted. So long as a child offers the narcissistic supplies for the parent, the parent's self-esteem is maintained and the system works. When the applause fails, the narcissistic rage erupts along with an inner experience of a fragmenting self. The "broken mirror-sensitive" adult needs others around him to function as selfobjects and help maintain his psychological equilibrium. He needs to feel respected, confirmed, validated, stimulated, and sometimes obeyed. It is the selfobject's job to make him feel worthwhile; when he does not see that positive reflection in the interpersonal mirror, he is left feeling vulnerable, helpless, and sometimes outraged.

The Power of Women

Kohut (1984) suggested that individuals with empty, depressive core selves depend on their relationship partners to shore up their vulnerable psyches; a partner's threat to leave the relationship is thus terrifying because of the unconscious fear of the deeply buried psychic pain the relationship has assuaged. The actual experience of feeling this pain ("fragmentation") can manifest as depression or as rage.

Even for a man who doesn't have an especially empty or depressive core self, the reflection offered by women as the mirrors in his life are especially powerful. He may find that he craves mirroring and affirmation from her. He may be extrasensitized, over the course of his relationship, to the ways that he and his wife and the life they have together have not sufficiently made up for gaps in his self-confidence or emotional well-being. He relies on her and on the relationship, as a selfobject, to compensate in some way for something he never quite fully received or a process that never feels quite complete.

When his partner seems (and the key word here is "seems") more interested in talking to her sister than to him or when their sex life wanes, he may become mildly depressed, his sense of self mildly fragmented. The glow from the positive mirroring selfobject has started to fade. When these responses are not forthcoming, he may start to feel dents in his sense of self-worth, self-esteem, or personal value.

Or, as my therapist once said to me: "You're still hoping for some repair and fulfillment of the emotions you have missed in your development, so when this fulfillment is missing in 'normal' ways from your adult life you overreact." I hated it when he told me that.

Pleck (1980) describes *masculinity-validating* power. Men often project this enormous mirroring power on women to remind them of their fundamental masculinity and masculine self-worth. In many situations, when a woman refuses to offer this validation, or when a man's unrealistic expectations and subsequent distortions convince him that she is withholding this validation, the man may feel fragmented and lost. He feels as if he has no reasonable psychological way to survive—other than desperately demanding the restoration of his virility, masculinity, self-worth, and ultimately self-cohesion by the powerful confirming source.

Dr. Alfredo Mirande, professor at the University of California–Riverside, tells a personal story about the power of women to shape men's views of themselves. "It is women who teach us to be men. They play a defining role in our development as men. When I was a child, I watched one time as my uncle was pushing around and threatening his wife. My mother, his sister, said to him, 'How can you call yourself a man if you beat up defenseless women?' My uncle was completely humiliated—she was calling him on his manhood. Women have this power. This had a profound effect on my masculine development" (Mirande, 2003).

Again, remember that men wrapped up in these interpersonal dynamics have made an unconscious decision to offer this power to women. These are not, for the most part, powers that women wish to hold. These are powers that men have projected onto them.

Some of this is extremely normal. No one ever escapes the need for positive mirroring, nor is this a desired goal or criterion for psychological maturity. But some people (for our purposes here, many men) have projected extensive needs onto their partners to offer this steady flow of positive mirroring, with little room for the inevitable gaps and depletions in this experience. This is especially true if, as a boy growing up, the man does not get "anointed" or fundamentally confirmed by his father. Then they get their sense of manhood only by affirmation from women (Pittman, 2003).

Author Terrence Real explained it like this: "When a covertly depressed man's connection to the object of his addiction is undisturbed, he feels good about himself. But when connection to the object is disrupted . . . his sense of self-worth plummets, and his hidden depression begins to unfold. . . . The difference between the normal and the addictive use of these substances or activities is the difference between enhancing an already adequate sense of self-esteem and desperately propping up an inadequate one" (1998, p. 60).

I was once interviewed on a radio show about one of my books and talked about these themes. After the interview was over, the male interviewer (off-air) said to me: "Damn! Now I get what happened to me yesterday! I came out of the bathroom after shaving and I had nicked myself a little on the cheek. My girlfriend looked up at me and said 'What happened to you? That's the second time you've done that this week' and I just went off. I started yelling at her, and then I stormed off, and our plans for the day were ruined. And it was all because I had a manhood attack, and I let what she said to me determine my sense of competence. I know she didn't mean anything like that, but that's what I heard. What the hell's wrong with me?"

What was wrong with this man is that he had been cut by the fragmenting pieces of his own crashing mirror. His girlfriend's comments felt like a stab at his own masculinity, as if she were saying to him, *What kind of loser are you that you can't even shave properly? Any man should be able to pull that off!* when, at worst, she was being a little critical. And at best, she was just pointing it out to him or affectionately teasing him. But to a guy whose self-esteem (particularly his masculine self-esteem) feels vulnerable (applicable to practically all men), this simple interchange can be perceived as an unbearable assault and threat. So he has to react, and reacting badly is usually the outcome.

Perhaps the most important thing to understand about relying on women in this way is how easily a man can misread his own inner experience. He may feel hurt—and then confuse this by ascribing intention to his partner *as if she meant to hurt him*. Sometimes, in some relationships, that might actually be true, but in most relationships it is not. He may have developed a dark view of his partner and others because he feels bad inside and seeks more mirroring and confirmation from the outside. That's the depressive self talking. The more depressed he is or the more empty he feels, the more susceptible he is to turning to his partner to fill him up. She may do everything "right" (or at least with good intentions) and he still may feel like the glass is half-empty or worse.

If he has been shortchanged in the positive mirroring department growing up, or if he is plagued with self-doubts, or if he is strongly attached to maintaining a strong masculine self-image, then he is especially likely to turn to his most intimate and trusted partner and crave the positive mirroring.

Faced with these emotions and these needs, a man can have a hard time admitting how emotionally dependent he is on his partner. He probably doesn't have as many close friends as she does, and so he looks to her to be his primary anchor. Women are often oblivious to this because a man who feels neglected doesn't often state it directly—he is more likely to deny it, escape from the feelings associated with it, or blame her for how he feels. None of these opens the door for resolution and integration of these complex needs.

In the course of many relationships, men become frustrated because their female partner is less interested in sex than they are. Often, we find that women tend to view the sexual desire of their husbands as a purely physical demand, without understanding how important sex is to men on other levels. When it comes to the psychological meaning of sex in a relationship, it is vital to recognize that there is no greater turn-on for most men than feeling deeply desired and arousing deep passion in their partner. Why? Because it is a mirror, a mirror that reflects back a picture of this man as being desirable. We, men and women both, need to remember that "what a man is looking for is the reciprocal experience of desire" (Epstein, 2005, p. 216). It's not just the passion. It's not just the fascination with the female body. It's not just the touching and connection. It is, for so many men, the profoundly deep, rich, and affirming experience of being desired. Unless the man is a psychopath or otherwise deeply pathological (and thus might get off simply by dominating a woman or experiencing personal pleasure), he is searching for that "look of love."

This does not suggest that women owe sex to men. It does suggest that women owe men, and men owe themselves, an understanding of what is at stake.

By itself, this is not a bad thing, nor is it doomed to failure or disappointment. We all need this. But some people are better at putting this in perspective and tolerating the inevitable disappointments and the inevitable imperfections of this search. In fact, when men get this concept, they often realize that having hot sex and experiencing her intense sexual desire and passion is not even required. It can be enough just for her to laugh at his jokes and respect his integrity or skills as a father.

The Broken Mirror Sequence Step 1: The Trigger Event

The broken mirror sequence is one of the most profound and powerful ways to make sense of the vulnerability of the men in our lives. Understanding this sequence gives us a clear map for how, when, where, and why so many men fail at essential relationship challenges. When these are small failures, we call them glitches or issues. When they are huge failures, we call them pathological or dysfunctional.

If a man behaves badly or simply cluelessly in a relationship, it is typically the case that he has experienced a narcissistic injury or mirroring breakdown preceding this outbreak. Something has gone wrong. His feelings have been hurt. He feels incompetent. His self-esteem has been diminished. He feels unimportant, or devalued, or disregarded, or rejected, or powerless, or helpless. These emotional states challenge his sense of masculinity. He enters a mood that, if left unchecked, leads him unconsciously down a slippery slope of toxic self-talk, dysphoric emotions, and dysfunctional behaviors.

Our contemporary understanding of male psychology helps us identify five stages in the broken mirror sequence. And it also offers us five different entry points to intervene, teach, and counsel; a successful intervention at any of these five points can make a profound influence in a man's life and in the lives of those closest to him. It can help bring out the best qualities in men, rather than hiding them behind fears, vulnerabilities, and defenses.

Various acting-out behaviors reflecting this fragmentation are at risk here: gambling, substance abuse, reckless sexual behavior, aggression, impulsive actions, workaholism; or simply pouting, emotional shut-down, avoidance of intimate relationships, sarcasm, or passive-aggressive behavior.

The trigger event in the broken mirror sequence is sometimes bold and blatant and likely to feel provocative to almost anyone. Other times, it appears (to the outside observer) to be a benign, only mildly negative, or actually even a positive event in that man's world. Idiosyncratic trigger behaviors can function as disinhibitors, thus "allowing" a man to say or do something that is not normally part of his behavioral pattern or values.

The wide variety of triggers have one kindred component: somehow, they lead to the man feeling diminished, anxious, powerless, frustrated, inadequate, incompetent, devalued, disregarded, ashamed, humiliated, hopeless, or unlovable.

One classic category of trigger is situational. Put a man in a situation where he does not feel successful, or where he observes others to whom he compares himself as lacking, and a broken mirror sequence may be launched. This could be observing another man's car or muscles, seeing other kids behaving better than his own at a birthday party, or recognizing that he is not successfully communicating to his wife in the way she needs him to, or when a man has a sexual performance crisis.

Some situational triggers are only relevant, or are exacerbated, depending on the audience. I could usually tolerate my kids' moderately rude treatment of me in private, but knowing that others were observing this "humiliation" in public would serve as a broken mirror and bring out the beast in me.

Another typical set of triggers involves key loaded language. A woman tells her boyfriend that "you're a lazy asshole just like your father." A teenage daughter tells her father that he is lame. Or, as in the movie *Back to the Future*, a man is called "chicken."

Sometimes the actual content of the trigger is astonishing until you hear the detailed description of what it meant to the individual. The following example may seem almost comical, but it reflects a desperate and vulnerable man. You need to know two facts to understand this outburst from Carlo: Carlo's wife was very attached to her pet parrot, and she had been trimming Carlo's hair throughout their marriage. Carlo, a handsome, balding man in his 50s, sat quietly in my office while he listened to his wife's complaints about their marriage. He stared her down without saying anything. He idly inspected his fingernails while she tried to get through to him. Finally, he decided to air his grievances and feelings toward her. Carlo began, "You offered to trim my hair, but you always forget to trim my ear hairs. What underlying psychological message are you trying to express? You groom that friggin' bird much better than you groom me. It's almost like you are mated to him. You're right—at first when we thought the parrot was a female, it didn't bother me so much. Then we find out it's a male, and it's like you have more of a bond with this male than with me!"

The broken mirror sequence was launched. What was the trigger? The wife's attachment and affection for her bird. Carlo actually felt threatened and displaced by his wife's attachment to her parrot, especially because it was male. It doesn't even take something obvious, like a man's wife taking on a lover. The smallest everyday events, when meaning is attached, can be powerful broken mirrors.

The Broken Mirror Sequence Part 2: The Wrong Story

As is clearly illustrated by Carlo, it's all about the story. In the end, events are just events. They become meaningful only when we try to make sense of them. Our brains are wired to create stories about what we experience, and these stories are the most powerful determinants of all that follows.

Famed psychologist Dr. Donald Meichenbaum so aptly described the fundamental task of therapeutic intervention: "We are in the business of *constructive narrative repair*" (Meichenbaum, 2001b).

The Secret, Silent Decision: Attributing Hostile Intent

The relationships we are in are governed by the stories we tell ourselves about them. When we are emotionally attached to people, and they really mean something to us, we make decisions about who they are and where we stand with them. We do this with our husbands and wives, girlfriends and boyfriends, parents and kids.

Men who seem to be most successful and most positively attached in these most intimate relationships are those who are telling themselves a story of their "others" that is essentially positive, hopeful, and compassionate, not perfect, but still fundamentally positive.

When men are not able to do this, the "others" suffer. When a man tells himself that his partner is fundamentally selfish or untrustworthy, or that his kids are purposely trying to make him feel impotent and unsuccessful, it sets the stage for everything from defensiveness to emotional withdrawal to passive-aggressive behavior to downright nastiness and even abuse.

Psychologist John Gottman referred to this as the "secret, silent decision" in which couples turn against or toward their partner. Once the decision has soured someone toward the other, he or she withdraws—and the person feels quite justified in behaving badly toward someone who (or so it seems) has been, is now, and will be behaving badly toward him or her. This story serves as the ultimate disinhibitor that can unleash destructive dysfunctional behavior in a relationship that might not otherwise emerge (Gottman, 2003a).

Sometimes these stories meet the litmus test of accuracy, and there is no reasonable alternative but for a man to tell himself this story of doubt, mistrust, and resentment. But, on many, many occasions, there are other stories that could be told, stories that fit better and lead to better outcomes. When the new stories are in place, new behaviors easily emerge that save broken repair relationships and further enhance the already good ones.

Misattribution (a flawed description of why behavior is occurring) research is especially valuable in identifying the impact of the personal narrative. As good researchers often do, Holtzworth-Munroe and Hutchinson (1993) quantified a phenomenon that most of us would have guessed to be true: a man who abuses his wife is much more likely to attribute the most negative intentions to her behavior. One of the most illuminating vignettes in the study involved a wife talking to another man at a party. Another involved a wife who was not interested in sex on a particular night. Consistently, abusive men were much more likely to be convinced that the woman was *trying* to make the man angry, hurt his feelings, put him down, get something for herself, or pick a fight. Furthermore, situations which activated the men's perception of abandonment or rejection were likely to generate dysfunctional, destructive, and distancing behavior—up to and including abuse.

All narcissistic injuries are strictly governed by the cognitive interpretation of the event. A nonabusive husband might interpret the same situation in a different, more benign way. If his wife were spending a lot of time talking to another man at a party, he might be a little irritated at her, or he might make nothing of it, or he might actually feel pleased that she was attractive and popular and having a good time.

In the classic opera by the same name, Otello starts to think of Desdemona as someone who is untrustworthy—and then everything she does (the missing handkerchief, the fragments of Cassio's conversation) just further serves to confirm what he has come to believe about her. There is no possibility of doubt; he cuts her no slack. There is no room for his perceptual error or her human error of imperfection.

In a fascinating Indiana University study focusing on men's empathic accuracy for females, researchers focused on the correlation between men's empathic accuracy and male abusive behaviors (Clements, Holtzworth-Munroe, Schweinle, & Ickes, 2007). Empathic accuracy means that the individual reads the other person's emotional state reasonably accurately—an unquestionably positive characteristic contributing to emotional intelligence and positive relationships. The research team also looked at the differences in men's empathic accuracy for strangers versus intimate partners.

Previous research by this team found that abusive husbands had deficits in accurately interpreting various types of wife thoughts and feelings, were more likely to attribute hostile intent to wife behaviors, and reported higher anger in response to the same partner behaviors.

McFall's (1982) model of social information processing identified three stages from event to action: *decoding*, *decision-making*, and *enactment* phases. The Indiana University findings have everything to do with the *decoding* stage: perceiving and interpreting incoming social stimuli.

In this study, the researchers found that abusive men reacted with defensiveness and hostility in response not only to aggressive wife behavior, but also to distressed and even facilitative statements. They did not discriminate between various types of wife behavior but rather were responding negatively to almost anything their wives said.

They were plagued with the curse of "attributing hostile intent."

Amazingly, in this study, the more abusive men were actually much more successful at empathic accuracy with women they didn't know: They were worse at inferring their female partners' thoughts and feelings than they were at inferring the thoughts and feelings of female strangers. This speaks to the emotional complexity of intimacy, especially for men who are less attuned to their own emotional states and needs. When the stresses and threats of attachment are activated, it is much more likely for many men to misread and misattribute because of their own emotional activation. In these emotionally charged, intimacy-generated, attachment-complicated states, they activate the wrong (and usually toxic) story that leads them to emotional distress and behavioral retaliation. The story launches all.

Gottman (1999) identified a pattern in successful couples in which men were much more likely to perceive complaints, suggestions, and even demands from their female partners as attempts to "influence" them—instead of the more typical male reaction (in dysfunctional and unsuccessful couples) that women are "so damn controlling." He found that men in successful relationships activated narratives that did not generate the broken mirror sequence and did not generate a profound suspiciousness or resentment of the partner. They could see past some of the negativity in the message and recognize the fundamentally positive intent of their partner.

In contrast, my client Jackie described his wife this way: *She's always gonna be the judge and jury about whether what I'm doing is good enough!* I had met his wife, and she was in the normal range of giving feedback and complaining in this relationship. Jackie could only hear it, however, as judge and jury. Jackie also told me: *I feel like she wants a straight gay man. I suppose I could be more like a girl.* His wrong story here: If my wife wants me to communicate more and listen to her better, she must be trying to emasculate me.

Emotional Reasoning

Emotional reasoning is a term used in cognitive therapy to describe the false conclusion that just because you feel something, then it must be true:

> *I feel guilty, so I must have done soothing wrong.*
> *I feel lonely, so it must be true that nobody cares about me.*

The reality, of course, is that sometimes our feelings serve as very accurate barometers of what is happening in our lives or how another person is treating us. And often they don't. The irrational beliefs associated with emotional reasoning often reflect empathic accuracy deficits.

This is particularly evident for men who "feel" hurt or betrayed or rejected or neglected or offended. Their emotional reasoning leads them to conclude: *Since I feel hurt, she must have been trying to hurt me!* Sometimes yes, often no. Everybody gets hurt, even in the best of relationships. Everyone feels disappointed and let down. Everyone feels deprived of attention. It doesn't necessarily mean that this was intended or that this represents a profound character flaw in the other person.

My client Richard put it that way: *When I can't get through to Sarah and she gets that hurt and scared look in her eyes, I feel really bad about myself. It's a broken mirror. I feel helpless and powerless. And I get convinced that since I feel this way, she must have been intending to make me feel this way. How could it possibly be any other way?*

Another client, Rocket (a perfect name for someone with an explosive personality, if I have ever heard one), had a history of substance abuse, stealing, manipulation of those closest to him, and failure at practically everything he ever tried to do. When he asked his parents for money—again—to help him pay for a new apartment, they refused, because they had been burned so many times before when they had given him things, and they had made a well-thought-out decision to no longer support him in this way.

Rocket whined and complained to his sister: *I'm sorry I made some mistakes, but I am sick of being punished for them!*

The reality is that Rocket *feels* punished. This is valuable information for him to understand himself and his own psychology. But it does not necessarily follow that because he *feels* punished that he actually is *being* punished. It just means, simply, that he has a feeling. He needs to be open to the possibility that he perceives every situation in which someone does not conform to what he wants from them as a form of punishment. And while this may sometimes be true, it usually is not.

Another example, a very common one, takes place in the bedroom: Jacob approaches Rosa for lovemaking. Rosa is not interested. Jacob is hurt and, because he feels hurt, he concludes that she must have been *trying* to hurt him. And, from his emotional center of hurt, he lashes out at her, because he used *emotional reasoning* and misread his wife's needs and motivations.

Overanticipating Broken Mirrors

Another pattern of creating the wrong story that leads to the broken mirror experience involves the anticipation of a broken mirror. Many people are convinced that a situation will lead to getting a negative response—usually in the absence of legitimate evidence that this is certain—and work up a head of steam, fueled by hurt and hostility, in response to a reaction that has not even taken place.

My client Jim told me about how he was struggling to lose weight. He had promised his fiancée he would lose weight before their wedding: *You know I have always struggled with overeating. Well, as Janice and I have gotten closer and we are actually talking about setting a wedding date, I have started up again. Then I get mad at myself about my eating and get really irritable with her. Part of it was that I just didn't like myself and I don't act well when I don't like myself. But it was also the old hedge-clippers story.*

I asked him what he was talking about: *What's the hedge-clippers story?*

You know, this guy in the suburbs wants to clip his hedges, but he doesn't own a pair of hedge-clippers. He knows that his next-door neighbor does, so he decides to go over and ask to borrow them. But on the way there he starts remembering that he had recently borrowed a power drill from the same neighbor and it had taken him a few days to return it. And he started thinking that his neighbor was probably a little irritated that it took a few days to get his drill back. And that he would probably resent being asked to loan out another tool. And that he probably didn't even want to see his face ever again. So he walks up to the door, knocks loudly, the neighbor opens up and greets him with a warm smile. And the guy screams out at him, "You can keep your damned hedge-clippers!"

That's me. Always anticipating that the neighbor will reject me, so I go on the offensive.

The other part of this is that I've always felt like I was selling Janice a bill of goods, that I'm nowhere near as well put together as she thinks I am. It's only a matter of time.

Another example of this is comically evident in one of Groucho Marx's famous songs from his movie *Duck Soup* (McCarey, 1933). Groucho plays the role of Rufus T. Firefly, ruler of the country of Freedonia, and he awaits the arrival of Ambassador Trentino of rival Sylvania. He hopes to make peace between the two countries, but he starts to anticipate that the ambassador might refuse his gesture of goodwill. Then he will feel snubbed. He tells himself (in song) that the ambassador must be a "hyena" and a "cheap four-flushing swine." So when the ambassador finally enters the room, Rufus says to him: *So, you refuse to shake hands with me, eh?* followed by *This means war!*

The Narrative of Shame and Blame: Fragmentation and Dysphoria

Men who have been exposed to shame will do anything to avoid it in the future (Dutton, 1998). The shamed boy becomes a hypersensitive man, whose radar is finely tuned to the possibility of humiliation. His reaction to perceived or real slights, and his desperate attempts to ward these off, represent a kind of phobia. Tragically, the very men who are especially desperate for affection and approval cannot ask for it, and they project blame and perceive the worst in others Sometimes the smallest signs of withdrawal of affection will activate their old wounds, and they will lash out at the perceived source of this new wound. In classic normative male alexithymia fashion, they can describe none of these feelings, and they usually are in the dark about where these reactions come from.

We have come to call this condition *shame-o-phobia*.

Men who have been repeatedly shamed about their emotional states and genuine needs turn to various forms of "addictive" behavioral patterns to escape the intolerable negative emotions. Terrence Real (1998) identifies the source of this condition as "the loss of the relational...that wound in boys' lives that sets up their vulnerability to depression as men" (p. 137). This relational impoverishment is the source of the feelings of shame, worthlessness, and emptiness that haunt many men.

One factor that engenders the development of shame-o-phobia is evident in the toughening-up process that boys undergo as they traverse the developmental stages of growing up male. Many fathers withhold from their sons or directly inflict emotional or physical abuse in the name of making a man out of them. Football coaches humiliate teenagers with the justification *He's got to learn how to take it*. Boys hear, in countless ways, the message that it is not acceptable for them to show weakness or worry, or even to care too much.

Of course girls are sensitive to shame, but boys are mortified by it. And boys and men will do whatever it takes to avoid, escape, deny, and mask shame. This is one of the central components in the broken mirror sequence, governing the stories that men tell themselves about who they are, how they are seen by others, and what is expected of them. This often is a trigger for good men behaving badly, leading to impulsive actions, escapist behavior, aggression, projection of blame, emotional withdrawal, relationship avoidance, desperate acts of bravado—anything to turn off the spigot of shame.

When the story goes wrong, bad things happen.

Some of these shame stories develop as a direct result of masculine gender socialization, when men have come to believe that enacting their gender role requires them to behave decisively and competitively, to develop strategies for power and control over others, and to curtail expressions of emotionality except for anger (Levant et al., 1992). So often, we see men who evaluate a situation as a measure of their masculinity (Levant & Fischer, 1996), especially if they *perceive* the situation to represent competition, self-reliance, or physical strength and endurance in which they expect to excel or to be dominant (Eisler, 1995; Pleck, 1981).

A series of studies testing how long, and under what conditions, men would keep their hands in ice water (cold pressor task) illustrates these points (Lash & Eisler, 1995; Lash, Gillespie, Eisler, & Southard, 1991). In these studies, men were randomly assigned to groups in which they were given different instructions about the task. Some were given "masculine gender relevant" instructions: How long they kept a hand in ice water was allegedly related to high levels of male sex hormones and an index of physical fitness. Some were given "neutral" instructions: Immersing a hand in ice water would allegedly allow the experimenters to obtain physiological measures of responses to cold water. And still others were given "feminine gender relevant" information about the task: How long they kept a hand in ice water was allegedly related to high levels of female sex hormones and to women's ability to bond with their children.

Results showed that under masculine gender relevant information, men kept a hand in ice water longer, showed greater cardiovascular reactivity, and reported greater performance expectations than they did under gender neutral or feminine relevant information. What does this tell us? How long a guy will suffer through keeping his hand in painful ice water is directly dependent on his appraisal of the task as relevant or irrelevant to his masculinity ideology!

This is where the problem lies: the distorted appraisal of situations as being masculine gender relevant. A man's masculinity becomes at stake here—because he is hypersensitive to the possibility of being shamed or "dissed." So the template that he uses to make sense of these interpersonal situations is severely colored by these expectations. If he defines everything as being gender-relevant, or pride-relevant, or as a potential broken mirror, then he will inevitably encounter many, many situations that threaten him. And he will be forced to withdraw (flight) or react (fight), or sometimes just freeze.

The Independent Center of Initiative

The antidote to the broken mirror story narrative lies in the capacity to recognize the other person's *independent center of initiative*. This is a concept developed from self psychology theory that identifies the process by which each individual makes personal decisions governed primarily by positive striving toward self-cohesion and competence—only secondarily by the needs of others, influences of others, or recognition by others (Basch, 1980). In other words, in most situations the other person has his or her own independent reasons for making a decision—reasons that have nothing to do with the man! They may affect him, but they are not *about* him.

The ability to activate an awareness of the other's *independent center of initiative* requires the capacity for *mentalization* (Fonagy, Gergely, Jurist, & Target, 2002): interpreting and responding to the behavior of others in terms of being attuned to their mental states, such as desires, needs, feelings, and beliefs. A person who can mentalize shows the ability to treat others as persons rather than objects.

We might also describe this process of *mentalization* when activating awareness of the *independent center of initiative* as empathy, insight, employing an observing ego, attunement, emotional intelligence, de-centering, psychological-mindedness, and so on. As psychiatrist Frank Pittman put it: "Intimacy means being able to read somebody else's mind" (Pittman, 2003).

The Broken Mirror Sequence Step 3: Normative Male Alexithymia

The next step in the broken mirror sequence involves *normative male alexithymia*, as described in Chapter 1. A man observes an event. He filters it through the wrong story. Then he experiences a set of emotions that he is either not very familiar with or finds totally unacceptable—or both.

This is a handicap. A man may be criticized by his wife, and he experiences this as especially shameful because it activates his history of being made to feel inadequate by his father. Most likely, the correct label for this emotional state is anxiety or insecurity. But this man may not have a well-developed emotional vocabulary. He may only have a vague recognition of dysphoric and agitated affect.

Consider this pattern in a man who came to see me a few years ago: Lewis was a good man who struggled with his moods. He would feel bad inside and, frustrated by his inability to understand what was happening to him and certainly frustrated with his inability to express it to his wife, would take it out on her. He would withdraw. He would get quietly critical. He would get that "look" that told her and the kids to stay away from the wounded bear. Finally, on an extended work assignment, he had an affair, which offered him a sense of vitality and excitement that he was missing in his regular life. The affair was exposed (he unconsciously set himself up to be caught) and the couple entered my office in the postaffair crisis.

In addition to all the other work that was needed to repair the damage of the affair, we focused on Lewis's *normative male alexithymia*. Frequently, when Lewis was feeling worried or hurt or depressed, his wife, Christine, would read the mood and ask him what was wrong. His standard reply? *I feel tired*. Finally she got sick of it and told him she couldn't stand hearing that anymore. Christine told me that she had outlawed the sentence *I feel tired* in their household. Christine was not being controlling—she was just being a leader in changing this relationship.

To his credit, Lewis did not immediately become defensive, nor did he use this as further proof that Christine was a controlling female. He got better and better at allowing her to "influence" him. With the help of her intervention and our couples sessions, Lewis began to find labels for his feelings. I introduced him to some new vocabulary words so that he could talk like this:

> *I'm feeling burdened by the kids—I just end up feeling like I get no time for myself.*
> *I can't get these worries about work out of my head, and I need some time alone.*
> *I feel so frustrated trying to get Danny to listen to me—I never could talk back to my father the way we let him talk back to me!*

Until Lewis developed some emotional vocabulary and overcame some of his *normative male alexithymia*, he was handicapped. He was mislabeling his experience, leading to the next stage of the broken mirror sequence.

The Broken Mirror Sequence Step 4: Emotional Flooding

The next step in the broken mirror sequence involves the rush of confusing and unbearable affect that follows the event, the wrong story, and the lack of emotional vocabulary and self-awareness to make sense out of what is happening.

Emotional Overload

One of the physiological curses of being a guy is the susceptibility to experiencing emotional overload more quickly and more intensely than women do. Gottman's studies (1994) described an especially male phenomenon in relationships that he called *emotional flooding*. His research team carefully examined the behavioral, emotional, and psychophysiological reactions of both men and women as they discussed difficult subjects in their relationship. This research showed that men consistently became more physiologically aroused during these discussions than their female partners did. Even in what most of us would consider to be mild areas of relationship conflict, men were more likely to become flooded with emotional agitation than women. Specifically, men were much more likely to react to criticism from their partners with this level of arousal. At a neurochemical level, men secreted more adrenaline into the bloodstream, and it took less provocation (as measured by a team of observers) to get there. Even worse, the recovery period—the time it took them to return to their baseline levels of arousal—was longer for men than for women.

This flooding elicits threat and fear. And threat and fear elicits sympathetic nervous system arousal, which in turn activates flight, fight, or freeze.

Steven Stosny (2001) illustrated what happens to men (or women, for that matter) in the face of emotional flooding by comparing a parent's reaction to a screaming baby to the destructive outbursts that result from emotional overload in adult relationships. Parents are physiologically mobilized by the distress cry of an infant. The nervous system reacts so intensely that the individual must either go to the aid of the child or get out of earshot; it is nearly impossible just to sit still and listen. As the cries get more intense, and as the sense of powerlessness likewise gets more intense, the internal distress signals skyrocket.

Under the best of circumstances, a very adaptive system shifts into gear. The baby is distressed, the parent becomes alarmed and activated, the parent offers soothing, the baby responds, and all is well. In fact, the baby learns one more time that distress is transitory, that help is available, and that the world is ultimately a safe and loving place. And the parent feels pretty successful.

However, as every parent knows, when the parent can't get the job done and the child is inconsolable, the distress alarm in both the parent and child intensifies. The available resources rapidly dwindle. Any parent in this situation is at risk for desperately turning to whatever it takes to turn off the alarm relentlessly screaming in his or her ears and inside his or her nervous system. Stosny compares this to hearing an alarm clock blaring when you are half asleep, unsuccessfully trying to turn it off, and becoming so enraged that you just hurl it at the wall to shut the damn thing up.

This is not unlike the experience of many men who get so frustrated with the complaints and criticism of their wives and girlfriends that they say, *I'll do anything to make her shut up!*

In these states of emotional overload, a man's experience is often one of powerlessness and concomitant narrowed behavioral options. So he emotionally or physically withdraws. Or he freezes with the "deer in the headlights" look and tries to function. Or he belittles his partner when she tries to bring up difficult topics, desperately trying to keep away from subjects that will flood him.

A common complaint from women is that the man in their lives is not empathic and is too quick to problem-solve. A man who reflexively tries to give advice or problem-solve in response to his partner's concerns is subtly trying to "manage" the emotional input. If he tells her that this is not a good time to talk, he is often motivated by his anxiety about emotional overload and resultant destructive behavior. This is not necessarily dysfunctional; in fact, it is often very respectful of the relationship. But it is dysfunctional when a man employs it consistently, particularly to avoid the tough stuff that relationships require. The net result is that his relationship partner feels alone and abandoned. The partner often ends up feeling like she has to dance very carefully around his tender ego and delicate sense of self.

Real's (1998) "I-don't-want-to-talk-about-it" syndrome, from an emotional flooding perspective, can be understood as a behavioral strategy for a nervous system that is simply overloaded. What may appear to be emotional coldness or power and control tactics in a relationship can also be viewed as a nervous system screaming out, *No more!*

Emotional Hijacking by the Limbic System

It is only in the last few decades that advanced research on brain functioning has given us a clearer working model for how impulsive and aggressive behavior is generated. *Magnetic resonance imaging* (MRI), *positron emission tomography* (PET), and *computerized axial tomography* (CAT) scans show us what is taking place in the brain as humans engage in a wide variety of typical activities: working, playing, arguing, meditating, worrying, creating. Most importantly for our purposes, these brain studies may be giving us greater clues about the neurophysiological basis for empathy. Researchers have identified individual neurons that fire as we observe the activities of others, helping us interpret their actions and feelings.

The *amygdala*, a tiny almond-shaped structure in the primitive limbic system, functions like a security alarm in the home. It governs emotional reactions and is particularly sensitive to perceptions of threat. Situations that our brain perceives as emotional emergencies stimulate the signals to the amygdala. The amygdala scans the information for potential danger: *Is this threatening to me?* The amygdala is very dependent on associational patterns; if something about the current event is similar to an emotionally charged memory from the past, the limbic system is likely to be activated in full force.

Some key regions of the brain normally help to maturely process information (*decoding*) and generate responses (*decision making* and *enactment*). The hippocampus helps to process information and lends time and spatial context to memories of events. How well it functions determines the difference between normal and dysfunctional responses to threat and trauma. The hippocampus serves as a valuable transport system, transmitting key information to the cortex, where it's then possible to make sense of the situation.

The hippocampus, however, is highly vulnerable to the stress hormones that are released by the amygdala's alarm, particularly adrenaline and noradrenaline. When those hormones reach a high level, the hippocampus is short-circuited and shuts down. This is not a good thing. Information that could make it possible to determine the difference between a tiger's roar and the wind howling, or between a constructive criticism and a profound character assault, never reaches the cortex. The guy can't properly decode.

This helps explain why all of us are vulnerable to reacting poorly when we experience interpersonal threat. If a man's partner says or does something that telegraphs *She doesn't love me* or *She is disrespecting me* or *She might be leaving me*, signals are activated along a pathway that serves as an express route to the amygdala. Once he determines that a situation represents a threat, the amygdala lights up the entire brain and body before the neocortex ever gets into the act. The narrative, or interpretation of the event, is a crucial factor here, because once the event is experienced as threatening, the neocortex—home of all of the most advanced functions and cognitive capacities—is bypassed. In other words, the male brain is emotionally hijacked by the limbic system. Once the moment passes, many people have a sense of not knowing what came over them.

It makes sense, from an evolutionary perspective, that our brains and nervous systems are wired in this fashion. This is an essential system for survival. The trouble is that, especially when a man is reacting so quickly and the demands of the moment seem so urgent, he may not realize that what was once the case is no longer so. He has lost sense of context. His emotional brain fails to recognize the distinction between current event and past traumatic event—it reacts to the present as though the present were the past.

Unfortunately, in our modern age, we react to a vast array of symbolic threats to our self-esteem as if they were saber-toothed tigers outside our cave. Men in particular are threatened by being "dissed," controlled, or emasculated.

Another way to make sense of the especially potent cocktail that tends to flood men is by recognizing the chemical effects of stress on the brain. When a man is in this state of heightened arousal, it doesn't take much more to put him over the top. The chemicals released, known as *catecholamines*, provide the immediate surge. But all kinds of stress—especially relationship stress—create a more general adrenal and cortical stimulation which keeps people in a state of readiness, like a military on alert. Although it only lasts a few minutes, this surge is potentially volatile, and to defuse it he must discharge the tension or cognitively reappraise the situation.

This leads to a "meltdown." This state of disorganization and suspension of judgment is known as *fragmentation*. Decision-making is significantly impaired. All that matters is dealing with the immediate, desperate emotional state. When the limbic system dominates, the individual is governed by brain processes that do not take into account good values, good judgment, and projection of future consequences. Zillman's research (1979) indicates that this level of brain and nervous system excitation even creates a mania-like state of grandiosity, power, and invulnerability which makes aggressive behavior more likely.

Head injuries, which are statistically much more prevalent in men than in women, can seriously erode inhibitory controls. This is especially true with damage to frontotemporal areas (Fogel, 1992). The ability to develop complex plans is impaired. Furthermore, injuries to the brain can affect his ability to make sense of interpersonal situations, and to read cues and develop an appropriate response. A man with a history of head injury who also abuses alcohol or drugs is especially likely to have trouble with advanced neocortical functioning.

The Broken Mirror Sequence Step 5: The Action Orientation

Finally, the ultimate link in the chain of men's broken mirror sequence is the action that results from all this. We wouldn't be spending so much time reviewing this, nor would so much theory and research be focused on this—except that this behavioral outcome is usually not pretty, functional, or respective of self or others. Nor does it usually lead men to feel more fulfilled in their lives and in their most meaningful relationships.

The social information processing identifies this as the *decision-making* and *enactment* phases (preceded by the *decoding* phase that contributes, in this sequence, to the wrong story). Holtzworth-Munroe (2000) has identified a deficit among abusive men in the ability to generate a realistic range of possible responses to difficult or challenging life situations. For any man who struggles to respond well, abusive or not, this perspective tells us that a man who has run through the broken mirror sequence loses much of his ability to think clearly and to choose wisely.

Acting Out and Broken Mirrors

A breakdown in the mirroring experience can be the trigger for desperate and often destructive acts. Try thinking of this emotional injury in terms of the experience of parents who overreact to their kids (White & Weiner, 1986). The parent experiences an emotional injury. The father needs to be respected and obeyed and made to feel worthwhile; when he does not see that positive reflection in the interpersonal mirror, he is left feeling vulnerable, helpless, and outraged.

This is not just a phenomenon found in abusive or extreme fathers. The seeds of this pattern are much more universal. In Walter Mosley's novel *The Man in My Basement* (2004), the narrator describes this process:

> Clarence and I had had these fights for more than twenty-five years. I could still get to him. I regretted it every time. . . . He'd always been better than I had. He held a good job as the daytime dispatcher for a colored cab company. He was married, but he still had more girlfriends than I did. He read the newspaper every day and was always referring to events in the world to prove a point when we were discussing politics or current affairs. Even though I had made it through three years of college, Clarence always seemed to know more. . . . So I tortured Clarence now and then, angry at him for proving my inadequacies. (p.12)

An adult female client of mine told me the story of her father's aversion to attending any parent-teacher conferences when she was growing up: *He never came to any teacher conferences at my school. Well, actually he did once. I think I was in first grade. My teacher told him that I was sucking my thumb. He felt so ashamed he never went back. Never went to any other school event or conference. Not once. Never.*

For this father, the shame and powerlessness he experienced at this school conference was a kind of trauma. He lost his ability to generate different possible adaptive responses to this. And he resorted to one of the few available coping repines to trauma: flight. He paid the price by feeling bad about himself and unsuccessful, and his daughter paid the price by feeling unsupported and unloved.

A Preference for "Action"

Research tells us that boys prefer to *do* things, more so than girls do. They prefer *doing* over *being*. Studies observing children on playgrounds show that boys are often involved in competitive, active play within larger groups. Girls are frequently involved in smaller groups of more relational, cooperative play. These sex differences appear to persist into adulthood and are thought to reflect externalizing defense styles (Gjerde, Block, & Block, 1988), distracting response styles (Nolen-Hoeksema, 1990), or externalizing ego defenses (Levit, 1991).

This pattern continues into adulthood and (although, as with all generalizations, exceptions are rampant) boys and men appear to prefer more action-oriented means of problem solving. They want to fix things. They want to feel effective. This style is extremely adaptive when it comes to active problem-solving, a willingness to take risks to protect others, and a capacity for hard work—qualities that are often ascribed to men. This style is maladaptive when these same men reck-lessly engage in high-risk behavior, have difficulty just "being," use escapist behavior to avoid, or engage in acting-out behavior to deal with uncomfortable affect.

A central component of emotional intelligence rests on the capacity for *distress tolerance*. Marsha Linehan, in her development of dialectical behavior therapy, defined distress tolerance as "learning how to bear pain skillfully" (1993, p. 96). Borrowing from the wisdom of Zen

Buddhism, she advocated the development of mindfulness skills, including the nonjudgmental observation of one's present emotional motional state, however distressing it may be. This capacity to tolerate painful feelings is an essential ingredient in emotional intelligence, and a deficiency in this skill is depressiogenic and a predictor of relationship dysfunction. The difficulties that men have in tolerating affective distress predisposes them to the only available action-oriented set of alternatives: fight, flight, or freeze.

Chapter 3

Approaching the Unapproachable

Over the years, we in the field of counseling and psychotherapy have not done a particularly effective job of creating a user-friendly environment for the mental health needs of many men. There is a mismatch between the relational style of traditional men and the social environments of counseling and psychotherapy.

Only one-third of voluntary psychotherapy clients are men (Vessey, 1993). Either men have fewer psychological problems and thus need fewer services—or else many men are simply less comfortable seeking the services they need.

"The man . . . is usually there because he believes there is no alternative. Few men come for therapy because they subscribe to its life-enhancing qualities. Even if they did they would likely not see it as something for them anyway. Men are in therapy because something, internal or external, has driven them to it" (Scher, 1990, p. 323).

There are exceptions, of course: Plenty of men, just like women, seek counseling or therapy voluntarily because they are unhappy with some aspect of their internal or external life. More often, however, men enter some form of counseling environment (groups, individual, couples, psychoeducational workshops, substance abuse treatment, etc.) because someone else told them to. Sometimes the outside pressure comes from social institutions, as when men are ordered into treatment for domestic violence, parenting classes, sexual offender programs, or anger management programs. Other times men are pressured to seek services by their workplace, such as when they are required to attend sexual harassment counseling, a substance abuse program, or stress management. And, last but not least, many men are "ordered" into some form of treatment by the women in their lives. When I ask men who come in for an initial therapy session my standard question, "What are you doing here?" the answer I hear most often is, "My wife told me I needed to be here."

In our field, that leaves us with two choices: We can wait around until men get more comfortable with a process that has traditionally been more user-friendly for females, or we can do everything within our power to reshape what we do and how we present it to increase the likelihood of reaching our audience.

Approaching Resistant Men

In general, men go to therapy less often than women, and they have more negative attitudes toward all forms of counseling and treatment. If we define a phobia as an excessive fear of a particular event, then we can define many men as suffering from *counseling-o-phobia*.

Factors That Inhibit Male Help-Seeking

To actually make an effort to seek out or simply take advantage of the opportunity for counseling or therapy, a man must first recognize that something is wrong. Many men, largely because of normative male alexithymia, gaps in emotional intelligence, or just good old-fashioned denial and defensiveness, may not recognize that they have a problem at all.

Humorist Dave Barry captured this experience in the following conversation between male patient and doctor:

> Doctor: *So what seems to be the problem?*
> Patient: *Well, the main thing is, I keep coughing up blood. Plus I have these open sores all over my body. Also I have really severe chest pains and double vision, and from time to time these little worms burrow out of my skin.*

Doctor: *It's just a sprain.*
Patient: *That's what I thought.* (1995, p. 149)

Researchers on male help-seeking patterns often identify the following sequence: "(1) realizing there is a problem; (2) deciding that therapy would be an appropriate way to try to solve the problem; (3) deciding to seek therapy; and (4) making contact with the mental health system" (Saunders, 1993, p. 556). It is important to note that, based on this sequence, just because a man gets through step 1, the recognition phase, does not necessarily mean that he will choose the therapy route. And, of course, just because he sucks it up and decides to give therapeutic services a shot does not necessarily mean that he is going to stick with it.

Our job is to understand these roadblocks, which exist for so many men, and do our best to alter what we do or how we present it to make it more likely that men will benefit from what we have to offer.

A recent research study from the University of Utah (Noyes, 2007) came to some valuable conclusions based on interviews with men seeking therapy:

1. Making the decision to attend therapy was very difficult, and often involved years of thinking about going. The final decision to attend usually involved encouragement by some important other (friend, spouse, family) and an acceptance that their problem was serious enough to warrant attending therapy.

2. The men were surprisingly uninformed about the true nature of therapy, and the majority based their impressions solely on those they gathered from the media. They attempted to gain more knowledge by investigating therapy thoroughly ahead of time through the Internet, asking friends about therapy, or even interviewing therapists, but still had little understanding of what it would actually entail.

3. Even after deciding to attend, the amount of emotional energy it took to show up (especially for an initial session) for therapy was very high. Men reported being very anxious about attending and frequently considered not showing up. They were keenly aware of the physical location of the counseling center and who might see them going in.

4. The men in this study continued to feel conflicted about attending therapy after they had attended for several weeks, but also reported that they gained a lot from their experiences. They particularly noted positive relationships with their therapists as being crucial to their positive experiences.

5. Despite gaining something positive from therapy, many participants still indicated that they would prefer not to have to attend therapy again in the future. They said they would rather be able to take care of their problems on their own. However, they no longer felt that attending therapy was in general a bad thing.

One of the fears that many men have about even entering counseling or therapy involves *stigmatization*. The labels of "psycho" or "wacko" or "mental"—or simply "needy" or "dependent" or "unsuccessful"—are enough to keep plenty of men away from the doors of facilities that offer counseling services. There are gradations of stigma. It's tough enough for a guy to admit having a problem. Even if he recognizes that something is wrong, this man must admit that he needs help. It is difficult enough to get a man to ask for directions, let alone seek assistance for psychological or relational distress. Even reading a self-help book about the problem creates some stigmatization. If it's a relationship issue, entering couples counseling is difficult, but going into individual therapy is even more threatening: It means the problem is more likely to be within. And taking medication often elicits an even more intense level of stigmatization for being really "defective" in some way.

Furthermore, even if this man is able to deal with these issues and still seek help, he then must rely on a professional to help fix his problems. While there are certainly many men who are quite comfortable turning to a professional for advice in many situations, there are plenty of other men who perceive this help-seeking behavior as a sign of weakness, dependency, and inadequacy. The very structure of this relationship functions as a broken mirror: *If I am relying on someone else to fix me, I must be failing at some important life tasks.* When this broken mirror is activated, this man is likely to avoid putting himself into this position, thus avoiding activating the dreaded broken mirror.

Another common male fear is the *fear of being changed against his will* by the counselor or the self-exploration experience. Men often worry that some fundamental aspect of themselves will be stripped away. They often fear becoming indecisive or self-questioning to the point of behavioral paralysis. It's a manhood thing.

Still another inhibiting factor is the *fear of not being understood* by the counselor or therapist. We often hear reports that men feel like the counselor or therapist will not really "get" what their life experience is like. Men often fear that they will be shoved into some sort of diagnostic box, based on preconceptions of what relationships are supposed to be like. This apprehension is especially apparent among minority clients who suspect—often quite accurately—that their therapists are rather clueless about the world they grew up in or the world they currently inhabit.

One more issue often overlooked by even the most informed and experienced therapists: the *confusion and anxiety* many men have about how the strange and mysterious counseling process actually works. Many of the men whom I treat in individual, couples, or group settings are entering uncharted territory. They are anxious about what they should disclose. They are not sure what is being asked of them, and as a result they wish to avoid coming in in the first place or they are defensive and wary sitting in that environment. I understand what that is like. I always want to have very specific information or instructions about new settings or environments, ranging from new social situations to snowboarding. This is anxiety-reducing, and it is incumbent on those of us who treat men to anticipate this anxiety and provide as much up-front information as we can.

In the movie *Analyze This* (Ramis, 1999), starring Billy Crystal and Robert De Niro, there is a hilarious scene in which the mob boss (De Niro) arranges a meeting with the therapist (Crystal) because of his persistent panic attacks. During the course of this interview, the mob boss first asks about problems his "friend" is having and is offended—and threatening—when the therapist suggests that he is really talking about himself. He is offended when the therapist identifies the symptom cluster as signs of "panic attacks." He then asks a series of questions about how this is supposed to work: who talks first, where they each sit, and so on. He is sure that the therapist will not really be able to understand—and is enormously relieved when the therapist does. And the punch line of the scene is when the mob boss is leaving the "session" and tells the therapist: "If I talk to you and it turns me into a fag, I'll kill you. You understand? . . . You turn me into a fag, you die."

In this scene, we see it all: the *stigmatization*, the *fear of being changed against his will*, *fear of not being understood*, and the *confusion and anxiety* about how counseling works.

The episode "Counseling" from the TV sitcom *Everybody Loves Raymond* comically highlights some of these issues. Raymond's wife, Debra, insists that they go see a marriage counselor. Raymond protests. When she tells him that the marriage therapist is a woman, Raymond howls with protest: "And whose side do you think she's going to be on?" So she agrees that if it makes him more comfortable, they can go see a man. This triggers a new anxiety for him. He is convinced that his wife will find this man more appealing than she finds Raymond. He sarcastically mimics what his wife will say: "Oh, you understand me SOOOO much better than my husband does!" (Rosenthal, 2002).

There are threats everywhere, if you are looking for them.

Getting Men In the Door

If you, as a counselor or therapist, have the opportunity to try to frame a man's decision to try the counseling route, there are certain strategies that increase the likelihood of success. And the same is true if you are in the position of advising others in this man's life about how to present this. The framing of this plan must be profoundly respectful of the issues that men struggle with—yet still make clear how important this is.

Here are some guidelines that I usually offer to wives, partners, children, parents, friends, and employers of the man who (according to those of us who believe in the counseling experience) could really benefit from the service we offer (Wexler, 2006a):

1. *Remind him that nothing is permanent: I would at least like you to give this a fair shot. If we try this for awhile and it's getting nowhere, we can stop.*

2. *Make sure he has a reasonable amount of control over the situation:* (a) *I've got a list here of people who have been recommended to us. Do you think you would feel more comfortable going to see a male or female therapist?* or (b) *Let's try going in as a couple and see what the counselor recommends.* Plenty of men are much more amenable to entering relationship counseling because the meta-message is that the relationship needs fixing—not the individual.

3. *Be creative and respectful with what you call this: I heard about a counselor who specializes in coaching men dealing with family issues.* Because of the stigmatization issue, many men would never enter therapy but they would go for "coaching." Or stress management. Or relationship/parenting classes. Or education. Or a consultation. I see one couple where the man would never come in the door for marital therapy. He labels it a "marital tune-up." I have never really told him that the work we are doing in the "marital tune-up" is the same that we would be doing in marital therapy. It doesn't matter, as long he gets in the door and does the work.

4. *His partner can offer a reasonable quid pro quo: You've been wanting me to go to a football game with you for a long time. I promise to go to a game with you—with a good attitude—if you'll keep a good attitude about this.* One caution: don't let the quid pro quo include anything that you would find distasteful or degrading.

5. *His partner can reframe the problem as something that HE wants to see changed: You know how you've been wanting me to stay on our budget? That's one of the things we can work on in these counseling sessions.*

6. *His partner can appeal to his sense of commitment to his kids: The ways we have been fighting are really harmful to our kids, and I know how much you love them. I think we owe it to them to work these things out.* Some men feel too defensive, threatened, or angry to do this for their partners, but they can suck it up to do it for the sake of their kids.

7. *His partner can let him know how important this is to her: I know how much you try to please me and how much it means to you to see me happy. This is something that will really mean a lot to me.* Most men are very sensitized to the happiness levels of their partners, and for you to acknowledge this will help him feel valued.

8. *His partner can lay it on the line: I am at the end of my rope with our relationship. I desperately want this to work, but if you do not go into counseling with me I'm leaving.* Sometimes this is all the partner has left. She should not say this unless she absolutely has to, and she shouldn't say it unless she really means it.

These guidelines are all meant to communicate as much respect as possible for the man's autonomy, personal concerns, and inhibitions—again, without forsaking the mission: whatever it takes, within reason, to get him in the door.

Discomfort with the Counseling Experience

Once men get in the door into a counseling setting, plenty of them do just fine. But plenty of men struggle.

In his review of the literature, Ragle (1993) found male gender role issues set the stage for men to be "controlling of the therapy process, to compete with the therapist, to be emotionally restricted, to avoid help in subtle ways, to demand tangible outcomes, to find the intimacy of the therapeutic relationship confusing and anxiety-provoking, and to misperceive the therapeutic relationship as sexual" (1993, p. v).

It goes against male gender role norms to reveal information to others in a way that might put the man at a disadvantage. So the natural, culturally trained response for many men in this setting is to keep it superficial and keep it defended. Sometimes we see men in this situation who will talk, but only in intellectual rather than more vulnerable emotional terms. Or they may say words that seem to be on target, but the words lack congruent body language, tone of voice, or emotional expression. Or they just say it and keep it short and then embark on a tangent.

Often, therapists (and wives, partners, children, etc.) become frustrated with men who sit in the room and reveal little, if any, emotion. They may see these behaviors as resistance that needs to be overcome rather than as an expression of the conflicting nature of dependent urges toward the therapist and therapy. More than one therapist (and more than one wife or girlfriend) has overtly or covertly accused these men of being cold and uncaring.

While sometimes these labels may apply, most times they do not. Most often, there are other narratives for why we are getting such little emotional response (or at least verbal expression) from the man in the room (Wong, 2005).

Sometimes, this restrictive emotionality may simply be because this man unconsciously represses his emotions. I have observed men listening to intense anger or pain from their partners—and when I ask the men the standard question ("How does this make you feel?"), I get the blank response: "Fine."

"But don't you feel resentful or worried or sad?"

"No, I'm fine, I really am, it's good that she can express herself."

In this example, this man is not consciously lying or withholding. He really isn't consciously experiencing the emotions we would expect him to feel, and he is really telling the truth based on his conscious access to emotional states. This is a symptom of normative male alexithymia rather than coldness or being withholding.

Other men in the same situation don't respond effectively to the question because they are lacking the emotional vocabulary. They know they are feeling something, that much is clear. But they can't find the right label, and thus they choose to say nothing at all—for fear of saying the wrong thing, sounding stupid or inadequate, or failing at the task of being a 21st-century relationship partner. Again, this is a form of normative male alexithymia.

Another explanation for the lack of responsiveness for these men in the counseling setting is that they are holding back from expressing the emotions they feel because the emotions are associated with a perceived failure in their internalized notions of masculinity. The situational demand to be more open and vulnerable does not sit well with many men because of the masculinity traps and because of the politics of intimate relationships. They are afraid that they will appear weak and needy. They are concerned that they will be less attractive to their partner and others.

At least one more typical explanation exists: Some men feel their feelings, can properly label the feelings, do not have shame about the feelings—but may sense that expressing these feelings in this context is genuinely dangerous or not in their best interest. They have examined the social context as being unsafe for expression. Sometimes they are correct in this assessment: Showing vulnerability or self-doubt in the workplace may not be appropriate. And there are certainly some intimate relationships that (regardless of what people might consciously claim) are not genuinely emotionally safe for expressions of vulnerability.

In other words, plenty of men either are not aware of having feelings, do not know what they are feeling or how to name the feelings they are having, do not know how to share the feelings, are afraid to show their feelings for fear of vulnerability, or withhold expressing feelings because they perceive this to be unsafe.

Rules of Engagement: Guy Talk

Once you know the particular issues and defenses that affect men as they try to deal with the emotional demands of their relationships and meaningful life issues, it suddenly makes sense to use language and imagery that men are more likely to understand.

Male-Friendly Motivations

I find it particularly helpful to reframe the requests for new behavior from men with language and metaphors in ways the best of masculinity. This allows men to "feel like a man" and still branch out to new behaviors that are more pro-relationship and pro-mental health.

When I work with men to react more maturely and rationally in the face of relationship conflict, I will often frame for them what we are looking for: *We want you to really take charge. We want you be really powerful. Not over others, but over yourself. We want to make sure that the everyday crap that comes up for all of us does not control you or provoke you into reactions that are not good for you or the others around you. We want you to be in charge, not the stuff outside of you.*

The outstanding campaign by the National Institute of Mental Health (2003) on male depression highlights the following two phrases to appeal to men:

It takes courage to ask for help!
It takes brains to ask for help!

The Veterans Health Administration has recently begun distributing flyers, posters, and magnets that read: "It takes courage and strength of a warrior to ask for help . . . if you're in an emotional crisis call 1-800-xxx-xxxx."

When you put it like that, what man could resist? Who wouldn't want to be identified as a man of courage, a man of strength, or a man with brains?

I remember Michael, a man sitting in one of my men's groups, angry at his wife, blaming others, and generally rather embittered in a pattern so characteristic of male-type depression. Very few of my interventions or the group's interventions seemed to have much impact, until one of the group members struck gold by saying to him: *Dude—your kids need you to turn this around.* Suddenly Michael's face softened and his eyes welled up. He asked the intervening group member what he meant, and the group member told him straight out how he was blowing up his family with his negative and angry attitudes. Michael listened for the first time. Why? Because someone had used motivating language that struck a chord for him. The content of the message hadn't changed, but the same message that everyone had been trying get across to him now had a chance of getting through

Male-Friendly Language and Metaphors

As already described, men often feel stigmatized by the labels assigned in the mental health world. In 12-step models, people are pushed to take full responsibility for their problems in unequivocal fashion right from the start: *Hello, my name is David, and I am an alcoholic.* And they are strongly confronted if they waver in their ability to make this statement. Many men in counseling environments, however, are much more reluctant to assign themselves labels of shame, and we do men (and the people affected by them) a disservice when we insist that they take on too much responsibility too soon. It's just not very practical, and we may lose the very people we are desperately trying to help.

This is especially evident in the label applied for the help-seeking process. Men (and the others around them) certainly don't have to call it *psychotherapy*. They don't even have to call it *counseling*. They can call it *stress management*, a *psychological tune-up*, *coaching*, or *consulting*. They may balk at being called a *patient* or, in some cases, may not even want to be called a *client*. *Consumer* or *customer* may be more user-friendly. It doesn't matter, as long as they walk in the door and start doing the work.

Male-friendly metaphors for change also come in very handy in capturing men's imagination and activating motivation (Englar-Carlson & Shepard, 2005):

> *I want to make sure that you are navigating your own ship* (for yacht club members and active duty Navy)
>
> *It seems like the two of you are coming in here with two strikes and two outs in the bottom of the ninth* (for baseball fans)
>
> *It appears to me that the foundation of your marriage may need to be repaired* (for men in the construction industry)
>
> *I wonder how you analyze the benefits and costs of continuing with the same patterns in the relationship?* (for men in the financial industry)
>
> *I think this relationship needs a tune-up, but you can be relieved to know that it doesn't need an overhaul!* (for the automotive crowd)

"What's in This for Me?"

It is also helpful to recognize—and respect—the fact that plenty of men are entering the counseling process truly wondering, "What's in this for me?" Part of your job is to pitch the benefits in a way that not only increases their motivation level, but also helps them feel less foolish about their involvement in the process. Men are more likely to change and to engage in a relationship when they recognize genuine self-interest.

Men who are attached to the traditional benefits of male privilege often feel like they have a lot to lose from therapy and particularly from any kind of couples counseling. The counseling process may demand of them that they share power in ways that they are not looking forward to, or that they offer more emotional depth and range in ways that make them feel uneasy. Only when they grasp the concept that their relationships stand to improve, that they may actually feel relieved to talk about things, and (most crucial for many men) that their kids will ultimately benefit, do they buy in. Then there is genuine perceived self-interest, and with this self-interest comes motivation and hard work.

Rules of Engagement: Communicating Respect

Reaching men effectively in this setting, in which so many men feel tentative and threatened, requires the communication of profound respect. Many men warm up to simple indicators of respect and reinforcement for their courage in walking in the door. When men do express emotionality—and it is not validated or rewarded—then they are less likely to try to again.

Empathic Responses

When a man in a therapy session is called upon to respond with affect but seems blocked, there are a number of user-friendly and engaging responses that can disarm resistance (Englar-Carlson & Shepard, 2005):

> When a man freezes up in response to a demand to express affect, the therapist can validate: *You're feeling a kind of blankness right now, is that it?*
>
> When a man is in couples therapy and he is reluctant to talk about his emotional states, the therapist can acknowledge the man's anxiety: *It's got to be difficult to talk about feelings in front of a woman who is "experienced" at this and a therapist who does this all the time!*
>
> If a man has a hard time expressing emotions and the therapist is male, the therapist can normalize with self-disclosure: *We were not trained for this, were we?*
>
> When a man is failing at the task of offering his partner the emotional connection she is seeking, the therapist can reframe for positive intentions: *You want to feel connected to your wife but it's just hard to find the right words!*
>
> If a man is ashamed of himself for being too possessive or jealous, the therapist can identify the positive component in this negative

behavior: *If you didn't care about her, and what she thinks of you, this wouldn't matter so much.*

Respect Resistance

There is a time and place to directly identify and confront male resistance and defensiveness. However, it is usually much more productive to offer respect for the defenses that we observe, keeping in mind the constructs about the vulnerability that men experience. Typically, when we adapt some of our styles to give men a little room to activate their defenses, they don't feel like they have to perform upon demand. The therapeutic outcome is better in the long run.

Permission to disclose gradually: It is easy for therapists to get impatient when men take awhile to warm up to the counseling experience. But it is essential that we respect, at least for a while, their anxiety or their unfamiliarity with plunging right in to the emotionally laden issues at hand. This also shows up in male "storytelling," as when a man relates a long, elaborate, excessively detailed account of an important event in his life, while the event itself lies buried in heaps of details. This is foreplay, leading up to the big event, and patience usually comes in handy rather than impatiently rushing him through: *You know, there was one particular thing you said in that story that really stood out to me, when you said you felt like you were on the outside looking in at all the family events.*

Personalismo and Schmoozing: These two words, from the rich languages of Spanish and Yiddish, both represent an interpersonal activity that many male clients value. They want to feel like this conversation is normal. Normal means that the therapist relates in a real, *personalismo* fashion, like there is a real person in the room who is not just playing a role. And normal also means *schmoozing* about little events that men talk about, like yesterday's football game, something goofy that happened on the way in today, a new contract that his company is working on, the latest BlackBerry gadgets.

Therapeutic transparency: As part of the campaign to make men as comfortable as possible with this unfamiliar process, it usually pays off to be as transparent and authentic as possible. If they ask about your credentials, offer all relevant information without defensiveness or without trying to analyze why they want to know. If they ask you why you got into this field or what it's like to work with "weirdos like me" all day long, self-disclose as much as your personal style and professional judgment allow. Reassure them that they will know what you are thinking of them, that you will never reveal any information about them without their consent (except for the legally mandated situations they have been informed about), and that they will know well in advance if you think they are not progressing in this treatment.

Triangle conversations: Some men have a hard time with the formal format of therapy, where they sit down and have a face-to-face, emotionally significant encounter at a designated hour with a mental health professional. This is especially true for teenage boys. Sometimes it works better to engage in an activity together, like going for a walk, playing video games, or shooting hoops. The activity forms one point of a triangle and the conversation, greased by lessened defenses against intimacy, sometimes flows more smoothly.

Respect for Men's Styles

It is easy to misread male humor and clowning as classic signs of denial, minimization, and avoidance. Often they are. But these behaviors also represent ways that men seek to achieve intimacy and affiliation, not just avoid it.

Another important consideration in treating men involves their anxiety about this foreign turf. It is very important to educate men up front about the counseling experience. It helps to let men know how long the sessions are, the roles that the therapist can and cannot play, and what is expected of them to do therapy right. When men enter our men's groups, we give them handouts with typical questions (and our answers) designed to anticipate their concerns, such as these: *Won't group counseling try and get me to let out all my emotions? I'm not comfortable with that!* or *I would rather have individual counseling because I don't like talking in front of other people and I can get more personal attention* (Wexler,

2006b). We also review exactly what we would identify as problem behaviors, so they don't feel blindsided if we later correct them.

One more strategy that shows respect for men's needs and learning styles: offering homework and action plans. Many men (although of course there are exceptions) feel anxious about the vagueness of therapeutic growth, and they want to know exactly what they are supposed to do based on these new insights or the emergence of new feelings. This is not resistance—this is actually the way many men demonstrate their commitment to the process. So be prepared with reading assignments, behavioral experiments, specific logs or journals that they can maintain, videos to watch, and so on. This shows respect for what men need and how they learn.

Rules of Engagement: Therapeutic Approach

The therapeutic alliance is vastly more significant in determining positive treatment outcome than any specific intervention or technique. Measures of therapeutic relationship variables consistently correlate higher with client outcomes than specialized therapy techniques (Lambert, 2002). This comes as no surprise to students of treatment outcome research in varied settings with many different populations over many years.

Often this alliance is generated naturally, if the counselor has an intuitive sense of how to foster alliance and if the male client is receptive. Most therapists are already skilled at this, but it helps all of us to recognize particular strategies that often enhance the therapeutic alliance with male clients, thus potentiating the positive effects of treatment.

Therapist Self-Disclosure

Therapist self-disclosure, carefully calibrated, can be effective in fostering this alliance and helping bring men out of their shell. Therapists often create an atmosphere of increased trust and intimacy by acknowledging that some of the same struggles and conflicts have taken place in their own lives and in their own relationships. This is a valuable tool in helping men normalize their experiences. Shame is our enemy here and therapist self-disclosure often defuses shame.

The rationale for therapist self-disclosure is best understood by the self psychology construct of the *twinship* (or *kinship* or *alter ego*) selfobject function (Basch, 1980; Shapiro, 1995). According to this model, an individual experiences increased self-cohesion through an identification with others. The more that someone feels kindred or has the sense of a shared human experience with others, the more emotionally integrated and centered he or she feels. This self-cohesion experience is the essential component of human experience that self psychology focuses on, and the *twinship* selfobject is (like the *mirroring* selfobject) one of the pathways that facilitates it.

There are two main types of therapist self-disclosure. The first is "here-and-now" self-disclosure, as in "When you talk like this, I feel really worried about you" or "I'm so excited watching you put together all these changes."

The second type, more commonly identified, is "extra-therapeutic" self-disclosure, as in bringing information about yourself into the therapy room that has actually taken place elsewhere: "I got stuck in traffic today" or "I was raised Catholic, too" or "I went skiing with my family last week" or "I have been diagnosed with colon cancer." All of these, ranging from the banal to the extremely serious, reflect the therapists' decision to reveal something about themselves that is not readily apparent to the clients.

The fundamental caveat of appropriate self-disclosure is this: Only do it when you are relatively confident that sharing this information is genuinely in the clients' best interest. The potential advantage with male clients is that they are more likely to relax their defenses if they experience a sense of affiliation and kinship rather than distance and inequality. I often tell male clients stories about horrendous blunders I have made with my kids or stupid things I have done or struggled with in my marriage. It serves to de-stigmatize what they have done. It opens up more possibility for them to self-reveal, without the excessive shame that tends to shut them down.

But you can only reveal what you feel comfortable revealing. And if you are not reasonably sure that it will serve a therapeutic purpose (even talking about traffic), then don't do it.

Although it is difficult to establish an absolute set of rules for when to self-disclose and when not to, you may assume that therapist self-disclosure is contraindicated in the following situations (Wexler, 2006b):

Revealing the "too personal": Be careful about revealing information that may place a burden on the client to take care of you, or may lead to a loss of your professional credibility if others in your field found out this same information.

Needing a friend: The reason to self-disclose is to offer something to help the man who is sitting across from you. If you find yourself talking about your recent divorce because you need to talk to someone about it and your client is very interested, you are making a grievous clinical mistake.

Needing admiration: Sometimes people in the counseling field, if they are not careful, use their clients to feel admired for personal accomplishments (famous people you know, a book you have published, an important position you have been chosen for). This is not the job of the client.

Losing credibility: If you think that revealing personal information may actually lead you to lose credibility with your client, then this would be a mistake. If you are a woman who was in an abusive relationship, and you reveal this to a man who has been abusive with the intention of letting him know that you know a lot about this area, he may suspect that you will not be able to see him clearly as an individual. If you have been happily married for 25 years, if you have raised kids successfully, then revealing this information may increase your credibility about families and relationships—or it may signal to the male client that you don't know enough about his tormented relationships.

Passing Tests

Control-mastery theory (Weiss & Sampson, 1986) is based on extensive research involving detailed observations of psychotherapy sessions. One of the most valuable findings from these studies is that clients often enter psychotherapy (or any relationship, for that matter) with preconceived pathogenic beliefs about themselves, about others, or about how the world works.

The pathogenic beliefs are formed directly from childhood trauma or ongoing dysfunctional family dynamics. For example, a boy growing up with an insecure or competitive father may develop the pathogenic beliefs fearing "outdoing": *If I am more successful than my father, I will be damaging him and I will be punished.* Or another child may grow up with the fear of separation: *I will do damage to my family if I am different from them and they will feel betrayed.*

According to this model, the client uses the therapy relationship and other intimate relationships to conduct a series of tests. Think of this as an unconscious scientific inquiry in which the client wishes to confirm or disconfirm a particular hypothesis. In this study, he enters into the investigation expecting to have his original and long-standing pathogenic beliefs confirmed—but he secretly hopes that maybe, this time, they will be disconfirmed.

Kohut (1984) said that narcissistic, vulnerable patients are particularly susceptible to anxiety about the re-experiencing of early trauma and early hurt. They anticipate the devastating repetition of early empathic failures if they open themselves up one more time. Their human longing for emotional fulfillment, they fear, will inevitably lead to potentially disintegrating disappointment. People expect to be disappointed and hurt again, and they expect that if they reach out to another person in any kind of open, trusting, or vulnerable way, they will be met with the same rejection, humiliation, lack of interest, or just plain cluelessness that they have experienced in the past. Why would it be any different?

The antidote for these pathogenic beliefs is the repeated discovery that, this time, things are different, or, in some cases, that this time the individual can handle the situations effectively. If a male client decides to reveal personal information about a childhood incident of being sexually abused, he is anticipating that he will make the therapist uncomfortable or that he will get some sort of message about his own culpability. When he gets neither, the test has been successful—or actually unsuccessful, because the null hypothesis has (in this instance) been disproved.

If he asserts his authority and challenges the therapist, he will be watching carefully to see if this will be met with a punitive attitude and power tactics in response; when he gets neither, this again disproves the null hypothesis. He is freer now to own the aspect of himself that is assertive and independent.

The therapist's job, in working with men, is to read and anticipate their tests and, if at all possible, to pass them. The therapist's job is, if possible, to respond differently than what the client is used to. If the therapist fails, then the alternate intervention is to name the tests, name the failures, and acknowledge the feelings and narratives associated with them.

Part of this testing process also involves helping the client design intelligent behavioral tests outside the therapist's office and also to recognize the inevitable accidental tests that take place all the time. Recently I directed a male client of mine to inform his wife that he had been secretly taking Cialis to prepare for sex with her. She had recently had an affair, and he was feeling enormous pressure to perform sexually in a way that she would never be tempted to stray from him again. His pathogenic belief? *My wife will humiliate me if I tell her the pressure I have been feeling.* It took tremendous courage on his part to conduct this test because the stakes were so high. But he found that, after some initial anger on her part that he had kept this secret from her, she was very understanding and genuinely appreciated that he had taken the risk to be open and honest with her. This is what she had been looking for from him, and this pattern of his hidden needs and feelings was one of the factors that had created the conditions for her affair.

In the end, she passed his test. And he was rewarded, not punished, for revealing something potentially embarrassing. This was integrating for him and enriching for his relationship.

Pacing and Leading

One strategy to bypass the inherent defensiveness of many men in therapy environments is called "pacing and leading." This approach, originating from the work of Milton Erickson and further developed by neo-Ericksonian practitioners (Erickson, 1979; Gilligan, 1984), carefully mirrors the experience of the other person, followed by a "leading" suggestion for a new way to think or act. Based on Erickson's original work with indirect, naturalistic hypnotherapy, pacing means first developing empathy and rapport for the client by careful delineation of his inner experiences, prior to making any correction or suggestion, prior to fostering a new perspective, and prior to guiding a new behavior.

Step 1: Offering mirroring responses that confirm the person's experience

Step 2: Then—and only then—"leading" him into some new ways of thinking, feeling, or behaving

In working with men therapeutically, *pacing* means carefully reflecting back an understanding of the men's experience:

> *When Karen was talking to this other guy at the party, you must have felt really threatened, like something very important was being taken away from you.*
> *And you must have felt betrayed, like "How can she do this to me?"*
> *Plus it was in front of other people, and your pride was at stake.*
> *And you felt powerless, probably thinking "I have to do something about this right now."*
> *You probably felt it all through your body, and it felt awful, and you didn't know what to do.*
> *It makes sense that you would feel this way, and that you would feel this urge to try to do something to feel powerful again.*

Then, and only then, comes the "lead":

> *And at that point, probably the most powerful thing to do would be to remember that you get insecure in these situations, and that it doesn't always mean that Karen is doing something to you. And to remember that you have ways to talk to her about it afterward. You can let her know what you need from her.*

79

There are three kinds of mistakes a counselor or therapist can make in "pacing and leading."

Improper pacing: If you tell a man that he is probably very anxious right now, and he is not (or thinks that he is not), then the pacing is unattuned.

Insufficient pacing: If you make a few pacing statements and the man is still guarded and mistrusting, it may mean that you need to spend more time with the pacing process, sometimes weeks or months.

Improper lead: Even though you may have paced very accurately and successfully, your "lead" suggestion may be something that doesn't make sense to him or feels offensive in some way to him.

When in doubt, return to pacing. It is hard to go wrong by doing this.

In the situation above, the therapist could have simply stepped in with the obvious "lead," but without proper pacing, the likely response from the guy would have been something like: *You don't know what it's like to have her treat me like this.* Without pacing, the counselor or therapist lacks emotional credibility. With pacing, the male client is more likely to feel understood—and then more receptive to the value of the advice, guidance, or correction.

Rules of Engagement: Male User-Friendly Services

Finally, not only is it important to engage men by communicating respect, but this atmosphere of respect is also communicated through the treatment environment that we design for them. The name of the service we are offering and the way we offer it are crucial.

We need to provide better education about what exactly is involved in therapy. This education should be dispersed in as many different media as possible so that men can safely investigate whether or not therapy is right for them. For example, as mentioned earlier, in 2003 the National Institute of Mental Health launched a national media campaign called "Real Men. Real Depression" to raise awareness of the fact that depression affects more than 6 million men annually. The NFL has tried to convince men to visit their doctors and proactively manage their health by developing a campaign in 2008 called "Tackling Men's Health."

Robertson and Fitzgerald (1992) designed a study on a college campus to find ways to "sell the product" of counseling services to students. They created two brochures for a campus counseling center and distributed them to community college students in auto mechanics, welding, and other mostly-male areas. One of the brochures described the center's counseling services in traditional terms; the other used terms like *consultations* (rather than *therapy*) and emphasized self-help and achievement. They found that the men who received the second brochure were more likely to say they'd seek assistance at the center than men who received the traditional one.

The services were exactly the same; only the labels were different— classic reframing.

Advertising services for men with specific skills-based labels like *stress management*, *parenting skills*, or *building better relationships* is much better at promoting the product and reaching the very audience we want to reach. It is not particularly complicated, nor should it be controversial, to try to make the service appealing to the consumer.

It is also important to recognize the learning styles of the men we treat and to design interventions accordingly. Psychologist Mark Kiselica (Horne, 1999) pioneered the use of flexible, male-friendly strategies to adapt to the needs and comfort zones of men, particularly boys and young men. He suggested offering flexible time schedules with the options for "drop-in" appointments and meeting in alternative settings, like coffee shops or basketball courts. He recommended having some snacks or drinks available to "break bread" together. Men also respond well to having male-friendly magazines in the waiting room (sports magazines are probably more appropriate than skin mags!) to give clients the clear message that men are welcome in this environment. He suggested that male therapists roll up their sleeves to relax the client and de-emphasize the gap between "doctor" and "patient." And he recommended triangle conversations: playing board games, playing video games, tossing a ball, and so on.

Chapter 4
When Women Treat Men

In the long run, issues of gender (like race or sexual orientation) tend to fade into the background in the therapeutic relationship. A good therapist is a good therapist, and a good therapeutic relationship is a good therapeutic relationship. Men in treatment, ultimately, care more about the quality and accuracy of the input from the therapist than the shape of the body or the nature of the chromosome structure of the person offering the help. Relationship and rapport trump gender differences.

But, until that point is reached, gender (like race or sexual orientation) is something we cannot afford to ignore. Much of the literature about treating men by forming a deeper connection with them assumes that the therapist is male as well. However, in the 21st century, the vast majority of therapists who treat men individually or in groups are female.

Women face especially complex transference and countertransference issues in treating men. They often struggle to reach defended and difficult men who don't respond emotionally the way that women generally do. And issues about women treating men in couples therapy are especially complex.

I am a little uncomfortable writing this chapter. I would feel presumptuous (as a white male) writing a chapter on the experiences African-American therapists face in treating white men, and this feels the same.

However, this subject is central to our field, and over the years I have supervised many female therapists, I have co-led groups with many female therapists, I have reviewed many articles on this subject by female therapists, I have been in therapy myself with female therapists, and I have a wife who is a female therapist. So here is some background and some guidelines based on all of these rich sources of information.

In HBO's *The Sopranos*, both Tony Soprano and his therapist, Dr. Jennifer Melfi, do their best to make the therapy successful. At times, they are just two imperfect people doing their jobs: client and therapist. At other times, issue of gender and gender roles become central to the work at hand (Sweet, 2002). Tony develops an erotic transference to Dr. Melfi, which masks the vulnerability he feels for depending on a nurturing female figure (his own hopelessly narcissistic mother failed to provide a lick of genuine nurturing). Then he turns on Dr. Melfi, sometimes violently, when she sets limits on their relationship. He is also determined to protect her when she is in trouble. Dr. Melfi, in turn, cares passionately and does some excellent work with Tony, but she develops an erotic countertransference to him that she works hard to manage, and she secretly longs to be taken care of by this strong masculine figure. Gender and sex make this relationship especially complex.

When Men Choose a Female Therapist

Sometimes a man ends up being treated by a woman purely by the luck of the draw. He comes in to a clinic and is assigned to the first available therapist. Or he is ordered into a treatment group and (because the field of mental health treatment these days includes so many more women than men), his group leader happens to be female. Or a friend of his doctor responds to his request for a referral by picking the best available and most trusted clinician, who happens to be female. The guy ends up with a female therapist, and he may not care one way or the other as long as he gets the help he needs.

Sometimes, men specifically request a female therapist or counselor. Why? Why would anyone specifically choose someone different from themselves? We could ask the same questions about a lesbian couple wanting to be seen by a straight therapist, or an African-American man choosing a white therapist.

It usually makes sense in these situations to put gender issues out front early: *Why did you choose a female therapist? Why did you think a woman might help you with this better than a man?*

Here are some of the most typical reasons that men are sometimes drawn to a female therapist (Johnson, 2005).

A safe place for vulnerability: A man who specifically chooses a woman therapist often carries with him an expectation that this will be an especially safe experience. In the presence of a woman, he can show his vulnerability and be comforted, accepted, and soothed. He will often perceive her as someone who will not tease, taunt, ridicule, or compete. He may have learned from his own experiences that he is most successful at accessing his deepest self within the interpersonal structure of a relationship with a female: his mother, his first girl-friend, his wife. He often carries a secret belief that women own the key to the Magic Kingdom of the vulnerable self and that through this connection he can safely explore what is buried within.

Less concern about competition: Sometimes a man will choose a female therapist because he worries that a male therapist will feel competi-tive and that this will unconsciously color the therapeutic responses. This man has had way too much exposure to male testosterone battles, and he may even have experienced male therapists in the past who had unresolved competition issues of their own. He worries that if he talks about his business issues, a male therapist will compare himself and be critical or withholding. He worries that if he talks about his multiple infidelities, a male therapist will either vicariously live through him or act more condemning because he feels secretly envious. He worries that the male therapist will have to prove some-thing to him about who's in charge here.

Perhaps more important, a man will often worry that sitting in a room with another man and talking about his life issues will inevitably activate competitive feelings and competitive behaviors within himself. He doesn't trust himself to drop his false self in the presence of another man because he will be compelled to prove something to this man. And, knowing himself, he believes this is less likely to happen with a female.

Women's special relationship expertise: Often, a man will choose a female therapist because he is struggling with relationship issues and he figures he might as well consult the experts on relationship: women. Here are some typical situations in which men might consult a woman not only because of her reputation and expertise but also because of her gender (Johnson, 2005):

1. A man wants a woman therapist because his son would not talk to him and he does not know how to open up the communication.
2. A man calls a woman therapist because he thinks a woman can help him understand why the relationship busted up. Later, he admits that he had hoped that a woman could tell him how to get his girlfriend back.
3. A man consults a female therapist because he is simply trying to figure women out. Who better to consult than someone who is a member of this mysterious club? Often, in men's groups led by a male-female team, the men turn to the female therapist and ask, "As a woman, what do you think? Would that have bothered you?" Most of the time, they are not being hostile or challenging; they just really want to know.

To please "the wife": Sometimes men choose female therapists because they think (or they have been told) that their female partner will be more comfortable. Or the female partners may want them to see a woman in individual therapy who will, allegedly, be better equipped to give the man a female perspective. I sometimes see men individually for relationship issues who ask me for a referral for a couples therapist. They specifically request a female because their partners have told then that only women will understand what the female partners are dealing with in these relationships. My clients, in these cases, do not really care; their goal in choosing the female couples therapists is to do whatever is most likely to succeed. In these scenarios, that means creating an environment that offers the greatest comfort level to their female partner.

Female Therapists Understanding Male Clients

If you are a female therapist and your goal is to offer men the best possible treatment, then the cornerstone of success lies in making sure that you understand the gender issues of men.

The first challenge is to make sure that you are educated about the distinctive issues of growing up male and how this affects male emotional responding and relationship functioning. This means recognizing the themes identified throughout this book: MGRS and the "broken mirror," understanding male covert depression, recognizing male "compartmentalization," respecting male fears of vulnerability, and being prepared for "normative male alexithymia."

"Getting" Men's Response to Emotions

As a female therapist, you should be knowledgeable about the reasons behind many men's resistance to understanding and feeling their emotions. As female therapist and author Dr. Holly Sweet said: "When I cry or need to ask for help, my behavior does not make me feel unfeminine and it does not go against female norms" (Sweet, 2006, p. 75). Not so for men. As discussed earlier, many men are alexithymic and are generally unaware of what they are feeling, and many more men may know what they are feeling, but experience anxiety about the self-exposure of revealing their feelings. This is often hard for many women to intuitively understand since the female socialization process is typically quite different.

Women may in fact assume that men are actively choosing to withhold feelings from them, but they need to remember that many men either do not know what they are feeling, do not know how to name the feelings, do not know how to share their feelings, or are afraid to show their feelings for fear of vulnerability.

Most therapists would understand a woman crying as she tells a story of loss or betrayal. What most therapists have a hard time with, and female therapists often cannot relate to, is that a man may display emotional stoicism or anger because of how he has been taught to respond to his sadness. It's not (usually) that he is unfeeling or uncaring. He has just been trained differently. Traditionally, women are more adept at identifying symptoms of depression in themselves and properly labeling the experience. Men, however, are more likely to deny, mask, and act out. They abuse substances, blame others, become resentful and angry, work excessively, or develop somatic complaints that are "safer" to complain about and to seek help for (Cochran, 2000). These are psychological defense mechanisms in action.

"Getting" Men's Resistance and Defenses

Furthermore, as a female therapist, you must be especially conscious of the ways that male clients tend to resist the efforts of therapists (and of partners and loved ones). They likely have more difficulty expressing emotions and more difficulty asking for help than the "typical" female clients. Male clients are more likely to deny problems and mask their distress with acting out.

It is essential to recognize that many men truly struggle when pressed to be more emotionally open. They are not just being cold or difficult; they fear failing at this task. This awareness can lead to less frustration for the female therapist and a more empathic connection to male clients.

I recently treated a couple in which the woman was extremely frustrated with her male partner's reluctance to commit to marriage. He had "agreed" to become engaged to her and he was open to having a baby together. But he wanted to "see how it goes" regarding actually getting married. She worked up her emotional courage in one of our sessions and told him point blank, clearly and respectfully, that she couldn't go on like this. She needed him to make a decision about their future together. And if he was paralyzed with indecision and could not make it, she would (at age 38, childless and wanting a child) need to leave him and move on.

He froze. He was not mad. He said later that he totally understood where she was coming from and respected her assertiveness. But he could not respond. He stared blankly into space with that deer-in-the-headlights look. He smiled nervously. We waited. She said to him, "Why aren't you saying anything? I have just poured my heart out to you and laid this big number on you and you just sit there? How do you think that makes me feel?"

I interrupted her to speak for him: "I know you deserve a response, but I think Gary is just frozen right now. That happens a lot, especially to men. That doesn't mean that he is not taking this very seriously or that he won't show emotions a little later, maybe in an hour, maybe in a week. But just because he is not reacting now doesn't mean that he's not feeling anything or that he doesn't care. This is actually kind of normal."

He looked at me with tears in his eyes and said, "Thank you. Thank you." And she nodded like she understood. This intervention reflected the perspective that all therapists need to help explain otherwise weird male behavior in relationships. And female therapists, not having the experience of being male and knowing what this moment is like, need to be especially aware of it.

I recently told this story to a female colleague. She said that her clinical instinct would have been to turn to the man and ask him if he could understand how his nonresponsiveness makes his partner feel. This intervention makes perfect sense, and at times I would go the same route, but it is potentially shame-enhancing at the very moment when he feels overwhelmed and vulnerable. Shame is not our friend.

It is common for female therapists, especially, to want to help men be more emotionally expressive. However, when a male client slowly begins to share his inner experiences, he frequently feels a rush of relief—followed immediately by a wave of anxiety and vulnerability (Scher, 1990). As a female therapist, it is vital to recognize that expressing his feelings breaks male tradition and may activate fears about his loss of manliness.

I always like to anticipate this: "So, when you started crying today, I imagine that it felt good but also made you feel kind of stupid." He can confirm or deny, but at least this issue is brought to consciousness and legitimized as a normal male reaction under these circumstances.

When a woman therapist is able to view male clients' responses less as individual pathology and more as a product of male socialization, she will be better able to move into the world of men. In so doing, she will increase her sensitivity to the pressures that shape men's behavior.

Tasks for Female Therapists Working with Men

Based on these perspectives, what practical changes do female therapists need to make in their therapeutic style and strategies in order to be better help men?

Welcoming men: Psychologist Holly Sweet reported this self-observation: "As I prepared for our first meeting, I became aware that the magazines on top of the table in our waiting room were *Martha Stewart* and *O*. I asked myself how I would feel if the magazines in my male therapist's office were *Guns and Ammo* and *Automotive Weekly*" (2006, p. 71). A female therapist recently told me that she took on a new male client and, as she walked into the office with him, she suddenly realized how feminine her office décor was: soft pastel colors, floral prints, and so on. This does not mean that you have to decorate your office with NASCAR posters or have copies of *Penthouse* in your office, but it helps to see the female therapist's office through the eyes of men. The initial impression goes a long way in helping all of us help the men we want to help.

Talking "guy talk": Although there are plenty of exceptions, many men do not respond well to typical therapy-talk like "getting in touch with your feelings." It is often helpful to use metaphors and images that are user-friendly to men, and both male and female therapists can facilitate treatment by having some available to help capture male clients' attention and get the message across (see Chapter 3 for details). Another form of "guy talk" is humor. Because therapy can be too emotionally intense for many men, humor serves to normalize the interpersonal experience and offer men some emotionally acceptable detachment from their feelings. It helps bond the client and therapist as equals (a "twinship" experience) (Sweet, 2006).

Male-friendly techniques: In general (and this is an enormous generalization that does not apply to all men), men are most receptive to practical, problem-solving interventions. This does not mean that men cannot feel or cannot go deep, but it is imperative, especially for female therapists, to recognize the comfort zone men experience when they have something concrete to do about the problem at hand. If you (as a male or female therapist) are philosophically opposed to this or if it just does not come naturally to you, then you run the risk that some men will not relate, will not stay in treatment, and will not benefit.

Homework assignments, bibliotherapy, and videotherapy are all examples of practical, structured interventions that men typically respond well to. Often, simply assigning a male client the task of complimenting his children once each day or recording one different emotion every day of the week helps relieve his anxiety about how to go about making the changes he knows he needs to make.

Transference Issues: How Male Clients View Women Therapists

Transference issues between male clients and female therapists are not always complicated. Sometimes men get into therapy and get right down to work. But in many situations, female therapists should especially be on the lookout for transference issues related to gender. For some men, this therapeutic relationship may be their first, or best, exposure to a genuine intimate emotional connection with a female (or to anyone), thus increasing the intensity of the transference (Sweet, 2006).

One classic transference reaction from male to female is when the male client views his therapist as the special, all-nurturing mother figure. Projected onto the therapist is the powerful capacity to both give and withhold essential love and nurturing. He may idealize her, based on an integration of his early emotional connection to his mother and his expectation of the archetypal woman who soothes and protects him.

One time, I was co-leading a men's group with a female co-therapist. One of the men, barely 20 years old, always lit up whenever he got attention from my co-therapist. As she was preparing to leave this group to take on some other assignments, the group was going through a good-bye ceremony and talking about their feelings about her leaving. When it was his turn, the young man smiled shyly, turned to her, and said, "I want you to be my mommy!" The group laughed, not derisively but actually rather affectionately. She handled it very well, reflecting that she knew how much she meant to him and that she had benefited so much from working with him, too. The moment sticks out not because the feelings were so unusual, but simply because this expression of what many men secretly feel was so pure and undefended.

With straight male clients, of course, women are often perceived as potential lovers, as "objects of desire." The normative male alexithymia issues that affect so many men often create emotional confusion when a man feels close to a woman: *If I feel close to her, that must mean sex*—since men are socialized to sexualize intimacy. The scene from *About Schmidt* (Gittes, Besman, & Payne, 2002) in which the Jack Nicholson character confuses friendliness and warmth from a woman with sexual interest captures this perfectly. Women therapists, of course, score extremely high in qualities like friendliness, caring, and warmth and are thus prime candidates for men to inject sexual overtones into the interaction—just like Tony Soprano does with Dr. Melfi.

A male client in treatment with a male therapist may find himself trying to display his strength and competence. With a female therapist, a man is more likely to try to display behavior that might make him feel attractive and important. He is driven to impress her in the way that men typically impress women. Both of these personas, though different in appearance, are attempts to overcompensate for a sense of insecurity and feelings of shame about having to admit to failing in some aspect of being a man (Rabinowitz, 2006).

Countertransference: When Female Therapists Treat Men

As a woman treating men, it is important to ask yourself a number of questions to examine your own gender-based countertransference issues. Dr. Sweet suggests that female therapists ask themselves the following questions (Sweet, 2006, 2002).

1. *How do you really see masculinity?* Do you consciously or unconsciously think of maleness as a sickness to be cured? Amusing as that may sound, female therapists sometimes approach male clients from this perspective, as if the features of males were inherently destructive to one's emotional well-being and to the success of interpersonal relationships. An alternative narrative, of course, is that some of the rules and roles that men have been bound by have value—and some are too rigid or overemphasized. And, although we are certainly focusing on many of the roadblocks that men experience in benefiting from therapy, any therapist who assumes that most men are inherently resistant and thus poor candidates for counseling is selling men short.

2. *Can you accept the fact that sexual feelings are a natural part of many male-female interactions?* Whether we are comfortable with them or not, sexual feelings are often aroused in the therapeutic relationship. If you are a female therapist treating a man, and his sexual attraction to you becomes apparent one way or another, can you find nonshaming ways to handle it? Likewise, if you notice your own sexual attraction, can you utilize this constructively? The clinical danger in this sexual minefield is for the therapist to be so uncomfortable with the sexual feelings that she withdraws or criticizes—or, perhaps even more dangerously, that she is *too* comfortable with the sexual feelings in the room and contributes to them.

3. *Are you afraid of men's anger?* Many men are quick to anger, but this surface anger is often just a mask. As Dr. William Pollack says, this is "their way of weeping"(Healy, 2005). For most men, the sadness, hurt, and vulnerability lurks just below the surface. The clinical setting needs to offer a sanctuary for a man to express his anger (with appropriate limits, of course). Often, a man is testing his therapist (male or female) to see if he or she can handle seeing his real self. If you are not funda-

mentally threatened (which is not the same as feeling undisturbed), you are less likely to respond with defensiveness or blame. As long as the behavioral expression of anger is not truly dangerous, then the clinical goal is to help him identify the weeping within.

4. *Are you aware of how previous experiences with men may be shaping your expectations of your male clients?* The defenses of male clients can trigger countertransferential reactions in you based on your past experiences with significant men. You may feel disconnected from men who don't share feelings. You may feel put down or pathologized by men for having vulnerable emotions or needing connection and security in relationships. You may feel guilty because you have not been successful in caretaking difficult men in your own life.

Maybe this gets expressed by becoming too quickly impatient with men who are limited in their expression of vulnerable affect. Or maybe you are too quick to side with the woman in couples' issues. Or maybe you too quickly bristle when men try to impress you or compete with you. Or maybe you try too hard to protect your male client from feeling pain.

5. *Can you handle being devalued by a male client?* Another risk factor for female therapists to be aware of when treating men: devaluation. Some men diminish the value of the female voice even if she is a professional he is depending on, and they may treat her with disrespect. Some men transfer the general cultural devaluation of women into the clinical office. "This devaluation can be subtle or overt, but if you react hostilely to it or ignore it, the therapeutic connection suffers" (Sweet, 2002).

6. *Finally, the Million Dollar Question: Do you genuinely like men?* If you have a solid history of good personal and professional relationships with men, your affection, interest, and compassion for men will more likely blossom in your clinical work (Sweet, 2002).

Other questions to ask yourself include the following:

7. *Do you favor women over men when working with couples?* Male therapists who treat straight couples have an inherent advantage in some ways. A male therapist has a slightly better chance of saying something direct and confrontive to a guy in a couple because it is more likely to be perceived as one guy respectfully busting another. Many men are

familiar with this and actually perceive this as a "loving" act. But if he heard the same thing from a female therapist, he is more likely to smell danger: *The women are ganging up on me.*

The biggest countertransference concern for women, of course, is favoring the woman in the couple. It is important to examine your assumptions and your potential countertransference: do you secretly (or not so secretly) automatically blame men for couples' problems?

Another twist on this countertransference problem is the opposite: Many female therapists have told me that, rather than favoring women in couples due to their allegiance or identification with their cohort group, they find themselves actually much less patient with and much less tolerant of women. Some of the harshest judgments about women who stay in abusive or otherwise destructive relationships come from other women, not men. Just like professional women on a jury are much more likely to judge an abused woman harshly for not leaving the relationship, many women therapists feel particularly impatient with women who are acting immaturely or selfishly.

8. *Do certain male behaviors disgust you?* As a female therapist, where do you draw the line? Can you work with men who seem to hate women? Can you work with batterers? Can you work with child abusers or sadists? A woman who can tolerate her disgust for these patterns of male behavior is potentially extremely valuable for these men—but there is no shame in recognizing that there is no way you can see these men clearly and offer them a fair shake. The worst is pretending that you can offer what you cannot.

When Male Clients "Come On" to Female Therapists

Every female therapist who has ever treated a male client has been on the receiving end of some form of sexually inappropriate behavior. This is no big revelation and, in fact, many of these same patterns also take place with gay male clients toward male therapists or female clients toward their therapists. It is essential, however, that female therapists develop a reasonable context to make sense of the particular patterns of these male client behaviors. Just as—in the field of domestic violence—a quick symbolic slap on the face should not be viewed through the same lens as a savage and systematic beating, these sexually inappropriate behaviors come in different shapes, sizes, and meanings. And they should, therefore, generate different clinical responses.

These sexually inappropriate behaviors range from mildly to severely inappropriate. Mildly inappropriate behaviors might include clients telling suggestive stories or offensive jokes, asking the psychotherapist to meet for coffee, winking, holding on too long during a handshake, or acting in some "overfamiliar" fashion (such as calling the provider "honey"). Severe inappropriate behaviors would include a male client making vulgar comments, pressuring the therapist for a sexual relationship, or intentionally exposing himself.

To help us make sense of this, researchers and clinicians at the Veterans Affairs Palo Alto Health Care System (Hartl, Zeiss, Marino, Zeiss, Regev, & Leontis, 2007) have classified these sexually inappropriate behaviors across two very significant dimensions.

Unintentional vs. intentional: The first dimension assesses *intentionality*. Is this guy aware of the inappropriateness of his behavior? Our understanding of the meaning and potential threat or pathology represented by this behavior depends significantly on this assessment. As the meaningful clinical relationship develops, male clients receive close individual attention, with high expectations for personal disclosure and high expectations for empathic attention from the female therapist. In these situations, some male clients will be disoriented by the positive emotional experiences, and they will harbor confused expectations about the nature of therapeutic relationships. As men are prone to do, they will often sexualize the intimate and act according to this narrative.

In contrast, some inappropriate actions are clearly intentional: The male client is sexually suggestive in an attempt to gain power or to intimidate the female therapist. Sometimes this is expressed through seductive and charming behavior, other times through behavior that is more aggressive and threatening. The implicit authority and power of a therapist—especially a female therapist—may trigger his resentment of the therapeutic relationship and the fact that someone else is in control of what is happening in this room and in this relationship.

Affiliative vs. distancing: The second dimension measures the ultimate goal—conscious or unconscious—of this inappropriate sexual behavior. These behaviors lie somewhere along a continuum of, at one end, an inappropriate attempt to actually be closer to the female therapist and, at the other end, an inappropriate attempt primarily designed to distance her. One behavior attempts to establish rapport, the other to damage it. *Affiliative* behaviors are those in which the client desires to bring the psychotherapist closer, whereas *distancing* behaviors are intended to disrupt the relationship between client and clinician.

Clinical Examples

A new client, after a few sessions, may comment on his therapist's attractiveness or even politely ask her to meet for coffee. This could easily be unintentional and an inept attempt to be affiliative. A long-standing client (who knows the limits of the professional relationship) engaging in the same behaviors might more likely be considered intentional yet still affiliative. If a male client in an uncomfortable situation (like being evaluated at a sexual dysfunction clinic) tells his female therapist, "I wouldn't have a problem if you were my girlfriend," we would probably label this as unintentional but clearly alienating and distancing. Finally, a male client who has been feeling threatened by the therapy experience with his female therapist (e.g., Tony Soprano) tells her that if she wants more information on his sexual functioning, she may just have to do some personal research with him privately. This is unquestionably intentional and unquestionably distancing.

If all we knew was the observed behavior, we might make the mistake of overpathologizing in some cases or writing it off as innocuous in others. These two dimensions help us assess the seriousness of the behavior and, most important, the intent. Intention is everything. For example, a male client says to his female therapist, "Wow, you smell nice today." He might be trying to get her to like him (affiliative). Or he might be trying to sexualize or exert power over the relationship (distancing). Understanding this context is crucial in knowing whether to take this behavior seriously and how—or whether—to interpret it.

Effective Clinical Responses

Hartl et al. (2007) identified different guidelines for responding to these sexually inappropriate behaviors. They vary according to the assessment of where these behaviors fall on the scales of intentional versus unintentional and distancing versus affiliative.

1. Sometimes a man will make complimentary comments about his female therapist's appearance. In most cases, this would be considered unintentional and affiliative. Sometimes the best clinical response is a simple polite "Thank you." If the behavior continues, a good clinical response is for the therapist to let him know that there are other more appropriate ways for him to let her know that he appreciates her: "Rather than complimenting me on how I dress, it would be much more meaningful to me to hear your comments about the work we are doing together. How would that be for you?" Again, the goal is to provide the client with clear education about what is appropriate for this professional relationship.

2. Furthermore, if the behavior is primarily unintentional and affiliative, usually a simple nonshaming clarification is in order: "I can understand that you would ask about what's possible in the relationship that we have formed. However, because our relationship is a professional one, you and I will never be able to have a relationship that is anything but professional. It would go against my ethics to enter into a personal relationship with someone who is, or ever has been, one of my clients."

3. Sometimes, when discussing intimate relationship issues including sexuality and sexual functioning, a male client may personalize the discussion: "Well, if you and I were having sex, I would probably . . ." This might (but not necessarily) be identified as unintentional but distancing (although, depending on context, history, and nonverbal cues, it could be intentional instead). An effective response to this might be, "Let's shift the frame. I really want to know about how this would be in *your* life, so think about an actual partner you might have . . ." When these kinds of behaviors are unintentional, then the clinical response should be carefully crafted to educate and set boundaries—and to avoid

shame or embarrassment for the client. The clinical intent of this type of response is to communicate that the therapist still wants to hear about the client's experiences, but in a way that is realistic and appropriate. It also subtly educates him about what is possible and what is not in this professional relationship.

4. It is often difficult to get a clear sense as to whether the client's behavior is actually an attempt to be affiliative or distancing or whether it is consciously intended to make her uncomfortable. When in doubt, it is usually clinically wise to simply get the subject out on the table: "What response were you hoping I would have when you told me I looked 'hot' today?" Clients may get flustered by this and have difficulty answering, but raising the question reaffirms that therapy is a safe sanctuary in which to explore behaviors and their underlying issues and motives.

5. Sometimes, when the behavior is clearly intentional, clearly distancing, and clearly repetitive, the best choice for the therapist is to indicate to the client that she must terminate the therapeutic relationship and refer him elsewhere. If a client persists in making vulgar comments, pressuring his therapist for a date, or acts downright threatening, then the therapeutic environment is toxic and unproductive. This is simply a time for limit-setting and self-protection.

Why Can't a Man Be More Like a Woman?

Finally, it is important to pay attention to how often men perceive a message that sounds like this: *Why can't a man be more like a woman?* This is Pygmalion in reverse, a symptom of our times. Whether they say it directly or not, clinicians—both male and female—often operate under this assumption and communicate this one way or another to male clients. Wives and girlfriends often communicate this to them in their lives as well. Those of us who work to reach men and bring out their best qualities must always remember the anxiety that many men experience about being turned into women. Our message, as we help men generate more emotional intelligence, is simply that we are trying to help them become better men, not to be more like women.

Chapter 5
Treating Men in Relationships

Probably the most complex and important role of therapeutic interventions for men involves helping male clients manage relationships more successfully and satisfyingly. Interpersonal conflict is one of the major complaints of males seeking treatment (Brooks & Silverstein, 1995). Our goal is to bring out the best qualities of men in their relationships while still holding them fully accountable for their relationship mistakes. How can we develop a deeper understanding of classic relationship challenges that men face and utilize specific strategies for managing individual and couples sessions that address these challenges?

Engaging men in the relationship counseling process requires three major tasks. The first is the creation of a safety zone, where men feel respected, understood, nonthreatened (or "tolerably" threatened), and honored—and in particular, a zone in which men understand what is happening and what is being asked of them. The second is making sure that the man has the skills to do relationships right, or at least to do his particular relationship right. The third primary challenge for all of us working with men in these contexts is to help clear out the roadblocks that get in the way of men accomplishing these tasks: bypassing resistance and defensiveness, identifying and adapting to insecure and/or dismissive attachment styles, and generating realistic expectations and narratives for what their most intimate relationships can reasonably provide.

Master Couples

A good place to start with most couples (and especially for most men who are looking for a structure and model to aim for) is to offer a framework for the key elements of a successful relationship. The best map for what a successful couple usually looks like can be found in the landmark research of John Gottman (1999) and his associates at the University of Washington. For the past few decades, Gottman's research team has studied couples' interactions in painstaking detail: verbal interactions, nonverbal communications, psychophysiological measures, and so on. The central goal of these massive studies has been to answer one primary questions: What do successful couples do that unsuccessful couples do not?

Successful Relationships

Gottman's studies showed that successful relationships are based on old-fashioned good manners more than anything else. These couples talk respectfully to each other. They are affectionate. Even when they are trying to bring up something potentially provocative, they find a way to do so with a reasonable degree of grace and respect. They are masters at de-escalating conflict and de-fusing hot subjects. They respond positively to the "bids for attention" from the other party. They believe in each other, and they can tolerate irritating behavior in each other because they fundamentally love and respect each other. And, particularly for men, they choose to accept influence from their partner rather than perceive the partner as being controlling. Each wants to make the other person happy, if possible, as long as this can be done without unacceptable sacrifice. In contrast, when one or the other feels treated unfairly, disrespected, or betrayed, we have a Middle East–style conflict that can cycle forever.

Gottman has identified an array of toxic indicators that predict, according to his research, almost certain deterioration of relationships. By examining the interaction of a wide variety of couples—including successful, happy couples—he and his team uncovered what they referred to as the Four Horsemen of the Apocalypse: criticism (or accusations), defensiveness, contempt, and stonewalling. When couples engage in these behaviors frequently, the relationship is much more likely to be dysfunctional and volatile. The researchers found that couples who regularly use these styles with each other are almost certainly headed for unhappiness, affairs, verbal or physical abuse, or divorce. (Gottman claims that his research team can predict this with 90% accuracy.)

The problem arising from the Four Horsemen is not only how emotionally beat up each person feels. The Horsemen also represent a painful and destructive decision that one or both partners has made about the other: *He (or she) is not a good-hearted person, is not truly on my side, and is a threat to me. I have given up.*

In dysfunctional couples, negative mind-reading runs rampant. It is as if each partner has made what Gottman calls a "secret, silent decision" about the other that he or she is an adversary and not worth respecting. Each assumes the worst about the other.

An ally's narrative goes something like this: *Oh well, he is in a bad mood. He has been under a lot of stress lately and needs more sleep.* An ally views negativity as unstable (highly alterable, fluctuating) and the cause as situational (external).

On the other hand, in an unhappy marriage, the same behavior is likely to be interpreted as stable (enduring, unchanging) and internal to the partner. The accompanying narrative might be something like *He is inconsiderate and selfish. That's the way he is. That's why he did that.*

What do successful couples do? Successful couples reframe. They change the self-talk, and they behave as if they trust and respect each other. One partner will soften, and the cycle of defensiveness is interrupted.

It actually doesn't take that much for the conversation to go differently—if both partners feel fundamentally charitable toward each other and have a few basic skills in their hip pocket.

In particular, men have a crucial responsibility to keep their defensiveness in check. They can interrupt the whole nasty sequence of bad behavior by generating a more compassionate narrative to explain the situation, not taking the (perceived) criticism quite so personally, and recognizing the independent center of initiative (that is, recognizing that she may have her own valid reasons for doing what she does and that these reasons may have nothing to do with him). I have repeatedly implored good men to keep in mind that it's not all about them.

The Relationship Respect Contract

Another important component in setting the ground rules for couples is the use of what I call the *relationship respect contract*. The fundamental purpose of the contract is to set the ground rules for what each person can and should expect from the other. Nobody can guarantee that they will never act out against the other person, but at least this contract helps couples develop a shared vision for what they would *like* to have in their relationship.

Many of the men whom I work with in couples therapy say to me something to the effect of, "Just tell me what to do and I'll do it." In the spirit of making it very clear to men what is expected of them, this contract lessens anxiety, and thus lessens resistance and defensiveness.

In the context of reviewing this contract, I explain to couples the concept of "relationship felonies" and "relationship misdemeanors." Felonies are behaviors that are potential deal-breakers in a relationship, and most relationships have a relatively small list of true felonies (such as infidelity or violence). Misdemeanors are behaviors that are frustrating or annoying or irritating, like not being a great housekeeper or watching too much television. They can usually be dealt with reasonably, or sometimes just respectfully ignored. One man in one of my groups pointed out that some of these annoying behaviors don't even reach misdemeanor status—they're just worthy of a "citation."

This perspective is especially valuable for men—who often perceive *any* frustration or rejection from their partner as a felony, no matter how minor. If a man is especially vulnerable to feeling disrespected or is especially sensitive to threats of abandonment or rejection, then even misdemeanors (or "citations") *feel* like profound injuries. Misdemeanors *feel* like felonies. Setting the record straight expands the couple's tolerance for relatively minor and relatively normal hurts, frustrations, injuries, and even mini-betrayals. These things happen, and they are not pretty, but they do not necessarily signal something profoundly flawed or doomed about this relationship. Instead, they signal being human.

Jason, in a men's group, told us the drama about his coffee mug. He regularly got up very early to get to work by 6:00 A.M. His wife would make him lunch the night before and have it ready for him. He also had a favorite coffee mug that he used every morning, and part of his wife's contribution to his early morning routine was to have the coffee mug cleaned and ready to go. With some frequency, however, she neglected her job of having the clean coffee mug ready, and this was an ongoing point of conflict between them.

So one morning Jason gets up and—again!—the coffee mug is not clean and ready. He responds by heading into the bedroom where his wife is still asleep, pulling the covers off of her, and berating her for screwing up again. Jason told the group this story, looking for sympathy. Fortunately, the group jumped all over him, and they were especially effective at reminding him of the distinction between a felony and a misdemeanor. Spacing out on cleaning the coffee mug is worthy only of a citation or maybe a misdemeanor. It is annoying. But it is not a felony, and Jason suffered from hypervigilance regarding acts of disrespect and significant betrayal potentially lurking everywhere.

Fortunately, in the context of relationship counseling, this is very often a correctable notion. Some of the most potent work with men in couples therapy centers on developing and applying the appropriate narrative for the situation at hand—in this case, classifying a difficult situation as felony, misdemeanor, or citation—or none of the above. Hundreds of times I have seen the lightbulb suddenly switch on for men when they learn a different story to apply to the relationship challenge in front of them: *I never thought of it that way before. Now it feels different.*

To further expand the narrative options for relationship dissatisfaction, it can also be extremely valuable to remind both partners (again, especially men) of the 80/20 rule. One of the characters in Tyler Perry's film *Why Did I Get Married* (Perry, 2007) described the rule: *I keep trying to tell you brothers about the 80/20 rule. . . . In most cases, in marriage, you only gonna get 80% of what you need. That's it. No more, no less. Most times, 80%. Now here comes this woman who offers you 20%. Now 20% looks real good when you ain't getting it. But the problem is you're gonna leave 80 thinking you're gonna get something better and you end up with 20.* I suggest to couples that if they discover that they are getting 80% of what they need in their relationship, they should (unless the 20% is bona fide felony material) get down and their knees, clasp their hands together, and thank the Lord for being so blessed.

Relationship Respect Contract

We agree to participate in couples therapy and recognize that this therapy will only have a chance to be successful if none of the following behaviors takes place:

1. No incidents of direct physical abuse or violence.
2. No direct or implied threats of physical abuse or violence (to self, other, or property).
3. No direct or implied threats to behave in a way that would be extremely harmful to the other person (such as exposing personal secrets).
4. No physical restrictions on either party's freedom of movement.
5. No significant property destruction as an expression of aggression.
6. No threats to leave the relationship (except for temporary "time-outs" to defuse a tense situation).
7. No pattern of extreme verbal put-downs, or character assassinations, or other humiliating acts.
8. No acts of infidelity or behaviors that suggest infidelity.
9. No pattern of lying or deception.
10. No pattern of abusing alcohol or drugs.

Other:

_____

_____

Both parties also agree to make all reasonable efforts to focus the therapy sessions on building the positive aspects of the relationship rather than using the session as an opportunity to simply report the bad behavior of the other party.

Four Pillars of Intimacy

Often, when I ask couples why they have come in to see me, I get this response: "We're having a problem with intimacy." And, until I dig deeper, I am never sure how that particular individual or that particular couple is using the word. For some (especially for many men), this is a code word for sex. "We're having a problem with intimacy" = "I'm not getting laid." For others, this same sentence means that they are having trouble communicating openly and honestly. And for others, this means that that aren't spending as much time together or that they seem to be incompatible in their interests and activities.

Particularly for men who are dealing with relationship issues, it is very valuable to expand the definitions of intimacy. I present couples with a handout called "Four Pillars of Intimacy." We review the multiple ways that couples experience intimacy—and only one of those categories includes passion and sex. Since men so often identify sex as the one tried-and-true method to experience this wonderful state known as intimacy, discovering the multiple ways that both partners actually can experience intimacy is illuminating.

Plenty of men *know* the rich feeling of intimacy that comes from shared experiences, from laughing at jokes together, from feeling really safe with another person, from knowing and from being known. They just never had a label for it, nor was the richness brought to consciousness. It is easy for couples to get stuck in a logjam: She feels like she is offering him plenty of intimacy, and all he notices is that she doesn't want to have sex as much as he does. So both feel like they are being "good partners" and that their needs are reasonable but unmet.

Sometimes it is helpful to work with the partner to help her recognize the importance of the sexual connection for him, but trying to get someone to have sex more than they generally want to is a tough nut to crack. More likely to succeed is to help the man recognize the bounty: There are already plenty of ways that he is loved and valued and plenty of moments that fill his needs for intimacy. Expanding the intimacy range takes the pressure off of sex, and it takes the pressure off the partner to provide something so meaningful in only one particular way.

Ironically, in couples with these dynamics, the less meaning and pressure he attaches to sex, the more likely he is to get it.

Four Pillars of Intimacy

Emotional Security and Safety
- Freedom from physical violence
- Freedom from threats of infidelity
- Freedom from threats of abandonment
- Freedom from humiliation or emotional abuse
- Trust in maintaining privacy and confidentiality

Personal Knowledge and Emotional Intimacy
- Knowing the details of the other person's everyday life and history
- Recognizing the personal vulnerabilities of the other person
- Knowing what is genuinely meaningful and rewarding to the other person

Expressions of Affection
- Genuine communication that "I like you"
- Everyday expression of physical affection
- Everyday expression of verbal affection
- Playfulness and humor together
- Shared meaningful and rewarding activities

Sex and Passion
- Compatibility of sexual drive and sexual behaviors
- Deeply connecting sexual experiences
- Consistent personal attraction

Empathic Accuracy and Empathy-Based Responses

For many men, the most profound roadblock to a reasonably successful relationship lies in their deficits in clearly reading the other person's experience and needs and responding in a way that is profoundly respectful of that accurate read.

The studies on *empathic accuracy* described in Chapter 1 are especially relevant. Empathic accuracy is an unquestionably positive characteristic, reflecting the ability of one partner in a relationship to accurately read and understand the partner's affective and cognitive state (Ickes, 1997). Empathic accuracy reflects the perceiver's ability and motivation to accurately infer the specific content of the thoughts, feelings, needs, and motivations of the "target" (the relationship partner).

What would explain why someone in an adult intimate partner relationship—a relationship with at least some degree of love and commitment and caring—would miss the mark in empathic accuracy? These deficits, of course, can be female-to-male, male-to female, parent-to-child, gay or straight, or any other combination. But since our theme is men and how understanding their relationship glitches guides us about interventions, let's start with the most obvious and benign explanation: deficits in emotional intelligence. Plenty of men, for reasons that have already been discussed, have not developed good skills in reading the emotional states of themselves or others. So when they are called upon to make sense of the thoughts, emotions, and motivations of their partner, they may fail because of this underdeveloped skill. Skills can be taught, and that's why every communication workshop and most couples therapy sessions focus on developing improved skills at active listening and accurate reading of the other person's state.

Other times, the deficits in male empathic accuracy and capacity to offer empathic responses have deeper roots. Many men fail to attend successfully to their partner's social cues because they rely excessively on preexisting biases to interpret partner's behaviors:

You can't trust women.
I can tell she was trying to disrespect me.
I can't let myself be controlled again.
I have been hurt before, and I won't let it happen again.

In situations like these, men are unfortunately plagued with the curse of "attributing hostile intent." They are guided by hostile or fearful attributions regarding their partner's behavior.

One other standard reason that a man may fail at the task of offering a response based on empathic accuracy is that he doesn't care. He may have the ability to accurately infer his partner's thoughts and feelings but he may not be particularly motivated to respond with anything resembling compassion, patience, or accommodation. If he is emotionally withdrawn from the relationship or if he feels victimized and resentful, he simply may not feel like generating an empathy-based response. More disturbingly, some men who fundamentally mistrust and resent women or who are characterologically psychopathic may have goals for their relationship that compete directly with compassionate responses. They may be more motivated to control or punish their partner rather than to maintain a healthy relationship.

Multiple Forms of Empathy-Based Responses

In couples, another issue often emerges that interferes with the successful implementation of accurate empathy-based responses. Sometimes the intent is good, but the form of expression is not user-friendly to the other party. In couples therapy, both parties need education regarding the man's conformity to masculine norms in his communication style, as well as the woman's conformity to female norms in her response style. Both partners need empathy regarding the other's relational standards instead of assuming that their partner's needs are the same as theirs.

Particularly for men, it is crucial to recognize that there are multiple types of responses that can reflect empathic accuracy or can communicate an empathic connection. We usually think of the most obvious, which is often identified as some form of "active listening": *Gee, that must have been so hard for you* and the like. And if we are guiding couples to improve the communication of empathy, that direct, straightforward verbal response usually does the job.

However, for many men, there are ways of saying "I love you" or "I understand and I care" without the words. Plenty of men, for whom direct verbal expression does not come as easily or as naturally, let their partners know that they understand by bringing them a cup of coffee or a piece of pizza and then cleaning up the kitchen afterward. Or they might say "Wow!" Or they might threaten revenge against the person who made their wife or girlfriend feel bad. Or they might choose to hang around the house that evening and watch a chick flick without complaining. These expressions of caring, based on a reasonable degree of empathic accuracy, are valuable even if they sometimes miss the mark. Even though we are always encouraging men to get more effective at offering attuned empathy-based responses, it also makes sense for his partner to expand her range of what she considers empathic.

One woman in couples therapy came into a session beaming with excitement: *This is really working! You know what he did? He was watching TV and I said I need to talk to him about something. Right away, he grabbed the remote and turned off the TV, turned his chair around, and looked me in the eye. And he asked me, "What's up?" That's exactly what has been missing, and it meant a lot to me. He's really listening.*

You may read this example and think that this woman has just been worn down so long that her expectations are way too low. I just see hope. Both of them are discovering that she is not that hard to please and that he has it in him to offer her some key responses that she needs. When I heard this story, I turned to him and said, "See? Now, how hard was that?" They both laughed, and they both felt like more was possible.

Confronting "Relational Dread"

In his work on men's experience of shame, Bergman (1995) described the anxiety that many men have in exposing their internal discomfort with the language of emotion. He coined the term *relational dread* to identify this male experience.

What's the dread? It is not fear of relationships per se, but fear of what often seems to be required of men (now more than ever) in terms of communicating about the relationship or the associated experiences of being in a relationship. Men often dread dealing with relationship issues and emotion-based conversations, privately or in the context of couples counseling, because of classic internalized male gender role prohibitions. They fear that they will fail at this task and that they will look foolish even trying. At its worst, this leads to a paralysis for men when they fear that something bad is going to happen if they become engaged in this relationship conversation. They fear failure at the task of demonstrating competence in relating to their partner.

The Seven Components of Relational Dread

More than anything else, a man may become flooded with negative thoughts about his inability to produce the feeling words his female partner may be asking of him. He may also experience feelings of shame associated with his incompetence. Here are some of the specific components of the *relational dread* experience, with typical cognitions that accompany them (Bergman, 1995):

1. Inevitability of disaster: *Nothing good can come of this. I am going to feel bad and so will she; I just have to endure this till it's over.*
2. Timelessness: *This is never going to end. We're going to be in this unbearable conversation for hours.*
3. Damage: *My self-esteem and our relationship are both going to be worse, and the damage will be immense and irreparable.*
4. Closeness: *I know this from past experience: More closeness like this in relationships inevitably leads to more pain—I DREAD this!*
5. Fluid process: *There's not enough structure here—I don't know what I am supposed to do.*
6. Incompetence and shame: *She is so much better at this than I am and I should be more successful. I am failing.*
7. Fear of aggression: *I am afraid that my anxiety and discomfort will lead me to become aggressive—I don't really trust myself.*

Because of this shame and dread, many men will not even try. They will squirm and deflect, avoid and defend. So when a man caught in the paralysis of relational dread is asked a simple question such as "How do you feel?" he will often freeze in his tracks and say that he doesn't know. For some men, this may genuinely mean that they don't know—but the *relational dread* phenomenon may tell us that they are just terrified of going there, which provokes frustration in the man's partner and distance in the relationship. Or this same man may respond by distraction: withdrawing, tuning out, changing the subject, making jokes, being nice or charming, and so on, which provokes frustration in the man's partner and distance in the relationship.

Relational Dread Intervention Strategies

Understanding the origin and nature of this relational dread is an enormously valuable clinical tool for therapists and a relationship tool for the partners of men who dread. It changes everything. It means that we can view this man's frustrating behavior in the relationship context with compassion and specific interventions that target the specific nature of the dread. This is not the equivalent of making excuses—it just means that we can intervene better.

The most important thing is to show some empathy for why this man may not be cooperating with the relationship program here. Even a straightforward reflective comment that names the experience can go a long way: *Jeez, you really hate this, don't you?* or *It is hard to talk about these feelings when your whole life you have kept this to yourself,* or even a teasing (but empathic) comment like *Man, aren't you glad you showed up today?*

If he fears that opening up a feelings discussion will lead to a marathon of processing hell, help the couple establish a time limit: *When you talk about this issue at home, set an alarm for 10 minutes. Discussion ends then, no matter what.* He will spend less time avoiding because it is not so aversive, and his partner gets more of what she needs overall.

For the man who dreads the lack of structure, make sure that he is fully equipped with very specific relationship-friendly communication strategies, like "active listening." Establish clear ground rules abut one person talking at a time. Identify any name-calling or characterological put-down statements as off-limits.

If a man is feeling shamed and unsuccessful, it can be very soothing and engaging to simply and compassionately state the obvious: *I know you don't feel like you're very good at this and that your wife is disappointed,* followed by words of encouragement like *I'm going to help you figure out how to do this and I know you can do it.*

Another valuable intervention to help men make the bridge between their positive intentions (*I really do want to have a better relationship*) and their task execution (*I can't seem to do this right and now I'm afraid to even try*) involves an old Virginia Satir family therapy technique known as "doubling." When a man in a relationship is having a hard time expressing himself, the therapist speaks for him. This works especially well when the therapist "gets" what this man is trying to do or longing to say but hasn't yet been able to present successfully. The therapist moves over to the man's side and gets very close (if you try this, make sure your client can handle this physical closeness), then positions his or her head near the client's, looking out at the partner. The therapist speaks in the client's more emotionally articulate voice: *I'm really trying to be more of the man you want me to be—I'm just freaked out that I might fail at this. That's why I shut down so much.*

When "doubling" is successful, it helps the client find words that he was unable to generate on his own, but now may be more able to. His emotional vocabulary is enhanced. For the partner, the man's behavior is now reframed as a good man struggling, rather than a cold man withholding. His partner often responds by saying something like *Now I get where you're coming from. How can I help you feel safe trying to talk more?*

If men express emotionality—and it is not validated or rewarded—then they are less likely to try to again.

Attachment Issues and Relationship Insecurity

As we try to make sense of the origins and the dynamics of male empathic accuracy deficits, normative male alexithymia, and male relational dread, it is valuable to look through the lens of attachment theory and attachment disorders—not only to understand better, but also to intervene better.

The development of attachment theory has had a profound effect on our understanding of child development, emotional self-regulation, and relationship dynamics. To activate the best qualities of men in their most intimate, attachment-based relationships, it is essential to understand the key elements of attachment conflicts and how these are expressed in relationships. Once we understand a man from this perspective, we can pass this knowledge on to him—or at least operate in the couples sessions informed by the wisdom of the attachment issues that we understand.

Peter Fonagy, one of the pioneers of the applications of attachment theory in clinical practice, said that attachment theory postulates a universal human need to form close affectional bonds (Fonagy et al., 2002). Attachment theory carefully identifies the nature of early experiences of children and the impact of these experiences on aspects of later functioning. Since attachment is the context within which the human infant learns to regulate emotion, this attachment style serves as a blueprint for adult experiences, particularly in the most intimate of relationships. Intimacy, of course, activates attachment issues.

To put it most simply, if a child in distress is soothed in a "good enough" fashion by a parent, the child develops a sense of secure attachment. If the parent is absent, inattentive, unattuned, or downright cruel and rejecting, distress disorganizes the child and desperate behavior escalates.

The categories of insecure attachments were initially classified as *anxious-avoidant* and *anxious-ambivalent*. A third category of insecure attachments emerged later in the research that was eventually called *disorganized*. Subsequent (and contemporary) corresponding terms for the three insecure patterns are *dismissing*, *preoccupied*, and *fearful*.

Secure Attachment
The image that captures the psychological and emotional functioning of the secure child is that of a child who seeks proximity and comfort from the mother but then returns to play when she is gone or when she reappears. The child cares, expresses that he cares, maintains a fundamental confidence that his mother will return, and responds to the distress of the absent and returning mother with a reasonable level of resiliency and adaptation.

What does this predict for men in relationships? They experience a more "cohesive" sense of self. They are more likely to have long and stable relationships. Self-esteem is greater, and they do not experience loneliness to the same degree that men who have developed from more insecure attachment patterns are likely to experience. They are more likely to cope with stress and distress by seeking social support and are more confident and comfortable with some degree of depending on others. Their capacity for self-disclosure is reasonably well developed.

Preoccupied (Anxious-Ambivalent) Attachment

In contrast, men whose psychological and relational lives have been shaped by a *preoccupied* style often try to please others in order to receive approval. As infants, these men were difficult to comfort or soothe after their anxieties had been aroused by the disappearance of their mother. These children sought contact with their mothers (as opposed to ignoring them upon their return) but also became angry at being abandoned or neglected.

Now, as adult men, they can present as extremely self-controlled in many life situations. But when they are in an intimate relationship and they perceive some threat of rejection or abandonment (which they perceive more often than others), they can become extremely clingy and angry. They are overwhelmed by their attachment needs and are unable to contain the anxiety and attachment-seeking behaviors.

Preoccupied men often carry a negative self-image, fearful and doubting as to their capacity to maintain the interest and attention of the loved partner. They are highly emotionally invested in their relationships, but also have a higher breakup rate. They are more obsessed than most other men with trying to please others and they worry excessively about rejection. They feel unappreciated. Most significantly, for those of us who work with men in relationships, they are excessively emotionally dependent, romantically obsessive, and jealous. They are "preoccupied" with their partners.

In working with men whose attachment styles are characterized by these patterns, it is essential to recognize their vulnerability to breakdowns in their experience of mirroring selfobjects; broken mirrors are more likely when you are living in fear of rejection and abandonment. As clients, these men need cognitive structures to make sense of their anxieties and the narrative distortions that trigger them. Practical self-talk strategies and self-soothing techniques are particularly appropriate here.

The preoccupied male client generates narratives that tend to be convoluted and saturated with uncontained affect about attachment experiences. He needs to learn how to better self-soothe so that his narrative will have more objectivity and cognitive structure to contain the appropriate degree of affect.

Dismissing (Anxious-Avoidant) Attachment

Men with a dismissing style come across as disconnected emotionally. The infants from whom these men grew up tended to avoid or ignore their mothers upon reuniting with them after a separation. It is as if these children made a major life choice as these patterns of development took place: *I will not let you hurt me again and I will seal up my heart to make sure and protect myself.* They seem to lack empathy. They often appear to others as if they are cold and uninterested in intimate relationships. They can vacillate between being distant and cut off emotionally and being critical and controlling.

When you explore the cognitions of dismissing men, you discover a preponderance of cynical and negative views of others: these men are particularly guarded and mistrustful in the most intimate relationships. They are reluctant to self-disclose. They seem less invested in relationships and tend to have more breakups. When the breakups do happen, they appear to experience less grief or distress than others; they just don't seem to care as much.

One man in one of my men's groups has the nickname of "Next!" His solution for every relationship problem that is discussed is simple: Get rid of her and find another one. Of course, it sometimes is appropriate to end a relationship that is marked by betrayal and profound disrespect. But he views all relationship flaws as felonies rather than misdemeanors and is remarkably expert at denying his own collusion in the relationship problems he has dealt with. Furthermore, he consistently chooses women who are unstable and who betray him, thus confirming his attachment-based life script that women can't be trusted and should be quickly discarded before they hurt him again.

Part of the therapeutic strategy in helping these men deal more effectively in relationships is, first of all, to help them (and their partners) recognize these roadblocks to intimacy. Then it helps to put this in a compassionate perspective, such as this: *It makes sense that you would have developed this attitude about relationships—look at your history. You had to do something to protect yourself.* This would be followed, of course, by *But we can all see that you have outgrown this. It's not working for you and the adult needs you have now.*

These men seem to lack an "emotional soundtrack" (Sonkin & Dutton, 2003). So another key therapeutic task is to help them develop one. More than anything else, this means creating a safety zone in the context of the couples counseling so they can redo the original attachment crisis. We want them to be able to turn to their partner and articulate what hurts or what scares them without pretending that it doesn't matter.

Fearful (Disorganized) Attachment

A third category of insecure attachment has also been identified, which includes elements of both the dismissing and preoccupied batterers, known as fearful (or disorganized). People in this category experience fear of rejection or betrayal if they are too close (and thus they dismiss and distance) and anxiety if they are too distant (and thus they become preoccupied and anxious).

The fearful children in attachment studies were particularly ambivalent upon reunion with their attachment figure, both approaching and avoiding contact. Bowlby (1969) described these children with his famous image of infants arching away angrily while simultaneously seeking proximity when reintroduced to their mothers. These children (and ultimately these adults) are anxious when cut off from their key attachment figure, yet uncomfortable and unsafe and discontented when they are attached. Men who fit this description expect the worst from relationships, but they need relationships to soothe their anxieties and to heal their damaged self-image.

Even more so than with other men whose relationship issues are influenced by insecure attachment, the therapist needs to address the early childhood trauma experiences and the disorganizing effects these experiences have generated.

Attachment-Based Anger

In trying to make sense of displays of anger in a man's intimate relationships, the attachment perspective can be especially valuable for the therapist, for the man, and for his partner. This is all part of the reframing process. Using the knowledge about attachment issues, we can identify excessive anger not only as destructive but also as a desperate attempt for contact and connection.

Bowlby's (1973) studies included observations of young children separated for the first time from their mothers. His studies identified an emotional and behavioral sequence of anger, despair, and detachment. This led him to the conclusion that the primary function of intimacy-based anger was actually to try to connect: to generate displays that would lead to the return of the absent mother. He saw anger as a signal to the mother that she was needed to help the child soothe tension and anxiety in ways that the child was not yet capable of doing for himself. The child (or the adult) fears loss and becomes angry in order to let the mother (or the intimate partner) understand and hopefully respond to the need.

According to Bowlby (1973), dysfunctional anger, occurring later in adult affectional bonds, is anger that distanced the attachment object (now his adult partner) instead of bringing the attachment object (now his adult partner) closer. Dysfunctional anger occurs whenever a person becomes so intensely and/or persistently angry with his partner that the bond between them is weakened—instead of strengthened—and the partner is alienated. The most violently angry and dysfunctional responses of all are elicited in people of all ages who not only experience repeated separations but are constantly subjected to the threat of being abandoned.

When these attachment bonds are highly insecure, the man converts anxiety to anger. He will often experience high levels of jealousy and use control to cover dependency. He eternalizes blame consistently: *She is making me feel like this.* The simple attachment-informed construct that can help men deal with anger issues in their intimate relationships is this: *Your anger once served a purpose, in letting the person closest to you know you were upset and needed attention and soothing. But now it has gotten out of hand and is destroying the very thing you want most: intimacy with the woman you love.*

Tasks of Attachment-Based Therapy

The therapist who is thinking of the male client's relational issues with these attachment themes should keep in mind several key tasks (in addition to the 10,000 other things a therapist is always trying to keep track of in a couples session):

1. *Create a safe place or "secure base":* The more you understand attachment issues and the dysfunctions that emerge from insecure attachment, the more vital it is to ensure that the client feels safe. This is basic and serves as the platform for all else. For men, this particularly means feeling respected, understood, not shamed, and encouraged in his efforts. It also means that the messages he hears are straight, true, and direct—even if they are presented in a respectful fashion.

2. *Educate about attachment issues:* This does not have to be a graduate-level course in attachment theory. Attachment theory can be made very user-friendly by using simple statements like this: *Your mother wasn't around much and your father fought with you a lot. So you made a decision at some point that you weren't going to let people hurt you or disappoint you anymore. Makes sense to me. Now that we get this, we can see how this is getting in your way right here and now.*

3. *Find new ways of regulating attachment anxiety:* Men in relationships whose attachment conflicts are activated (getting preoccupied and possessive, acting like they don't care, getting angry to maintain attachment, etc.) need specific skills to regulate this anxiety. It is here that the couples therapist functions as an educator or coach: teaching self-talk strategies, relaxation techniques, distraction strategies, and so on. Perhaps most important, we can train this man to recognize what is being activated within him and to generate a new narrative: *I am feeling like Stacy doesn't love me any more, but it might just be that she needs her own space. Repeat the mantra: Stacy is not my mother!*

Jeremy Holmes (2001) suggests that attachment-based psychotherapy is a process of story-making and story-breaking. Our interventions need to break the rigid, unemotional, and unrelated story of the *dismissing* man and create a story with greater emotional content, better balance of positive and negative experiences, and a more descriptive and realistic narrative description of relationships. With the *preoccupied* man, our narrative task is to break the emotional dysphoria by creating one that is also infused by logic and perspective and balance of affect and reflective understanding. And with the *disorganized* man, the task is to do both.

Gay Couples: Similarities and Differences

Gay men are raised in the same masculine society as straight men—and thus they incorporate some of the same strengths and weaknesses, the healthy and unhealthy aspects of growing up male, as do their straight counterparts. Longitudinal research on gay, lesbian, and heterosexual married couples by Kurdek (1998) and his associates has generally concluded that gay and lesbian individuals in relationships operate on essentially the same principles as straight relationships. They struggle for power and control. They have conflicts about emotional commitment. They compete over who makes more money, who has a more prestigious job, who attracts more sexual interest, who is more competent or smart—just like straight couples (Bepko & Johnson, 2000).

John Gottman and associates (Gottman, Levenson, Gross, Frederickson, McCoy, Rosenthal, et al., 2003; Gottman, Levenson, Swanson, Swanson, Tyson, & Yoshimoto, 2003) conducted a 12-year study of gay and lesbian couples at the University of Washington. Using the same models for examining subtle patterns that distinguish successful from unsuccessful heterosexual couples, this research studied 21 gay couples and 21 lesbian couples. As in their other classic studies of couples, here they recorded gay and lesbian couples interacting and coded partners' expressions to learn more about their emotions and behavioral outcomes.

One striking pattern in these findings had to do with the universality of relationships: Overall, relationship satisfaction and quality are about the same across all couple types (straight, gay, lesbian) that Gottman and his associates have studied. Gottman and Levenson concluded that "gay and lesbian couples, like straight couples, deal with everyday ups-and-downs of close relationships" (2008, p. 1).

Of course, the observations about similarities and universality between straight and gay couples always must be understood with some major qualifiers, just as is true with any ethnic minority or social subculture. After outlining the similarities between straight and gay couples, Gottman and Levenson also made this comment: "We know that these ups-and-downs may occur in a social context of isolation from family, workplace prejudice, and other social barriers that are unique to gay and lesbian couples" (2008, p.1).

Although many gay men typically view their committed relationships as seriously as heterosexual couples do, an inevitable pressure on a gay relationship stems from the lack of official societal sanctioning of this union (Bepko & Johnson, 2000). At the time of this writing (although the option for gay marriage may be in transition in some states), the historical absence of society's blessings simply makes gay relationships more complicated. This adds extra layers of complexities to gay relationships, especially if each partner has different ideas about how visible the couple should be to the outside world. Kurdek's (1998) studies found that, compared to married straight couples, gay partners reported more autonomy, fewer barriers to leaving, and more frequent relationship dissolution.

Much of the most recent Gottman research (Gottman, 2000) highlights ways in which gay and lesbian couples handle conflict more successfully than straight couples. Overall, compared to straight couples, the research showed that gay and lesbian couples are more upbeat in the face of conflict. They often use more affection and humor when they bring up a disagreement, and partners are more positive in how they receive it. Gay and lesbian couples are also more likely to remain positive after a disagreement. They are more successful in activating one of the hidden strengths in successful couples, the use of "repair mechanisms."

Furthermore, gay and lesbian couples use fewer controlling, hostile emotional tactics. Gay partners display less belligerence, domineering, and fear with each other than straight couples do. In a fight, gay and lesbian couples take it less personally. In straight couples, it is easier to hurt a partner with a negative comment than to make one's partner feel good with a positive comment. Remarkably, this research suggests that this pattern is reversed in gay and lesbian couples. Gay and lesbian partners' positive comments have more impact on feeling good, whereas their negative comments are less likely to produce hurt feelings. Gay and lesbian partners, according to these studies, have attributes that are quite valuable for the success of relationships: the tendency to accept some degree of negativity without taking it personally.

Another trend that distinguishes gay and lesbian couples from straight couples, in a positive and hopeful way, is that "unhappy" gay and lesbian couples tend to show lower levels of physiological arousal during conflict. This is just the reverse for straight couples. This physiological arousal—including elevated heart rate, sweaty palms, and jitteriness—is an indicator of frustration and aggravation and often a predictor of hostility and aggression. The research suggest that gay and lesbian couples have lower levels of physiological arousal during conflict, which correlates with an increased capacity to soothe each other.

One warning sign for gay men in particular emerged in this research. If the initiator of conflict in a gay relationship becomes too negative (the "harsh start-up"), his partner is not able to repair as effectively as lesbian or straight partners. Gay men may need extra help to offset the impact of negative emotions that inevitably come along when couples fight and to do whatever possible—even more than everyone else—to avoid negativity in conflict.

Educating Partners

Ultimately, in addition to all the ways that counselors and therapists can address the challenge of bringing out the best qualities of men in intimate relationships, it helps to enlist the aid of his partner as the central ally in this task.

This does not mean that she is responsible for healing him. (Although I use the pronoun "she" throughout these guidelines, most of these same principles apply to gay male relationships as well). This does not mean that she should tread carefully to protect the fragile male ego. This does not mean that her emotional needs should take a backseat to his. It simply means that, if we are all in this together, it is simply smart, pragmatic, and productive to approach one's partner in a way that is most likely to elicit the most pro-relationship response—as long as this does not involve an unfair or unbearable sacrifice to the approaching partner.

The Broken Mirror and Softened Start-Up

A woman who is "informed" about broken mirror issues and the particular sensitivities that men have about feeling unimportant or disrespected is in a better position to approach her partner. She can contribute to the health of the relationship, and to the likelihood of drawing out the good man rather than the good man behaving badly, by perfecting the art of what Gottman (1999) has described as the "softened start-up." Softened start-ups might otherwise be described as good old-fashioned good manners. The harsh start-up sounds like this: *Why am I the only one who ever does any cleaning up around here?* It may seem true at the moment—but it is an exaggeration of the truth, it does not honor the positive qualities of her partner, and it is usually communicated in a hostile tone of voice.

Some men, who are blessed with patience or tact or who avoid conflict or who are simply having a very good day, can accept the harsh start-up and deflect it. More typically, they respond defensively and prepare to retaliate. The harsh start-up communicates her distress but does nothing to contribute to the atmosphere of generosity and mutual respect that both people ultimately want in their relationship.

The softened start-up sounds more like this: *I am really feeling overwhelmed with how messy the house is. Can we spend some time tonight working on this together?* Isn't that how anyone would like to be addressed? Although many men need a shove sometimes, most men do best if they feel fundamentally respected and appreciated. Then they are much more likely to feel generous.

The softened start-up is concise. It may register a complaint, but without much blame or accusation. It comes with a softened tone of voice and nonconfrontational body language. It usually starts out with something positive, includes a message of *We're in this together and I care about you,* and is more descriptive than judgmental. To put it most simply, it is polite, and someone who is on the receiving end of this may—on good days, at good moments—actually experience it as a gift. As in *Thank you for sharing.*

Disqualifications

One of the patterns in couples' counseling that often derails progress occurs when the woman complains about a man's behavior and requests that he change. He integrates this (sometimes reluctantly and defensively) and actually tries to make some movement in the requested direction.

And then she finds fault with him and his efforts. She usually finds fault because of her anxiety that the changes are not real, genuine, or likely to last. No matter what the understandable reason for her criticism and skepticism, it kills his momentum. Here are some classic negative reactions from a woman in response to the changes a man is trying to make (Wexler, 2006b).

1. *His behavior:* Upon her request, he has made an effort to demonstrate more affection and appreciation toward her.

Her discounting self-talk: "He never would have done this on his own."

Negative reaction: "Yes, you've been showing more affection and appreciation lately, but it's just because the counselor told you to. You don't really mean it."

Or she could use constructive self-talk: "I can tell he's trying. This is more of what I need from him."

Which would lead to a more rewarding response: "It feels great to me that you've been touching me more. It's starting to feel like the old days."

2. *His behavior:* Upon her request, he has made an effort to socialize more with her family when they come over to visit.

Her wounded self-talk: "I don't think I can forgive him for letting me down so much in the past."

Negative reaction: "Why do you even bother? I know you don't want to be here with them, and so do they!"

Or she could use constructive self-talk: "I like seeing some of his new behaviors, and I can't let myself stay stuck in the past."

Which would lead to a more rewarding response: "It really means a lot to me that you've been trying so hard with my family."

3. *His behavior:* Upon her request, he has been helping out more with the kids at night.

Her discounting self-talk: "What good is it to me if he doesn't do it the way I think it should be done?"

Negative reaction: "I know you've been giving the kids baths more often, but you're not doing it right."

Or she could use constructive self-talk: "This is really new for him to help out more."

Which would lead to a more rewarding response: "I love it that you've been taking over the kids' baths. Can I give you a few tips about what I've found that works well?"

4. *His behavior:* Upon her request, he has made an effort to be less self-involved and listen more to what she is going through.

Her fearful self-talk: "If I don't stay on his case about making these changes, he's just going to get complacent. I can't let up."

Negative reaction: "Of course you're listening to me talk more about my feelings now, but that's only because I'm watching you so carefully. As soon as I take the pressure off, this will all go back to the way it used to be."

Or she could use constructive self-talk: "I can tell he is trying."

Which would lead to a more rewarding response: "It means a lot to me that you are listening to me more. I feel closer to you."

5. *His behavior:* Upon her request, he has been revealing more of his business worries to her.

Her fearful self-talk: "Oh my God, this really scares me!"

Negative reaction: "Oh no, we're going to lose our house!"

Or she could use constructive self-talk: "I know this scares me, but I am really glad he is not keeping this all to himself."

Which would lead to a more rewarding response: "Thanks for letting me know what you are going through. This really means a lot to me."

Expecting Immediate Nondefensiveness

Another classic situation that occurs in couples counseling goes like this. The woman confronts the man about something. It could be relatively minor and she may be presenting it to him in a way that is relatively user-friendly, with a relatively softened start-up:

You are yelling at the kids way too much. I don't think you realize how you're reacting and you need to chill.

The ideal response from the most self-actualized man would be something like this: *I know, I know, you're right. Damn, I've really got to work on this!*

Instead, what we typically hear is a defensive response like this: *What the hell are you talking about? The only reason I have to yell at them is because you spoil them and make me the bad guy. You're the problem, not me!*

So when she hears this, she is very likely to give up. This confirms her worst fear about his man: he is stubborn, defensive, and blaming. She can't get through. There is no point.

What I usually point out to women in this encounter is that this defensiveness is frustrating, immature, and obstructionist—and very normal. Women do the same thing. The vast majority of the men who initially respond with defensiveness like this are demonstrating a knee-jerk reaction to a broken mirror experience. An hour later or a week later, many of these same men either apologize directly with their words or alter their behavior as a tacit apology and a tacit acknowledgment that they are taking the feedback seriously. My advice to her: Be patient here. Recognize the broken mirror experience. Rely on the likely possibility that the message got through, at least somewhat, despite the outward defensiveness. And I would give the same consult to a man frustrated with the same response from the woman in his life.

Multiple Forms of Expressing Love

For both the therapists and the partners of men, it is very important to recognize the multiple forms that we all have for expressing love. Many women get hurt and frustrated because their male partner doesn't tell her he loves her or offer romantic demonstrations of affection. And while a woman's frustration in this situation is understandable, her narrative that her boyfriend or husband is thus uncaring or unloving is not necessarily the right story.

Not all men are like this, but there are certainly many men who express their deepest feelings of connection and caring through behavior—or through the self-control of undesirable behavior:

I washed—and waxed—her car!
I went with her to her parents' house after they had been so rude to me!
I haven't been watching as much football as I used to!
Hasn't she noticed how I have cut way back on smoking pot because I know it bothered her?
If those things aren't love, what is?????

The key component here is to recognize positive intentionality whenever and wherever it can realistically be recognized, rather than just complain because the behavior was not delivered in the proper package. This is simply practical and pragmatic: If a woman tells a man *I really appreciate how you have handled everything with my difficult family— this really tells me you love me*, he is likely to demonstrate more and more expressions of love. He feels encouraged, not hopeless and ashamed. Again, I would give this same consult to a man. It's just practical. When people feel loved and appreciated, they just feel more generous and are more open to hearing other ways to express their generosity.

Chapter 6

Treating Male-Type Depression[1]

Recent research on patterns of depression have uncovered a set of symptoms that appear to be uniquely male. This "male-type depression" is characterized by desperate attempts to escape dysphoric moods, denial of problems, reluctance to seek help, projection of blame for bad moods, and increased aggression.

Categories of Depression

First things first. Before identifying some of the specific issues in depression that are especially relevant in understanding and treating men, any clinician needs to know the wide range of depression diagnoses and constructs. Without going into extensive detail, here are some of the most obvious and universally recognized, based on *DSM-IV* (2000) descriptions and other popular labels for depressive symptomatology:

Major depression (or *major depressive disorder*) is characterized by a combination of symptoms that interferes with the ability to work, study, sleep, eat, and enjoy once-pleasurable activities. A major depressive episode may occur only once but, more commonly, several episodes may occur in a lifetime. Major depression often includes thoughts about suicide or actual suicide attempts. Chronic major depression may require a person to continue treatment indefinitely.

---

[1]Much of the material in this chapter originally appeared in *Is he depressed or what: What to do when the man you love is irritable, moody, and withdrawn*, D.B. Wexler, 2006. Reprinted with permission by New Harbinger Publications, Inc., www.newharbinger.com

Dysthymia (or *dysthymic disorder*) is a less severe type of depression, involving long-lasting symptoms that do not seriously disable but still keep the person from functioning well or feeling good. It describes a condition that we all observe frequently: mild to moderate depression that goes on for a long time but never quite pushes somebody over the edge to suicide, total despair, or incapacitation. Many people with dysthymia also experience major depressive episodes at some time in their lives.

Bipolar disorder (or *manic-depressive illness*) is a type of depressive illness that is characterized by cycling mood changes: severe highs (mania) and lows (depression), often with periods of normal mood in between. Sometimes the mood switches are dramatic and rapid, but usually they are gradual. When in the depressed cycle, an individual can have any or all of the symptoms of depression. When in the manic cycle, the individual may be overactive, overtalkative, and have excessive energy. Mania often affects thinking and judgment, and leads to feelings of invincibility and grandiosity. This is followed by social behaviors that cause serious problems and embarrassment: reckless business decisions or physical risk-taking; gambling sprees; reckless, unsafe sex; aggressive and violent behavior, and so on.

Acute, temporary depression is also known as reactive or situational depression. In everyday language, this describes a reasonably understandable depressive reaction to life events. If someone is clearly grieving and melancholic after the breakup of a relationship, the loss of a job, or even his team's breakdown in the Super Bowl—and he is neither severely debilitated nor afflicted for more than 6 months—then this category applies. Many people get through this kind of depression without treatment, but for many others therapy or medication is indicated. This category specifically rules out bereavement depression, because it is so normal to be depressed when grieving the loss of a loved one. But the intensity and duration of the low mood can reach levels where it would qualify as "beyond normal" and meet the criteria for one of the previously defined clinical categories of depression (even in the case of bereavement).

Seasonal depression (often called *seasonal affective disorder* or *SAD*) is a depression that occurs each year at the same time, usually starting in fall or winter and ending in spring or early summer. It is more than just the winter blues or cabin fever. People who suffer from SAD have many of the common signs of depression: sadness, anxiety, irritability, loss of interest in their usual activities, withdrawal from social activities, and inability to concentrate. They often have symptoms such as extreme fatigue and lack of energy, increased need for sleep, craving for carbo-hydrates, and increased appetite and weight gain. This illness is more commonly seen in people who live at high latitudes where seasonal changes are more extreme. It is estimated that nearly 10% of Alaska residents suffer from SAD. The influence of latitude on SAD strongly suggests that it is caused by changes in the availability of sunlight. One theory states that with decreased exposure to sunlight, the biological clock lock that regulates mood, sleep, and hormones is delayed, running more slowly in winter. Exposure to light may successfully reset the biological clock.

Depression secondary to a medical condition is another category of depression that is often overlooked. This would include specific symptoms, including reactions to medications, that were primarily generated by a physiological condition—not depression, which is simply a psychological reaction to the idea of suffering from this physical condition. Medical illnesses such as strokes, heart attacks, thyroid imbalances, and Parkinson's disease are all known to be risk factors for precipitating depression. Although many depression symptoms can be relieved from psychological understanding and clinical interventions, depression in these cases probably will not abate very much until the source of this physiological problem is treated.

Male hormonal depression (also known as *male menopause, andropause, male climacteric,* or *testosterone-deficiency depression*) sometimes begins to insidiously take hold during the male aging process (Diamond, 1997, 2004). This is the only form of depression that, by definition, only applies to men. Although the male response to aging and hormone changes has very little consistent pattern, sometime during a man's fourth or fifth decade of life (and sometimes as early as his 30s), his body's production of testosterone may begin to slow. This gradual decline can produce a variety of changes and effects on the male body, including:

- Erectile dysfunction;
- Decreased libido;
- Mood disturbances, including depression, irritability, and feeling tired;
- Loss of muscle size and strength;
- Osteoporosis (bone thinning);
- Increased body fat;
- Difficulty with concentration and memory loss; and
- Sleep difficulties.

Male-Type Depression

In addition to all the standard categories above, new conceptions of depression are emerging. In recent years, both research and theory have offered us a new clarity about the particular ways that many men experience and express depression—patterns that have often gone unrecognized and misread in the past.

This is called *depression–male type*, or *male depressive disorder*, or *covert depression*.

Studies (Potts, Burnan, & Wells, 1991) highlighted the profound underdiagnosis of depression in men. Comparing physicians' diagnoses of depression with the administration of specific standard depression questionnaires found that 65% of men's verified depressions went undetected and undiagnosed. In other words, almost two-thirds of men who were actively suffering from depression (even when assessed by an instrument that is actually designed for typical overt depression rather than the unique symptoms that we are discovering in male depression) had their illness undetected and untreated. Depression really looks different in men than in women. Men and women can have the same disease but symptoms can vary greatly.

In this pattern of male depression, men do not usually report sadness, but they do report feeling irritable or tremendously fatigued.

They don't have a name for the feelings, but there's a sense of being dead inside. Something is missing. They feel restless and agitated and unsatisfiable. They lose their vitality. Vague, persistent physical symptoms show up, like headaches, mysterious pain, and insomnia. These men often attempt to self-medicate with alcohol or drugs—or gambling, sexual affairs, workaholism, and reckless physical risk-taking. And, most disturbingly for men's relationships, they blame others for their vague feelings of unhappiness and for their bad moods.

The experience and expression of depressed mood in men are "masked" by culturally derived norms that encourage acting out and self-medication and prohibit grief and sadness (Levant & Pollack, 1995). Pollack gave a wonderful description that captures the tragedy of male acting out as a an expression of internal distress: *That's their way of weeping* (Healy, 2005). Women cry, while men engage in anger, bullying, and blaming. Pollack also captured how the male experience of depression is strongly associated with feelings of vulnerability and shame: *It's the equivalent of being psychologically castrated.*

Acting-Out and Male-Type Depression

Although some depressed men may be plagued by impotence and loss of sexual interest, many others become hypersexual (with their partners or with others). Many complain of depression's physical symptoms—sleep troubles, fatigue, headaches, or stomach distress—without ever discerning their psychological source. Compared to women suffering depression, depressed men are more likely to behave recklessly, drink heavily or take drugs, drive fast or seek out confrontation.

Instead of acting like they are filled with self-doubt, depressed men often bully and bluster and accuse those around them of failing them. For many men, anger—a masculine emotion that one "manages" rather than succumbs to—is their mask for deep mental anguish. Winokur (1997) suggested that alcoholism and antisocial behavior disorders are likely masculine expressions of underlying depression with a genetic basis.

Intense depression is often associated with extreme acting-out problems: suicide and homicide. Suicide is a significant mortality risk for depressed men (Mosciki, 1997). Despite reporting half the depression that women acknowledge in epidemiological surveys, men commit suicide three to four times more frequently than women do (Cochran & Rabinowitz, 2000). This risk rises even higher with increasing age (Metz & Lowinger, 1995). Men act. And men externalize. In addition to suicide, homicide is associated more frequently with men. This, too, often occurs in conjunction with a depressive episode.

To put it very simply (and very generally, because gross statements about men and women are always somewhat misrepresentative), women tend to think and process their feelings when they are depressed, and men tend to act. Acting in the face of depression can either be extremely adaptive (such as going out looking for a job if he is feeling depressed about being unemployed) or extremely maladaptive (such as picking a fight and getting drunk to escape the angst and helplessness of feeling bad about himself, or becoming suicidal). Research studies (Nolen-Hoeksma, 1992) report that when women describe what they actually do when they are depressed, the most typical pattern involves responses like "I try to find out why I feel the way I do" or "I try to analyze my mood." For men, the patterns are typically quite different. Most men report that they turn to an activity they enjoy or simply decide to distract themselves from the bad feelings: "I decide not to concern myself with my mood." Of course, many people (especially men) are likely to respond with "What do you mean, depressed?"

Seligman concluded that "men and women experience mild depression at the same rate, but in women, who dwell on the state, the mild depression escalates; men, on the other hand, dissolve the state by distracting themselves, by action or perhaps by drinking it away" (Seligman, 1998, p. 87). Again, while distraction can come in very handy, the particularly male pattern of avoiding uncomfortable emotional states often leads to avoidance, denial, minimization, and acting out. The distress is there, but it has no name. It is unnamed and unclaimed.

Components of Male-Type Depression

When a man is depressed, he may very well demonstrate the typical clusters of depressive symptoms as delineated in the *DSM-IV* (2000):

depressed most of the day, diminished interest in almost all activities, significant weight loss/appetite changes, insomnia or hypersomnia, psychomotor agitation or retardation, fatigue or loss of energy, feelings of worthlessness/guilt, concentration deficits/indecisiveness, recurrent thoughts of death/suicide, and so on. But he is just as likely to score relatively low on many of these classic symptoms and instead show patterns of many of the newly recognized symptoms of male-type depression. These symptoms can be generally classified in the following four categories.

Antagonistic and Blaming of Others

The covert, underlying depression that these men experience, when unnamed and unclaimed, often lead down a dangerous path of blame. If a man is locked into this pattern, others are likely to notice some of the following characteristics:

- Blames others for his depression/attacks when hurt
- Is overly hostile or irritable
- Believes his problems could be solved only if his wife (co-worker, parent, friend) would treat him better
- Has increase in intensity or frequency of angry outbursts
- Feels suspicious and guarded
- Creates conflicts with very little provocation
- Demands respect from others, especially those closest to him

Exaggerated Behavior

Hidden depression in men, even if it only barely leaks through into consciousness, presents a profound and intolerable threat to traditional masculinity. In response, many men unconsciously turn to exaggerated, hypermasculine behaviors. It's as if they have to consistently prove to themselves and everyone else that they really are NOT depressed— NOT weak, NOT vulnerable, NOT emasculated. It's as if they are desperately turning to behaviors so they can scoff and say to everyone: *Look at me: Do I look like a guy who's depressed?*

Although many people of both genders live interesting and exciting lives by taking risks and seeking out stimulating life experiences, the covert depressed male will often turn desperately to excessively stimulating experiences to try to shock himself out of his depression. He hates feeling bored. He hates feeling down. He hates feeling dull and empty and deadened inside. So he unconsciously administers a kind of shock therapy to himself by generating high-stimulation experiences.

These patterns of male depression typically include the following:

- Tries to fix the depression ONLY by problem-solving
- Becomes compulsive about time and order
- Has a perfectionistic need to master tasks/workaholism
- Makes increasingly rigid demands for autonomy
- Desperately craves sex
- Tries to maintain a strong male image

Avoidance and Escape

When it is obvious that a man is acting erratically, or withdrawing emotionally, or making poor judgment decisions to prove to others that he is a strong and independent person—in other words, when he is probably going through *male-type depression*—then we are probably observing a pattern of behavior designed to avoid feeling bad or escape feeling bad.

There is nothing inherently wrong or dysfunctional with this, in moderation. Finding a way to avoid or escape feeling bad can represent a very resourceful set of skills. But when he's feeling depressed, anxious, alienated, lethargic, unmotivated, and pessimistic, he may have a vague awareness that something disturbing is taking place within, and he may feel woefully ill-equipped to recognize it, name it, express it, and productively deal with it. Or at least live with it until it passes.

This sets the stage for unhealthy avoidance and escape. Avoidance patterns are evident when he carefully selects situations that he does not want to find himself in and carves out a lifestyle engineered so he does not have to go there. Psychologically, this make perfect sense. Who wants to put themselves in a situation that is likely to make them feel bad? Except that the life restrictions we are talking about here are ones that cripple his life. The following are more examples of these patterns:

- Having "I Don't Want To Talk About It" syndrome (Real, 1998)
- Leaving or avoiding intimate relationships for fear of failure
- Feeling terrified of confronting weakness
- Having the incapacity to translate feelings into language: normative male alexithymia (Levant, Good, Cook, O'Neil, Smalley, Owen, et al., 2006)
- Being unable to grieve/denial of sadness
- Using alcohol, TV, video games, the Internet, or sex to self-medicate

Discontent with Self

Another primary feature of male-type depression is a profound unhappiness with himself. He is likely to display signs of the following:

- Being shame-sensitive/shame-phobic
- Having a strong fear of failure
- Being harshly self-critical, often focusing on failures as a provider or protector
- Feeling ashamed for feeling depressed
- Being plagued by "imaginary crimes" (Engel & Ferguson, 1990) and fears that he is disappointing or hurting others

Relationship Judgement Impairment in Male-Type Depression

In the movie *About Schmidt* (Gittes, Besman, & Payne, 2002), Jack Nicholson plays the lead role, Warren Schmidt, who is recently widowed, lonely, and depressed. But he doesn't know what to call this or what to do. To the audience, it is plain as day that this man is depressed and lost. We can see that something is wrong with him and that he is profoundly disconnected from himself and from others. If anybody in his life were to suggest this to him, they would likely get a denial and a "No, no, I'll be fine" response. And he would not be purposely lying or deceiving. He really would not have the language to describe his experience or make sense of it in the language that makes sense to others.

In one scene, Schmidt meets a very nice couple living in a trailer who befriend him. When the man in this couple goes out to pick up something from the store, and Schmidt is left alone with the youngish woman, she tells him that he seems so sad and lonely. He is touched by her compassion and understanding. He softens, opens up to her. He even puts his head on her shoulder. She is a little surprised. Then he starts kissing her passionately—and she jumps up, outraged, and screams at him to leave. It is so painfully obvious that he is not a sexual predator and means no harm. He is just emotionally clueless. He has had no clue about how depressed he has been, and thus he is overwhelmed with gratitude that a kind soul has identified this pain in his heart. And he is so inexperienced with his emotional life that he confuses friendliness and understanding—and the flood of good feelings that accompany them—with sexual interest. So, because he has a depression with no name, and because he experiences warm feelings of connection with no proper name, he turns this into one of his few known male pathways for meaningful connection: sex. Many men have an underdeveloped ability to make these kinds of discriminations. Their portfolio for feeling warmth for others is not fully diversified, just like their inability to distinguish between irritation and rage, or minor rudeness from profound betrayal and threat.

In the Woody Allen movie *Hannah and Her Sisters* (1986), Elliot (Michael Caine) struggles with a classic midlife depression. He feels empty, restless, unfulfilled by his competent, loving, but (to him) "too perfect" wife Hannah, played by Mia Farrow. So he develops a mad, insatiable crush on Hannah's sister, Lee (Barbara Hershey). He sneaks around desperately trying to woo her, eventually wreaking havoc in the lives of himself, his wife, and his sister-in-law. What is missing from his capacity to behave any way but stupidly is some deeper recognition of his depression. He doesn't know what to call the demon within. It should be called "Elliot is going through a midlife depression and needs to find more meaning in his life and in his marriage, if possible." Elliot's narrative instead is "If I only I had Lee in my life, I would feel better and this crappy feeling would go away."

My client Raul told me about what he went through earlier in his marriage that was chillingly similar: *I was so depressed in my marriage. I felt totally disconnected. I could tell she didn't care for me anymore, and I felt lost. And then I started to develop a thing for her sister. I couldn't stop thinking about her. Finally, after I had a few drinks at a family gathering, I took her aside and told her, "You're the one I'm really in love with!" She was shocked. She told her mother, who told my wife, and the shit started rolling. It was just like in that Woody Allen movie. It was like I was on drugs, except the drug was depression. It set the stage for me to lose all judgment and do something so stupid and totally passive-aggressive.*

Another depressed man, Terry, drifted away from his marriage and had an affair. The shock of what he had done forced him to wake up and put words to the innermost of the miserable feelings he had been carrying around inside: *Don't you realize I just don't have much time left? I got cancer two years ago! Fucking cancer! The big C! Everybody thinks I'm recovered but who knows? My father died last year. My mother's on her way out. Our relationship has slipped away. So that's why I felt so much urgency! And I guess my head was in the clouds. I just didn't see how it would affect you or the kids or anyone else. Now I get it a little more. I have been depressed and worried! I've got to talk about this. I can't just keep making impulsive decisions with my head up my ass.*

For each of these men, the depression here—unnamed and unclaimed—serves as a profound disinhibitor. It distorts their judgment, and it releases them to do things that they would not normally do. They desperately want to find some salvation from the feelings that are so fragmenting. If they can be drawn out of the alexithymia and actually put some words to their feelings (all the feelings, not just anger or blame), there is hope that they may quit projecting responsibility for their unhappiness onto others.

Author Terrence Real put it this way: "One of the ironies about men's depression is that the very forces that help create it keep us from seeing it. Men are not supposed to be vulnerable. Pain is something we are to rise above" (1998, p. 22).

The Emotional Blackmail of the Depressed Male

Sometimes the partner of a depressed man experiences guilt, not only because she feels blamed for his unhappiness, but because of the inevitable by-product when he feels really bad about *himself*.

Sometimes this emerges naturally, with no intent on his part, but other times the depressed man may find ways to subtly and passive-aggressively make his partner feel sorry for him in a way that controls her mood and behavior. Misery loves company.

The Threat of Suicide
The most obvious and destructive form of this is the suicidal threat: *I will kill myself if you leave me.* He may be saying this in all sincerity, simply stating the facts. Or he may be saying this in a desperate, manipulative, and calculated way, knowing that his partner would never want the blood on her hands if he actually did something so horrible to himself and to her and to the others around him.

No matter what his motivations, this is a pattern that the loved ones of a depressed man should be warned about if there have already been any hints of it. They need to keep their own narratives in check. If he kills himself, horrible as this would be on a thousand different levels and to a thousand different people, it would be his decision, no one else's, and his fault, no one else's.

The risk here is especially significant when a man is in the grip of the angry and blaming components of the male-type depression. Because he finds his own unhappiness and impotence so unbearable, he must find a source for this condition outside of himself. These threats have a three-fold purpose: They project blame, they control the behavior of the other person, and they enact revenge. These tactics, conscious or unconscious in the angry, depressed male, can even be used with some effectiveness in his relationship with counselors and therapists.

When the other people in this man's life have their own narratives straight in their own minds, they are then equipped to deal with this calmly and effectively. They need to be clear about what they need in a way that is least likely to be punishing or destructive to him: *I pray that you would never do something so horrible to yourself. I would miss you horribly, and so would so many others. But if you choose to do this, it will not be because of me, and I will not run my life in fear that you might take that step.*

The Threat of Feeling Horrible

Another form of manipulation (again, sometimes intended and sometimes not) takes place when a man describes how bad he feels. And then he retreats into painful guilt and excessive self-recrimination. The emphasis here is on the word *excessive*.

For example, my client Aaron, moody and depressed, came into the couples therapy session saying that he really wanted to hear some of the things about his behavior patterns that were bothering his wife. So far, so good. She was reluctant, because he had a history of defensiveness and counterattack when she would bring up issues like this. But, with a therapist in the room to help guide the discussion, she gingerly told him some of the hurt and resentment she had been keeping in.

Aaron did not become defensive. He did not counterattack. Instead he went the other direction: *Oh my God! Everything you say is true. I have been a horrible husband to you. You don't deserve this. I screw everything up. I can't see how you can stay in this relationship, because I know I'll never be able to change.*

She hated hearing this. She liked it when he took some responsibility, but this wave of shame was the last thing she was seeking to provoke and the last thing that gave her comfort. She found herself starting to console him, telling him that it was not as bad as he was making it out to be.

And, of course, it really wasn't as bad as he was making it out to be. But the net effect of his self-flagellation was the same as if he had yelled, threatened, or pouted: Aaron's wife shut up and shut down. Now she felt like she couldn't tell him this kind of information because she didn't want to precipitate this over-the-top reaction in him. She wanted him to take her concerns seriously, but she didn't want him to become so devastated. She felt guilty for making him feel bad. And she was left with the nagging realization that, just when the spotlight was on *her* to talk about *her* feelings, Aaron had found a way to get the spotlight back onto *him* and what *he* was going through.

I don't think Aaron consciously planned out this maneuver, but that didn't change the effect. His wife's best response? Assertively insist that the communication pattern change: *Aaron, wait, you're taking this too far. When you get so devastated, I feel like I can't tell you these things. Let's try this again, and I just want you to listen to what's bothering me, let me know if you get it, and maybe try to problem-solve. That's all.*

In working with the emotional blackmail patterns of male-type depression, I find it helpful to equip his partner and the other important people in his life with clear, respectful responses that establish healthy boundaries declaring who is responsible for what. Although these are written in the voice of his partner, the principles of these responses are relevant for counselors and therapists as well:

Emotional blackmail	**Good response**
I will kill myself if you leave me.	*That would be horrible, but it would be your choice, not mine.*
I know that nobody loves me.	*I don't think that's true, and I want you to know that being upset with you doesn't mean that I don't love you.*
I can never do right for you and the kids—this just proves it.	*I want you to be able to hear what I have to say without making it worse than it is.*
You're right—I do terrible things. I don't know why you stay with me!	*Some of the things you have done have been very hurtful to me. But I stay with you because I love you, and I have to keep telling you when you are treating me badly.*

Midlife Issues and Male Depression

The confluence of midlife issues and depression in men is often a powerful one that requires a special level of awareness—for both therapist and client.

At the core, most men are seeking to find passion that has been lost or misdirected in unhealthy ways (Englar-Carlson & Shepard, 2005).

Context and Education

For some men, good old-fashioned education helps immensely. Many men respond especially well to simple and straightforward labeling of their internal experiences. As long as the label is credible to them and is presented in language that makes sense, they are often very relieved to get a context. With context comes action plans.

Midlife is sometimes referred to as the "third individuation" (Colarusso & Nemiroff, 1981), after the first individuation of the "terrible 2's" and the second individuation of adolescence. It is an opportunity, one more time, to break free of previous patterns and self-definition and for some new aspects of the self to emerge. Midlife offers still another chance for sharper self-other differentiation and new aspects of identity.

But with this opportunity for men, of course, comes upheaval (or at least the potential for upheaval) and a profound potential for experiencing losses. Physical bodies are deteriorating. The physical bodies of spouses and partners are deteriorating. Parents are aging and dying. Dreams about work achievements are fading—or they are fulfilled and they have not brought ultimate happiness. Marriages and the expectations from relationship partners are often in flux. Children are leaving the home and often are not turning out exactly the way that their fathers hoped they would.

Hart (2001) listed a cluster of crises that midlife men are susceptible to. With crisis comes both danger and opportunity:

1. *A crisis of values:* Questions about the meaning of life and how fulfilling the satisfaction of material needs may or may not be become prominent. As in adolescence, all beliefs are up for scrutiny (more examples of the "third individuation").

2. *A crisis over primary relationships:* Closeness and intimacy may have been eroded by familiarity and/or long-standing irritation and resentment. The couple may have steadily drifted apart over years of dissatisfaction or feeling misunderstood.

3. *A crisis over children:* Fathers notice how well the kids are turning out and feel unimportant or that their task is primarily complete. Or

they notice that their children are far different from what they envisioned and they feel profoundly helpless to engineer the outcome they wanted. Their "dreams" for their kids may be turning into "nightmares."

4. *A crisis with aging parents:* Midlife men often experience a role reversal, becoming the guardians of aging parents. Or they experience the death of their parents and feel the weight of being responsible for the next generations in ways they have not faced before.

5. *A crisis of letting go:* A man at this stage may recognize that the sense of unlimited opportunity and possibilities is fading.

Throughout the struggle with these issues, it is important for us to help midlife men recognize this fundamental hopeful attitude about intimate relationships at midlife. Love handles are depressing, but genuine intimacy and wisdom trumps all. Learning how to appreciate and value long-standing relationships (rather than the more youthful gratifications of the physical self and nonrelated sex) is a key component of the truly adult self and a major developmental step of midlife. The main issue in the male midlife crisis is *relatedness* (Davidson, 1979).

Rybarczyk summarized the impact of male midlife crisis: "The consequences of these changes can be positive (e.g., new roles, new goals) and negative (e.g., feelings of disappointment). For men whose self-concepts rely heavily on youth-oriented masculine traits, these changes undoubtedly force a redefinition" of their identities (1994, p. 114).

The "Dream" Crisis of Midlife

One especially powerful crisis that complicates the emotional and psychological issues of midlife men centers around what researcher Daniel Levinson (1978) refered to as the "Dream." Levinson identified male young adulthood as a period with a vision for how a man's life should be. This stage of adult life is dominated by a push toward productivity. This sense of purpose, while challenging and often difficult to fulfill, is very organizing. He is guided by clear goals and themes. The obstacles are tangible, the achievements (for the most part) measurable.

For men, however, the increasing awareness of their ticking clock at midlife often causes disorientation and disillusionment.

The first type, the unfulfilled dream, strikes when he wakes up one day and realizes that the Dream is not going to happen. He faces the often sobering realization that what he sees is what he gets and what he is going to get. He will probably not achieve significantly higher levels of career success than he already has. If he hasn't yet written the great American novel or become vice president of his company, he probably never will. The rock band that he has been trying to put together for years may never quite make it in the way he dreamed, and he may need to settle for producing music rather than performing it. His idealized visions of his family life, how successful or wonderful his kids would be, how loving and appreciative his relationship with his partner would be, how nice a home and lifestyle he would be able to create, may not have quite materialized. In some cases, they may be very painfully unmet. He may fear that there is nothing to look forward to except for a slow deterioration and narrowed possibilities.

Men often develop a nagging sense that aspects of their personality that they once had have faded away, or that aspects that they might have had will never flower. Marlon Brando, speaking the famous line from *On the Waterfront*, laments, "I coulda been a contender" (Kazan, 1954). Although he is hardly in midlife, he is speaking for all men who realize that a golden opportunity has passed them by, never to return. Or so it seems.

The second type of crisis, the crisis of meaning, affects men if they have achieved their dream but suddenly find it meaningless. It does not fulfill him: "So what? Now I am successful. I don't feel any happier. I don't have the approval of my father. I still can't relate to my kids the way I want to. I feel alone. The fundamental struggles never really change!"

The excitement and organizing principle of building something (career, family, reputation), even if it has been fundamentally accomplished, no longer holds everything together. He wonders, now, if this is all there is.

Moods and Feelings

Midlife depression is often fueled by the onset of dark and brooding moods. The men we work with need to understand the power of moods and the difference between moods and feelings. Moods are not feelings. Jungian analyst John Sanford (1979) identified the origin of a mood: when a man is having powerful feelings but is not "attending" to them.

When the mood strikes, the man knows something is wrong, but he doesn't know how to make sense of it. Given the tendency of men to act on their feelings rather than discover them, moods can be dangerous and destructive. Men become itchy and action-oriented, and they tend to project blame. They feel like they have to do *something*, but they don't know which direction to turn.

Moods, with their dark clouds, projection of blame, and emotional withdrawal, are signs of stagnation. When a man is enveloped in a mood, according to Sanford, he can have no real relationship with his partner: *She can't understand, she doesn't care, she's a bitch, it's all her fault anyway.*

The onset of complex emotions and inner conflicts serves as a breeding ground for moods. In a mood, he can't move forward. Feelings are not always pretty, but they are signs of vitality and generativity. Feelings open the door to new energy within himself and new energy in his relationship. Most women can relate to honest expression of feelings, but they are alienated by moods.

Any of the following could be a trigger for a mood:

- feeling injured or upset by something
- feeling embarrassed or humiliated by something his partner, or someone else, said
- feeling unhappy with his work
- feeling frustrated and ineffective as a parent
- feeling a vague sense of lack of fulfillment in his life

Moods come with their own characteristic thoughts, feelings, and behaviors. Any of the following may be an indicator of a mood:

144

- believing that there is no point in talking to anybody about how he feels
- thinking that everyone is just out for themselves and no one really cares about what he is going through
- telling himself that he will just have to work this out on his own
- believing that his partner is determined to make him feel bad about himself or to deprive him of things he really needs
- acting cool toward his partner, finding fault with her, or putting her down
- feeling sorry for himself
- noticing that other people seem to be very cautious about approaching him
- exaggerating and overreacting to slights from others
- trying to make others feel guilty for depriving or hurting him

The strategy for diminishing the tyranny of midlife moods is ridiculously simple and hopelessly hard. Moods dissolve into good old-fashioned complicated feelings when you find the words and talk about them.

First, the man needs to identify the feelings. He needs to develop a language to describe exactly what is bothering him and how it makes him feel. He needs to think about it, write about it, meditate or pray to get clarity about it.

Second, he needs to muster every resource he can so that he does not project blame for his unhappiness, his dark mood, anywhere else. This does not mean wife or his job or his football team are without fault. But men are notorious for desperately avoiding this responsibility for their unhappiness. A man may make this statement to his wife: *Of course, I'm in a bad mood because you are on my case all the time and you never have time for me.* Which is a very different statement from I am feeling really cut off from you. *Let's figure out ways we can do more stuff together.* The first is a mood talking, and is "unrelated." The second expresses feelings, respectfully, and opens the door for genuine problem-solving. It is "related."

Third, he needs to find a way to express his feelings in a respectful way—then (in many, but not all, cases) share this with someone who cares. Ideally, this would be his partner, but if that seems impossible or unwise, he needs to find someone else who gets it: a family member, friend, therapist, clergy, co-worker, support group, or chat room pal. The chosen witness and listener, of course, cannot be someone who represents a threat to his primary relationship. In other words, finding a lover who will listen to how he feels is a path wrought with risk.

Helping Men Get Help for Depression

We already know that in general, men are reluctant to acknowledge that they have a psychological or emotional problem. This label serves as an unbearable broken mirror that they are not self-sufficient and competent.

This self-labeling issue is especially complicated when it comes to depression. The definition of a successful man in this culture does not include being depressed or not functioning well. Men feel as if they can't afford, psychologically, to label themselves as having a problem that connotes weakness, ineffectiveness, indecisiveness, and lack of success and productivity.

Another important issue regarding the labeling process is reflected in the contemporary definitions of male-type depression. Often, men look at traditional symptom lists of depression and don't recognize themselves. So they conclude that they must *not* be depressed because the lists are not sufficiently inclusive or representative.

When Men Can't Call It Depression

If you are working with a man who seems to be depressed, the way you label his "condition" can determine whether he will comply with the treatment plan or vigorously resist it. Here are some labeling guidelines, valuable for counselors, therapists, wives, partners, and parents.

1. *Call it something else:* You don't really have to call it depression if that is going to alienate him. You can call it stress, which is a more male-friendly term. Or burnout. Or tension. Or moodiness. Or a funk or a

slump. The goal is not to break through his defenses and convince him of everything you are sure you know and understand about him. There is only one simple goal: to do anything that will facilitate him taking some actions that will help him and the people who love him.

2. *Labeling can be a relief:* As usual, no rule applies in all situations. For some men, the labeling issue has just the opposite effect. They respond extremely well to calling this experience depression because then they have a label with an action plan. This label can serve to organize the vague cluster of distress they have been experiencing and can be an enormous relief.

3. *Make sure he knows what's heroic:* Remember that all of us have a very valuable role in helping to shape the male client's narrative about masculinity. The more he can get the message that seeking help in changing these patterns is an example of *relational heroism* (Real, 1998), the more likely he is to engage. The goal here is to employ the values and constructs that this man has in ways that are most likely to expand his options and be of help to him.

Other important people in his life can also be employed in this task. My client Enrique agreed to come in for treatment after his father told him that he, too, had suffered from depression—and that the counseling and medication he received was the best thing that ever happened to him. So now Enrique was released to do this, too. In Pat Conroy's novel *The Great Santini,* a mother writes a letter to her son on his 18th birthday and tells him, "I wanted to tell you that gentleness is the quality I most admire in men" (1976, p. 203). If a man clearly gets the message from the important women in his life that talking about his feelings or taking responsibility for his bad moods are profoundly masculine (not just his wife's attempts at emasculation), he may feel like a *relational hero* as well.

Men's Myths of Depression
A poll of 1,000 men asked the question: *Why do men say they are less likely to seek treatment for depression?* The poll found that 41% of the men iden-

tified one of the reasons as "the attitude that a man can or should tough it out" and 24% reported the reason as "embarrassment or stigma associated with depression." Another 16% said that the main problem was that men "don't recognize the symptoms" (Hales & Hales, 2004). Note that the most prominent reasons are inextricably connected with classic masculine self-image: *I cannot admit that I have thing called depression or that I actually need help.* And the other response reflects the normative male alexithymia problem: Many men don't even recognize what is taking place inside in a way that they can make sense of it and develop an emotionally intelligent action plan.

Many of the reasons for denying the problem, keeping it to himself, and not seeking help even when he recognizes that something is wrong stem from long-standing misconceptions men have (and many women, too) about the nature of depression. Here are some of the most common misconceptions, along with specific guidelines for how to best respond to them.

Remember to always lead with the positive and affirm the man's positive values, even if you are determined to challenge his constructs and you are encouraging him to do something different.

1. *This depression thing is just biological or biochemical—there's no point in therapy or anything psychological.* This is sometimes true, but usually not. Even when the problems clearly stem from biochemical disturbances, such as in classic bipolar disorders, psychological interventions can still be a valuable weapon in the treatment arsenal.

Best Response: *I know that's true about the biological part. But these things are all mixed together. We both know that your thinking still gets way too negative and offtrack sometimes. And all the research indicates that thinking like this becomes a habit after a while, even if the primary cause is biochemical. All the studies recommend getting help on both ends.*

2. Or the opposite: *Depression is all in my head.* Although this is often true, in the sense that the cognitions and narratives that a man uses have the power to either generate or diminish depression, there are many situations in which the symptoms of depression are clearly traceable to

bona fide medical or biological conditions that reflect nothing about the man's strength of character or personal choices. For example, steroid reactions, diabetes, brain tumors, aftereffects of chemotherapy, fibromyalgia, and testosterone depletion are just a few physical conditions that can cause depression.

Best Response: *You make it sound like you just made this thing up and it's not real. First of all, it IS real, even if it is just in your head. And there are so many physical conditions that can be causing this, too. I think it's good that you think of it as being in your head, because it means that you can try to change what's going on inside of your head—but I hate to see you using that as a way to blame yourself more or make it seem like it's not a real problem.*

3. *Even if I know I am depressed, I should be able to slug it out myself. Like a man.* Most men are raised to be self-sufficient and to know where they are going without asking for directions. So it stands to reason that a man would believe that asking for help—by talking about his feelings with someone—would go against the Boy Code or the Guy Code. And since most men have little history with this working very well—in fact, they may have plenty of experience with feeling worse or at least embarrassed when talking about problems or weakness in the past—why they should believe that asking for help makes any sense? The reality, however, is that most people with depression do benefit from some sort of counseling or psychotherapy, with or without medication.

Your Response: *I have no doubts whatsoever about what kind of "real man" you are! But you know what goes into my definition of being a "real man"? The kind of man who can ask for directions sometimes. The kind of man who is secure enough to be able to ask for help when he needs it. Haven't you seen all those articles about Terry Bradshaw and his depression, Joe Namath and his drinking problems, and Mike Ditka promoting Levitra? If they're not "real men," who are the real men?*

4. *Okay, even if this is depression, I shouldn't need a pill as a crutch!* We can all respect this position. And it reflects some of the best qualities of masculinity (independence and determination), along with some of the worst (stubbornness, fear of dependency). But it is often misguided and limiting.

Best Response: *I respect that you feel that way, and I probably would, too. But you might want to think about this like diabetes or something. There's no shame in taking insulin if your body needs it. And all the experts in depression say that you should try to do anything that breaks the cycle, or all the habits of depression just sink in deeper and deeper. You can always stop if you don't like it or when you've been better for a while.*

Stories of "Real Men" and Depression

One of the most powerful media messages that actually counteracts this programming is evident in the current wave of ads for erectile dysfunction medication. As just mentioned, Levitra uses as a spokesman Mike Ditka, former coach of the Chicago Bears and the New Orleans Saints, who has a reputation for being one of the toughest "man's man" there is. The implicit message, of course, is that if Mike Ditka can acknowledge imperfections in what we usually consider to be the pillars of manhood, so can the rest of the guys! Masculinity is redefined as encompassing the capacity—based on personal security in one's manhood—to recognize that you need help and to go for it.

In fact, the men who we usually think of as being the toughest—the "real men" whom we often turn to for strength and protection—are at an especially high risk for this kind of depression. Soldiers. Firefighters. Police officers. These men utilize traditional male strengths to put aside their fears and rise to the occasion. There is no way that our society should aim at eradicating these strengths. But the very strengths that are invaluable in these emergency situations also inhibit their ability to acknowledge fears, doubts, indecisiveness, or regrets in other types of situations.

It can be especially effective to steer reluctant male clients to stories of "real men" who have the personal strength and wisdom to seek help. Firefighter Jimmy Brown, 37 years old, ran into the World Trade Center minutes after the first plane hit on 9/11 (Hales & Hales, 2004). He found himself buried in rubble and ash. He was sure this was the day he would die, but he miraculously survived with only minor physical injuries. The trauma was not over, however. The posttraumatic stress from what he had witnessed and experienced plunged him into an emotional hell and a paralyzing depression. He spent days never leaving the house, then finally, at his wife's insistence, he sought out a psychologist and began the emotional healing process. Brown is now developing a peer counseling program to help police and firefighters deal with stress and depression.

Business mogul Philip J. Burguières, once the youngest chief executive of a Fortune 500 company, reports that he was a highly successful businessman. But he never slept more than a few hours at a time—and he was plagued with anxiety and distress inside: "I almost wanted to peel my skin off" (Healy, 2005). Burguières passed out in his office after a particularly stressful week. He was referred to a psychiatrist, and he got the word that he was "clinically depressed." He received the treatment plan: medication, psychotherapy, and participation in a mental health support group. Burguières never followed up. Several years later, his depression returned, and (citing "health reasons") he resigned his executive position. He had been fantasizing obsessively about committing suicide. Now owner of the NFL's Houston Texans, Burguières has spoken to many business groups about his depression and how he eventually got the help he needed.

More visible still are the athletes who have gone public. In November 2002, Milwaukee Bucks power forward Jason Caffey announced he needed time away from basketball to get treatment for his depression. Surprisingly, Milwaukee fans and sportswriters were sympathetic and supportive.

Baseball slugger Mark McGwire publicly acknowledged his experiences in psychotherapy and how much benefit this has been to him. One of the great baseball managers of our times, Joe Torre, founded an organization called "Safe At Home"—because of his personal history of living in a family plagued with domestic violence and how deeply he struggled with its aftereffects all of his life.

In May 2003, four-time Super Bowl quarterback Terry Bradshaw embarked on a multicity campaign sponsored by GlaxoSmithKline, maker of the antidepressant Paxil, to discuss his own lifelong depression and urge sufferers to get help. "Taking the first step toward a diagnosis and treatment was one of the bravest thing I've ever had to do," said Bradshaw.

More recently, Eric Hipple, star quarterback for the Detroit Lions in the 1980s, "came out" about his own depression and the tragic story of his 15-year-old son who committed suicide. Hipple is the spokesman for the highly successful "Men Get Depression" campaign (Men Get Depression, 2008).

If these men can acknowledge depression and can seek out help, other men can find it easier to go the same route.

Chapter 7

Treating Men Who Are Fathers

The world of fatherhood (not to exempt motherhood, but simply to focus on the particular issues that challenge men) is filled with good fathers sometimes behaving badly. Most of the fathers I know who have made tragic mistakes or simply subtle, everyday blunders have been operating out of a well-intended but unattuned effort to be a good dad.

The breakdown between a man's intentions and the effect of his actions can sometimes be attributed to bad timing, like when a father ineptly tries to have an important conversation with a son who is concentrating on a video game. Or it can be attributed to lack of skills at communicating, like coming across sounding judgmental when he's just trying to contribute some ideas to help his daughter deal with the social crisis of the week.

We will review how to help men develop good parenting skills and get better at the most important job in their lives. But when men who are fathers are seeking counseling because of problems related to how they father, nothing is more responsible for their errors than their own emotional needs, narcissistic injuries, overidentifcation, and broken mirrors.

Broken Mirror Issues: Good Fathers Behaving Badly

One of the key factors in problematic father-son relationships is the father's unresolved hurt feelings from his own childhood (Sanford &

Lough, 1988). This type of father lives with a hurt little boy within himself, one who is always ready to be rejected, and this makes the father oversensitive to what he perceives as rejection.

In our clinical work with men who are confronting their issues in being a father, this is the one of the first places to go. The man who *needs* something from his children in order to feel whole, loved, or successful himself will inevitably get tripped up by the complex demands of parenting. It is normal to (at least once in a while) reap the rewards of parenting and feel more whole, loved, or successful; it is neither normal nor functional when the man needs these too much. It sets him up to try too hard, to expect too much, and to be much too sensitive to perceived failures or moments of incompetence as a father.

Helping men identify the ways that their children function as a mirroring selfobject (and how easily this can trigger the broken mirror sequence) helps them become better fathers.

Broken Mirror Issues: Taking It Personally

The most profound problem that directly and painfully sabotages a father's positive impact on his kids lies within his own personality and his own personal history. Men tend to overpersonalize situations because of their own unresolved emotional issues. They perceive their children's behavior as if it is a direct—and very negative—reflection of themselves as men and as fathers.

The problem here is the inability to appreciate the child's independent center of initiative (see Chapter 2). Wade Whitehouse, the protagonist in the book and movie *Affliction* (Banks, 1989), gets sarcastic and critical with his daughter because she is not having a good time at the Halloween carnival that he has brought her to. He can only make sense of his daughter's unhappiness as a personal reflection on him, and he responds accordingly. The child loses big here, but so does the father.

When a perceived broken mirror reflects a fragmented image back on a father, he is likely to lose access to his wiser judgment about what is happening with his child and what to do about it. Suddenly—and worst of all, unconsciously—the issue becomes one of validating and protecting his own sense of self. At those junctures, he is quite capable of rationalizing the destructive response to his child as being justified, deserved, or for the kid's own good, when it is really only to make the father feel temporarily better or temporarily less powerless.

One time my son, when he was nine, was trying to do this bike stunt where he would have to make his bike jump in the air and then come down over some boards. He couldn't do it. He was scared. I really got on him: "You're a baby, you're chicken, you're weak. I'm going to take your bike away from you!" I kept thinking he was letting me down! It was like he was disrespecting me.

Tom told me this story as his marriage was unraveling. He had become a lot smarter by the time he told me this story; back then, he had actually been able to convince himself that boys needed to be pushed by their fathers or else they would remain permanently stuck in the clutches of overprotective mothers. He was determined not to let his son become "feminized."

But it was all bullshit. It was really just about me! My kid was timid; so that meant I was a loser as a dad. All I could think of is what my old man would have said to me, and what he would have thought if he saw me "letting" my son get away with backing down from a challenge. You see? It was all about me! I couldn't see past my own shit and see that the kid was just scared. And he really needed me to be understanding more than anything else.

I remember the story of another man, a second-grade teacher who felt chronically ineffective in his work. His 5-year-old daughter was clearly a handful, as 5-year-old daughters tend to be. One day he came home and her toys were scattered throughout the house. He told her to pick them up, and she ignored him. He raised his voice and told her again, and she had a 5-year-old smartass answer. Then he picked her up and sat her on her bed, screaming at her that she had better listen to him, now!

His next words have always stuck with me: *I let these second-grade kids run all over me all day long, but I'll be damned if I'll let that happen in my own home!* It was all about him. When he heard himself say these words out loud, in front of me and his concerned wife, he started to cry. He told us that it just sounded so pathetic.

Stuart, another client, felt powerless, not only in managing his two kids, ages 13 and 11, but throughout his life. He came by these feelings honestly. Injured in Vietnam, he had lost a leg. And he had spent many of the subsequent 30 years fighting with various VA clinics about problems with his prosthetic leg. He felt frustrated and helpless. In his job, he felt insignificant: he was low on the totem pole, not earning the respect that a man of his age and experience should have.

One day he came home from work to the wailing of his 13-year-old daughter. Apparently, his daughter's "best friend" had been spreading rumors accusing her of being promiscuous. Stuart listened to his wife as she told him what had triggered all this. And he came up with a plan, in the spirit of being a good father who feels the pain of his kids and wants to do everything he can to come through for them when they are hurting.

Stuart announced his plan: "Okay, here's what we're going to do. We're going to call your friend's mother and insist that she get her daughter to apologize. And especially to go back to the kids that she told this to and tell them that she made it up and that she is sorry!"

His daughter's response to this plan was to wail "Noooooooooooooooooo!" even louder than before, the way only a 13-year-old girl can wail. Stuart's wife turned to him and quietly stated the obvious. "I don't think she wants us to do that."

Stuart's response was to stand up and lay down the law: "I know what I'm doing here. It's time that you all listened to me for once! If you don't go along with my plan, it's a sign that you don't respect me—and I'm outta here!"

Neither wife nor daughter said anything. Stuart stormed out of the house and actually spent the night in a hotel. He came back the next morning rather sheepishly, realizing that he had thrown an adult version of a temper tantrum.

To his credit, Stuart—a good man behaving badly if there ever was one—understood what had happened. He had simply become unbearably overwhelmed with feelings of powerlessness. At the time he didn't know how to recognize it, name it, or express it. He just felt compelled to escape it through a grandiose attempt to feel powerful. He lost his perspective; suddenly the unfolding drama had turned into a drama only about himself.

His daughter's distress had become a broken mirror, and her drama had become merely a reflection on him. He had not been capable of recognizing that this was actually a potential twinship and bonding experience. They all felt powerless together.

Rob, an introspective doctor in his 40s, came in to see me, distressed by his frustrations and his excessive criticism of his 14-year-old son. First, he wanted his son to see me, then he decided he wanted me to see the two of them together. He finally settled on the core of the problem: himself. We compared notes and war stories about the frustration of fatherhood. It was a twinship experience, and it helped him normalize what he was going through. The centerpiece of the challenge for Rob was to recognize how hurt and resentful he felt because his son was not playing his part in Rob's vision of the father-son relationship. And, as with a marriage crisis, we worked on ways to take care of these emotional needs elsewhere—or at least recognize that it was not his son's responsibility to meet them.

Rob came to see himself as a very good parent tripped up by his own emotional needs, occasionally behaving badly.

Broken Mirror Issues: Overattachment and Overidentification

A classic chapter of the broken mirror story is this: a man, previously wounded, turns to another person—this time his child—as a mirror to confirm his self-worth and to offer him a sense of well-being. Sanford and Lough (1988) pointed out that fathers who are laboring with these personal issues tend to either avoid relating to their children or go out of their way to be good fathers, but then feel hurt when they don't feel properly appreciated or rewarded. They experience the child's rejection of their help or their values as a fundamental rejection of their own self. And, in their own overt or covert way, they blame the child. They blame the mirror for breaking on them.

In the 1990 movie *Parenthood*, starring Steve Martin, this pattern of men overidentifying with the fate of their own children is dramatically and hilariously portrayed (Howard, 1989). Martin plays the role of Gil

Buckman, a concerned, well-meaning, and slightly neurotic father with a 9-year-old son. Kevin is a sweet but very anxious kid who does not exactly meet his father's idealized image of a bold, adventurous, and confident boy. But Gil, a good guy, does his best to put aside these expectations and love his son just as he is.

Gil is the coach of Kevin's Little League team. In a crucial game, he encourages Kevin to fill in at second base. The movie then veers off into Gil's fantasy of Kevin's college graduation. Kevin, of course, is handsome, confident, and the chosen class speaker. In his speech, he informs the audience of the key to his past. "When I was nine years old, I had kind of a rough time. A lot of people thought I was pretty mixed up. But there was one person who got me through it. He did everything right. And thanks to him, today I am the happiest, most confident, and most well-adjusted person in this world. Dad, I love you. You're the greatest!" The camera focuses in on his father, standing up in the crowd to the wild admiration of all.

After this fantasy dissolves, reality sets in. Kevin muffs a pop-up that allows the other team to win. He storms off in tears, screaming at his father, "Why'd you make me play second base?"

Now the dark fantasy takes over. Gil imagines a future with Kevin in a university clock tower, randomly picking off students. Someone cries out, "It's Kevin Buckman! His father totally screwed him up!" Kevin screams out to his father in the crowd, "You made me play second base!"

The moral of the story for male clients who are fathers: Your kid is who he is. Your role is to be the best father you can be, which means deeply appreciating him as he is. If his behavior does not match your standards, adjust your standards. If your own issues about proving yourself as a man take over when it is time to offer yourself to your kid, think first and act second. Parenting is not about you.

Broken Mirror Issues: Dysfunctional Parental Syndromes

The father with narcissistic injury and broken mirror issues is always scanning the child's behavior and the interactions between father and child with the primary question in mind: *What does this say about me?* The job of counseling a father involves helping him become aware of this question and finding ways to defuse it, or at least to put it in about fourth or fifth place.

When a father suffers from *parental helplessness syndrome*, he is overwhelmed with the unbearable feeling of powerlessness in getting his child to do something, feel something, think soothing, or be something. The best alternative narrative: *Welcome to the world of parenting.*

When a father suffers from *what would my parents say? syndrome*, he is preoccupied with the nagging worry that his father would scoff at what he is letting his kids get away with. For example, his son whines and complains that "this family really sucks." The father lets it go and does not react, but remembers that he probably would have been slapped by his parents for saying such a thing. He is haunted by the fear that he is looking foolish or weak in the eyes of the previous generation (dead or alive). The best alternative narrative: *I am my own man now and I have decided this is the best way to be a good father to my kids.*

When a father suffers from *what would the neighbors say? syndrome*, he lets his preoccupation with how he will be viewed by his parental cohort dictate his decisions. This is more broken mirror syndrome. I once worked with a father who struggled with how to handle his teen daughter's decision to dye her hair purple. He knew that, given everything that was in stake in his family, this was not a battle to fight. It fell in the category of temporary (he hoped!) rebellious behavior about her own physical self. But he couldn't stop himself from getting in an all-out war with her—because he couldn't bear how he as a father would be viewed by his neighbors and fellow fathers. The best alternative narrative: *I am making my own decisions about what is truly best for my daughter and our family and nobody else is in a position to truly understand or judge.*

When a father suffers from *parental guilt syndrome*, he cannot bear to see his kids unhappy or resentful of him. Divorced fathers or workaholic fathers are especially vulnerable to this syndrome. They feel like they have let their kids down (and any signs of this generates a broken mirror experience), so they act desperately to make up for the perceived damage. They become Disneyland dads or they refrain from enforcing any limits when the kids are in their care for fear of making the kids unhappy. The best alternative narrative: *I may have been responsible for causing pain for my kids, but right now my job is to be the best possible father I can be—which does not mean overindulging them.*

The Legacy from Father to Son, Father to Son

In the novel *The Great Santini* (Conroy, 1976), Bull Meecham is a demanding and charismatic Marine colonel pilot who runs his family the way he runs his squadron. Bull Meecham (a.k.a. the Great Santini) plays against his eldest son, Ben, in an annual one-on-one basketball game in their backyard in front of the whole family. Ben, now 17 and the star of his high school basketball team, has finally reached his father's level and actually beats him in this game. But this leads to very disturbing consequences. Bull has never been able to bear to lose to any of his children. When he senses that his son is besting him in this game, Bull cheats and plays dirty, but to no avail. Desperate to regain some sliver of self-esteem after his defeat, he insults his daughter, strikes his wife, and launches a relentless attack of verbal humiliations on his own son. He calls him a mama's boy. He keeps taunting him, telling him to go ahead and cry.

He starts to bounce the basketball repeatedly off his son's head. "You're my favorite daughter, Ben, I swear to God, you're my sweetest little girl!"

Ben, to his enormous credit, stands his ground and refuses to lower himself to his father's pathetic level. He walks calmly away, withstands the blows to his head, and finally yells at him, "Yeah, Dad, and this little girl just whipped you good."

Bull's response to his son hits the jackpot for humiliating punishment. It is random and irrational. It is public. It is global. And it is highly shaming.

There is a direct correlation between boys who are treated like this and grown men who are especially sensitized to experiences of rejection and humiliation. A boy who experienced this kind of parenting often grows up to anticipate shame and to find it even more unbearable than the rest of us do. This man is likely to hear *You are an inadequate loser!* when his wife makes a comment about how she wishes they lived in a bigger house. He is likely to hear *I'm ashamed of you!* when his son ignores him at back-to-school night.

This hypersensitivity is especially destructive because there are so many situations in which men actually *are* rejected or in which they actually *are* put down. These are painful enough! Boys who experience especially high levels of paternal rejection or humiliation grow up to be men who perceive put-downs or rejection in even more situations—and it is essential that fathers who are in counseling or therapy recognize the impact of this style of parenting.

Wounded Fathers, Wounded Sons

When I think of men who have become hardened by the wounds of their childhood, I remember listening to a radio talk show caller several years ago. It was December, and the focus of the show was the state of the Christmas spirit in our society. The caller went off on a rant. He complained that the problem with our entitled, narcissistic society begins in childhood when kids receive Christmas presents without having done anything to earn them! All I could think was this: *Who wounded him growing up?* What deprivation must this man have experienced to generate a social philosophy blaming unearned Christmas presents? And how sad that he has developed a life philosophy to justify the pain he had experienced, rather than recognizing the pain and building a philosophy based on something more than trying to deny trauma.

Breaking the Chain: Cognitive Dissonance Theory

One way to help fathers break the chain of shame, put-downs, and emotional withholding is to help them identify (and challenge) their own *cognitive dissonance*. Cognitive dissonance represents the conflict created when a father's self-image conflicts with the negative and intolerable reality generated by his own behavior. This creates profound discomfort and threatens his sense of well-being. Following the sequence identified by cognitive dissonance theory, he then adjusts his narrative to reconcile this internal conflict.

If a man has an image of himself as a good father, and he yells at his kids, he is stuck with a disturbing dissonance. Psychologically, he is left with two choices:

1. He can tell himself that the yelling behavior is actually a good thing so he doesn't have to face the self-image of behaving badly as a father.

2. He can tolerate recognizing the mistakes he has made and the destructive effects, and he can acknowledge that even good fathers sometimes act badly and that he (like all fathers) needs to learn from this.

The son or daughter, faced with a father who threatens and shames, is left with similar choices:

1. She can tell herself that the yelling behavior is actually a good thing—so she doesn't have to live with the idea that her trusted father is betraying her.

2. He can acknowledge how much this has wounded him, consciously experience disappointment in his view of his father, and maybe even acknowledge that even good fathers sometimes act badly.

The first choice, in both examples, is the more popular and the path of least resistance. It is so much easier to go this route because it maintains a fundamental identification between father and child, which is crucial to children and emotionally seductive to adults. The second choice requires more psychological maturity—certainly far more maturity than most children can be expected to have. It requires the capacity to tolerate ambivalent feelings toward a person whom you have idealized. And it requires the ego strength to integrate the different aspects of your personality and behavioral patterns.

Children are usually not developmentally capable of taking the second route; they almost invariably assume that they deserve the abuse or tell themselves that it is somehow a good thing. Terrence Real (1998) called this *empathic reversal:* the boy who has been traumatized adopts a relationship to himself that mirrors and replicates the dynamics of his early abuse. This is the link between trauma and depression. Boys who experienced emotional or physical abuse often develop into men who resolve the cognitive dissonance that comes from this abuse by convincing themselves that their father's behavior made sense. Instead of challenging the narrative of the trauma, they justify it. To protect their fathers, or at least their image of their fathers, they develop a narrative that this rigid treatment of children actually represents the cornerstone of being good, responsible, and loving fathers. This boy turned into a father rationalizes these values and often, disturbingly, repeats these behaviors in his own interactions with those closest to him and most vulnerable to him.

Clinically, many fathers benefit from recognizing how desperately they have chosen the easiest route to reconcile the cognitive dissonance—and, surprisingly, how capable they actually are of tolerating the emotional distress of seeing themselves and their personal history clearly. Those fathers who can do this are better positioned to generate acts of *relational heroism*.

Breaking the Chain: Releasing Children from "Imaginary Crimes"

Some children are never released from the burden of their fathers' messages. Many sons who were shaped (consciously or unconsciously) by shaming fathers, or by fathers who unconsciously relied on their sons to provide a mirror for them as fathers, grow into men who are always swimming upstream and always trying to reinvent themselves. Some men get stuck. They perpetuate the legacy. Sometimes they see themselves doing it but feel powerless to stop it.

Any father, however, who has come to recognize the damaging effects of his own childhood experiences, and the consequent struggles this has generated for him as a man and as a father, now has a tremendous parenting opportunity. He can talk to his children about himself and release them from the burden he has placed on them.

In order for a father to do this, he must come to a fundamental psychological realization: It is not the child's job to take care of the parent's emotional needs.

Control-mastery theory (Weiss & Sampson, 1986), popularized as theories about "imaginary crimes" (Engel & Ferguson, 1990), posits that children often experience an unconscious pull toward taking care of the unconscious emotional needs of their parents (see Chapter 3). A child believes she is guilty of imaginary crimes of success, separation, or survival. When she believes that something good about her or something that she has done well has turned out to be hurtful to others, she feels guilty of the "crime" of success. The same feeling may emerge when she has succeeded where others have failed. And she may feel guilty of separation or survival when she has individuated successfully and a parent feels abandoned, or when she has been blessed with good fortune (like brains or beauty or good health) when her parent or sibling has not.

The worst imaginary crime of all is the crime of existence. This is the "criminal" experience that is engendered in children whose parent communicates this message: *I wish you had never been born.* Children who hear this, or who sense it even without directly being told (like being abandoned by a father or a mother), develop a fundamental shame about their very being. They feel ashamed not only for something they have done but ashamed for who they are.

Zack, a man in his late 20s committed to staying clean and sober, told me about his conversation with his father about drinking. "I have been trying to stop, because I have seen how much this has messed me up. I'm going to AA meetings. My father has tried this off and on but never stayed with it. He says to me, 'How long is this not-drinking thing going to last?' Like there's something wrong with it or it's kind of silly."

Zack is on the receiving end of an imaginary crime message. His father sees Zack taking charge of his life by controlling his drinking. This serves as a broken mirror to the father, who is reminded that he himself has a problem but has not been successful with it.

So Zack's father has two choices. He can be thrilled with his son's success and even use him as inspiration. Or he can demean what his son is doing so that he won't have to acknowledge that there is something worthwhile in the task Zack is accomplishing.

The second choice is easier, and this is what he does.

Zack unconsciously learns that he can be loyal to his father and keep his father in a better emotional state if he does not surpass or outdo him. Zack may actually believe, at some level, that success with his own drinking patterns is a crime against his father. He doesn't want to be his father's broken mirror. It's not difficult to see how Zack's guilt over his imaginary crime could lead him to sabotage his own success.

When a father recognizes the ways that he has cursed his son or daughter with an imaginary crime, he then has the option of not only changing his ways but also directly clarifying the message to his child (of any age). He can offer his blessing.

Terrence Real told the story of his lifelong struggle with his father and talked about his sense of being cursed by his father's warped values about masculinity. Finally, as his father was dying—with rigid defenses softening, emotions and regrets flowing, a reordered sense of priorities emerging—he sent his son this message: "May you and your brother reach your fullest potential in every regard. My blessing to you is this: May nothing in my past, or in the family's past, hold you back or weigh you down. If there are any encumbrances on you, I release you from them. You hear me? I release you. I want you to be free. Happy, strong, and free. That is my blessing to you, son" (1998, p. 333). He went on to tell his son, "It's no small thing." And it's not.

A father who can reveal himself as a real person with flaws and limitations, rather than projecting the message that his disapproval or emotional withholding are indicators of the child's inadequacy, can free his child and free himself.

Helping Fathers Understand Kids

Sometimes well-intentioned fathers are unsuccessful because of lack of awareness about a certain subject, like why his 7-year-old boy wets his bed or why his 12-year-old girl has to rush home to start instant messaging with her friends—or the fact that his child may be constitutionally very difficult to parent.

Many fathers overreact to or disconnect from their kids simply because they apply the wrong narrative to the child's behavior. The father's behavior makes more sense based on the context that he has created cognitively, but the context is distorted.

One time, in a public restroom, I heard a young man talking to his child behind a divider. I could overhear him saying to his child, "There was no reason for you to be throwing that tantrum in there! There was no reason for you to behave like that in public! You can probably get away with that now, but when you're a little older, that kind of behavior will get you a good whipping! I'm really mad at you!" I sneaked a peek at this man. The child he was addressing was an infant, no more than 4 months old—and he was changing his diaper! I had been sure he was talking to an older child, who would be at least somewhat able to cognitively integrate these corrections and instructions. If it hadn't been so sad, it would have been hilarious, this father trying to talk sense into his 4-month-old and threatening him with future consequences. I didn't know this man, but I suspected that he was like many other young fathers I have come to know: wanting desperately to be a good and responsible father, but needing education both in skills and in capacity for empathy. He did not yet know how to do it differently than it had been done to him.

Meichenbaum (2001b) worked with parents by helping them reframe their expectations for child behavior. He challenged them to develop a reasonable quota for negative behaviors: *You are driving to Grandma's house, which is 400 miles away. You have two boys in the backseat. How many fights do you expect to have in that time? If you expect zero, you are in for frustration. How about one fight every 50 miles?* Since parental frustration is directly related to the gap between expectations and reality, helping parents develop more realistic expectations can bring out the best qualities in parental responses. If they no longer label the child behavior as offensive, immature, or excessively defiant, they can chalk it up to the behavior of a "normal kid" in a stressful situation. This changes everything.

Meichenbaum (2001b) also quoted studies of child compliance to help parents adjust expectations. His review of the literature concluded that "normal and healthy" kids only comply with 50–66% of parental requests! So the message to a father who feels like his child's noncompliance is a sign of poor child behavior and ultimately failed parenting is this: You are not alone. It comes with the territory of parenting. Identifying moderate noncompliance as pathological would be like identifying marital arguments as pathological.

Fathers who are in counseling regarding their own skills or identity as a parent often benefit tremendously from the reframing that comes from learning more about childhood development issues and reasonable expectations. Author Ross Greene wrote about the impact of parents developing new and more informed perspectives on the difficult behaviors of their difficult children: "There's a big difference between viewing inflexible-explosive behaviors as the result of a brain-based failure to progress developmentally and viewing them as planned, intentional, and purposeful. That's because your interpretation of a child's inflexible-explosive behaviors will be closely linked to how you try to change these behaviors. In other words, your interpretation will guide your intervention" (1998, p. 14).

The message to fathers: *Your interpretation will guide your intervention.* It will also guide your self-esteem as a father and your susceptibility to dangerous broken mirrors along the treacherous path of parenting.

Family adviser Jane Nelsen succinctly identified four guidelines for parents to live by as they think about their teenagers that, she found, lead parents into being more compassionate, empathic, and ultimately successful—not to mention sane:

Show an attitude of faith in the basic goodness of your teen.
Let him know specifically what you appreciate about him.
Try to understand her reality by making some guesses about what it might be.
Count on teenagers to be obnoxious. Step back and try to see it as cute
(Nelsen & Lott, 1994, pp. 92, 149).

Guidelines to Help Father Connect with Their Kids

When helping men bring out their best qualities as fathers, I usually find it helpful to give them a list of specific guidelines to keep in mind. These tips, developed from many years of clinical experience, personal experience as the father of two, review of the research literature, and the wisdom of other clinicians (Pollack, 1998, 1998b; Straus, 2006; Taffel, 2001) can help men focus on what they need to do to do it right.

Making Conversation

1. At least once a day, give your child your undivided attention. You are not on the phone, you are not cleaning up, you do not have one eye on the computer or the TV. Even if no earth-shattering conversational breakthrough emerges, you are still there, and your son or daughter knows it. When fire lookouts in national forests stand guard at their lookout post, most of the time nothing happens. But they are ready for the very important moments when it does. Don't demand too much, don't withdraw. Just be waiting in the wings.

2. Set the stage for conversation through activity. Boys especially are usually most comfortable with triangle conversations, with people making up two points of the triangle and an activity making up the third: watching TV together; listening to music together; playing basketball or a video game; taking driving trips so you're forced to talk and you can both stare at the road.

3. Toss a softball together. Then talk about what the world record is for most times tossing a softball back and forth in this neighborhood without moving more than one foot. Then start to steer the conversation to how things are going at school. Just getting the heart rate up seems to intensify thinking and communication, making it more likely that the words exchanged will stick in a child's memory.

4. Get to know your kid's friends. If nothing else, it will give you more to talk about. Turn your house into the site where kids want to hang out.

5. When your child is hurting, don't hesitate to ask her whether she'd like to talk, but avoid shaming her if she refuses to talk with you. If she blows you off, no matter how hurt or frustrated you feel, do not say, *You're never gonna get any help from me if you won't even tell me what's going on!* You must respect what author William Pollack (1998a) called the "timed silence syndrome." Boys, especially, often are not ready to talk right away or when you think they should. It may come later, and it is your job to pay attention to the signals and windows of opportunity.

6. Be receptive to any opportunity to listen to her, even if it is inconvenient. When your daughter seeks reconnection, try your best to be there for her. Maybe she wants you to hang out with her as she's falling

asleep, and her defenses are down. Even if you're dead tired or resentful that she has waited so long, try to find a way to seize this golden opportunity anyway.

7. Know when your child is most open to conversing with you. Adolescents tend to be more talkative at night, so take advantage of their "inner clock."

8. If you are in a conflict or disciplining your child or teen, avoid "parental" body language like leaning back with arms folded. Other body language and nonverbal communication to avoid are the scowl, the raised eyebrows, the rolled eyes, the smirk, and the heavy sighs and groans.

9. Be proactive about bringing up complicated subjects, like sex, drugs, teen suicide, and so on. Your kids will eventually take their cues from you.

10. Take a chance. When in doubt, guess: *I'm not sure about this, but I know your coach has really been on your case lately. Are you feeling down because of that?* If you do this, there are three possible outcomes and two of them are good. The negative outcome is that your child will blow up at you, tell you you're totally clueless, and banish you from his or her room. But sometimes you will guess right, and this will stimulate the conversation. And, at other times, you will guess wrong—and in her disgust with how stupid you are, she will blurt out the real reason for her distress.

Accepting and Encouraging Feelings

1. Listen empathically. Don't lecture or judge, just relate. It seems impossible, but you can do it.

2. Find a way to talk to your child that is not shaming. In particular, when a boy expresses vulnerable feelings, avoid teasing or taunting him. If he starts to tear up watching a sappy movie, say nothing about this or maybe just touch him lightly on his shoulder—quietly, discreetly. If he expresses an opinion about something he has been thinking about, do whatever it takes to take it seriously, no matter how ridiculous you find it to be. More than anything else, you want to establish his home life as a safe sanctuary: a shame-free zone.

3. Tell your kids about your own experiences. They need to experience "twinship" about feeling insecure, foolish, and incompetent.

4. Encourage the expression of a full range of emotions. When your child tells you about getting hassled by a teacher, find labels for the feelings besides *pissed*. Try *embarrassed, misunderstood, disrespected.*

5. However, avoid using shaming language in talking with your child, especially with your son. There are words that girls are more likely to accept than boys ever could. I have learned to stay away from words like *afraid* and *threatened* and *intimidated* because you usually get a response like, "Afraid? No way? What are you talking about?" It doesn't matter if you're right. *Worried* and *frustrated* are a little more palatable and less of a violation of the Boy Code.

Building Self-Esteem the Right Way

Good, well-meaning parents want to help build their children's self-esteem. It is obviously good parenting to reinforce your children for their skills and accomplishments and to communicate in thousands of little ways how much you value them, appreciate them, and believe in them.

But recent research has informed us that many parents have been accidentally approaching the self-esteem issue incorrectly, sometimes doing more harm than good. In a series of tests conducted by researcher Dr. Carol Dweck (2007), grade-school children were randomly assigned to two groups. Everybody, in both groups, received the same easy test. Then the researchers took every child aside individually and praised them. The students in the first group were praised for an innate ability: their intelligence. The researchers told the kids in this group: "You must be smart at this!" In contrast, the students in the second group were praised for their effort: "You must have worked really hard." Then the researchers gave both groups another, much harder test. The results? *The group that had been praised for effort significantly outperformed the group praised for their brains.* Since they believed that they were good at effort, they apparently tried harder and performed better.

Here are some guidelines for appropriately fostering self-esteem in children, based on contemporary research:

1. Praise *effort*, not outcome.

2. Praise *effort* much more frequently than praising innate talent (like brains, athletic talent, creativity, looks, etc.).

3. Remember that inauthentic, excessive praise lowers credibility and motivation. Say it sincerely and simply. Saying *You are so wonderful!* is sometimes oaky, but saying *I can tell how hard you worked on this paper because it is really clear!* is even better.

4. Tell kids *You should feel proud of yourself* a lot more often than *I am so proud of you.* You don't want to excessively encourage relying on external reinforcement as the payoff for effort and achievement (not that there's anything wrong with that). Instead, you want to encourage relying more on the rewards from within.

5. Look for opportunities to praise for things that run counter to your child's temperament or comfort zone (being generous, being bold, reading a book, taking a risk).

6. Look for opportunities to praise your child for random acts of kindness (catch them doing something right).

7. Remember that eye-to-eye praise is usually the most effective and appreciated.

8. If your child gets interested in something, don't overdo your enthusiasm (*Oh my god, that's so great, let's sign you up for daily piano lessons right now!*). But do show your interest in what they are interested in!

Also remember, however, that when it comes to raising kids, there are no rules that always apply. This reminds me of a story I once heard from the mother of a son. She had learned, from reading all the best books, that the preferred way to help build true self-esteem in kids was to say, *Wow, you should feel really proud of yourself!* instead of *I feel so proud of you!* as mentioned above. Except that one day, when her son was 14, she said this to him and he looked at her, vulnerable and stricken, and said, *How come you never tell me that YOU'RE proud of me?* She explained her philosophy, reassured him of her pride in him—and was reminded that no advice about raising kids is always right.

But even your imperfect role in nurturing self-esteem in your child's life is one of the greatest gifts you can offer him.

For Boys Only: Messages About Being Male

1. Talk openly about the Boy Code. Your son needs some education about what other people have learned about the life of boys and how complicated it is. Give him some labels for these experiences.

2. One of the best ways you can help your son develop a broad definition of what masculinity is all about is by talking about your experiences in relationships with girls and women. Tell your son about the women you have loved and why.

3. Do whatever you can to ensure that the model of masculinity that he is exposed to is broad and inclusive. Introduce the concept of relational heroism to your son so that he expands his concept of heroic male behavior to include acts of integrity, taking personal responsibility for his emotional life, treating his loved ones with respect, and offering glimpses into his own emotional life to others even when he doesn't feel like it.

4. In your adult relationships, help create a model for men who are not just caricatures of masculinity. Share cooking and cleaning. Don't refer to parenting as "helping out with the kids" or "I'm babysitting my kids tonight." Do whatever you can to discourage the use of "gender privilege" (from both genders!) in your relationships with women: *I'm the man and I will decide how we spend our money* or *I'm the woman, and you should stop interfering with how I want to raise these kids.*

True Father-Love

When all is said and done, it is important to remind men that true love from a father means loving children the way they really want and need to be loved—not the way fathers would want to be loved, not the way fathers think children should be loved, and not the way fathers want to love kids that would make the father feel better. The father who is reasonably self-aware of his own mirroring needs and who is reasonably educated about the true developmental needs of this particular child stands a much better chance of offering true love to his child. There is nothing more important.

Chapter 8
Treating Men Who Abuse Women

One reason that men show up in clinical settings (voluntarily or involuntarily) is because of a pattern of aggressive behavior toward their intimate partners. Contemporary research and clinical practice now help us identify the wide variety of motivations, personality patterns, personal histories, and relationship patterns that trigger men's aggressive and abusive behavior.

The skills and strategies used in effective intervention with abusive men are complex, controversial, and changing quickly. But there is one central principle that is the key to any effective intervention in this important work: We need to engage these men in the healing process. In most situations, it is not enough to offer lectures about gender politics and sexist attitudes or simply to incarcerate. You don't win the battle against intimate partner violence by inciting a gender war. If the mission is to stop intimate partner violence, then the challenge is to learn as much as possible about what goes wrong for the people who generate this violence—and then use this knowledge as a lever for change.

Typologies of Domestic Violence Offenders

"Who are these guys?"

The most important factor to recognize in working with men who have been identified as abusive toward an intimate partner is that one size does not fit all.

Recent research has yielded valuable insights into how and why domestic violence takes place. The research has been conducted almost exclusively on adult male heterosexual offenders and should not automatically be extrapolated to domestic violence offenders who are adolescent, female, or gay (although many of these issues certainly overlap). We know now that the men who commit these acts have a wide variety of motivations, triggers for aggression, personal histories, and personality styles. And they operate in different kinds of relationships.

Some of the most valuable research in this field has been generated by Michael Johnson (Johnson, 1995; Johnson & Ferraro, 2000; Johnson & Leone, 2005) at Penn State University. This research suggests that that there are two distinct forms of male violence against female partners. The theoretical foundations of Johnson's control typology are grounded in the ostensibly mutually contradictory analyses of feminist theory and family systems theory. Feminist theory (Dobash & Dobash, 1979; Stark & Flitcraft, 1996; Stets, 1988; Yllo & Bograd, 1988) conceptualizes intimate partner violence as a matter of *control*, rooted in patriarchal traditions of male dominance in heterosexual relationships, especially marriage. Family systems theory sees intimate partner violence as a matter of *conflict*, rooted in the everyday stresses of family life that produce conflicts that may or may not escalate to violence (Straus, Gelles, & Steinmetz, 1980; Straus & Smith, 1990). Johnson asserted that although these theories have generally been framed as alternative conceptualizations of the same phenomenon, they are better understood as explanations of two essentially different forms of intimate partner violence: one rooted in an attempt to exert general control over the relationship and the other arising out of particular conflicts.

Intimate Terrorism

The basic pattern in what Johnson now calls *intimate terrorism* or *intimate partner terrorism* (originally labeled *patriarchal terrorism*) involves violence that is embedded in a general pattern of controlling behaviors, indicating that the perpetrator is attempting to exert general control over his partner. Johnson suggested that this form of violence is what is typically intended by terms such as *battering*, *wife-beating*, and *spousal abuse*.

The operating theory here is based on feminist narratives of gender politics focusing on control. In these, the most toxic, dangerous, and intractable cases of interpersonal violence, the primary abuser is almost always male. Compared to the *situational couple violence* category, the violence is more frequent and severe, and is much less likely to stop. The abuser holds power over his partner not only through direct physical violence but also through a systematic pattern of *coercive control*: nonphysical tactics including intimidation, isolation, economic control, controlling her activities and decisions, emotional abuse, and ultimately the erosion of independence and self-esteem. Women who are subjects of abuse in these relationships often describe the experience like this: "All he had to do was look at me that way and I would do whatever he wanted."

In these relationships, female violence is primarily understood as an act of self-defense, or at worst, retaliation after experiencing relentless emotional, physical, and sometimes sexual abuse. The paradigm in these relationships suggests that they represent a microcosm of a larger social system of subordination and control of women by men, which trickles down perversely to the specific abuse between this one man and this one woman.

Situational Couple Violence

In contrast, the intimate partner violence that Johnson now calls *situational couple violence* (originally labeled *common couple violence*) involves violence that is not connected to a general pattern of *coercive control*. This pattern of violence involves specific arguments that escalate to violence without any significant relationship-wide evidence of an attempt to exert general control over one's partner.

This narrative for violence in a relationship is based more on family conflict theory, including a systems and psychological perspective rather than the more sociocultural perspective. Data from multiple community-wide surveys indicate that this type of violence is actually initiated just as frequently by women as it is by men. (This is a major controversy in the field of domestic violence and could consume an entire chapter all by itself. Suffice it to say that although the actual reported incidents in community-wide samples are approximately equal, upon closer examination there are significant differences: Women are injured more, they are killed more, they live in fear more, and the psychological impact of a man even mildly assaulting a woman generally carries more implied threat of harm than the other way around. Nevertheless, the notion that there is such a thing as women physically abusing men should no longer be discounted.)

Compared to the patterns in intimate terrorism, the violence in these cases is usually less frequent and not as severe. Most important, the violence here is not conceptualized as representing a pattern of coercive control. Instead, the violent acts are understood as one of many tactics used by partners to express conflict and disagreement. One set of researchers (Prince & Arias, 1994) identified acts of interpersonal aggression in these relationships as expressive, misguided, cathartic responses.

Distinguishing Between Typologies

In trying to make sense of these different models for interpersonal violence, it is important to look at the sources of the data. Johnson (1999) reported that less than 10% of domestic violence identified in community samples were characterized by intimate terrorism; in other words, approximately 90% of the noncriminal population that anonymously reported incidents of domestic violence in their relationships could best be described as situational couple violence. In contrast, the vast majority of cases identified among battered women's shelter samples (74%) were characterized by patterns of male intimate terrorism. These data confirmed for him the proposition that situational couple violence is what is typically found by family violence researchers in their population-based surveys and that intimate terrorism is most often found in the clinical samples favored by feminist researchers.

The two types of violence are not defined by the nature or frequency of violent acts but solely in terms of the relationship-level control context in which they are embedded. Simply put, intimate terrorism is violence that is embedded in a general pattern of control; situational couple violence is not.

The two groups differ in levels of dangerousness, the dynamics of violence, and the presence of *DSM-IV* Axis II personality disorders. Based on these perspectives, the intervention of choice may range from incarceration of a "terrorist" perpetrator, court-mandated treatment aimed at rehabilitation and reform, or even interventions for couples focused on relationship patterns and dynamics.

These distinctions are central because they have implications for the development of theories of interpersonal violence, the design of educational programs and intervention strategies, and the implementation of public policy. Furthermore, these distinctions between different forms of partner violence are also important for understanding the effects of violence on victims.

Johnson and Ferraro (2000) argued that our attempt to understand, prevent, and successfully intervene in domestic violence will never be powerful as long as we do not distinguish between behaviors as disparate as a feminine slap in the face, a terrorizing pattern of beatings accompanied by humiliating psychological abuse, an argument that escalates into a mutual shoving match, and a homicide committed by a person who feels there is no other way to save her own life.

Dutton (2005) argued that intimacy and psychopathology rather than gender alone generate relationship violence. It is because of intimacy conflicts that straight and gay rates of abuse are similarly high; the impact of attachment-related distress and related anxieties contribute significantly to generating anger and abuse in intimate partner relationships.

Similarities

While we now know how different domestic violence offenders can be, it is also important to first summarize the factors that they (adult male heterosexual domestic violence offenders) have in common. Here's what the research tells us:

- Hold attitudes that evaluate the use of force less negatively
- Distort causes and consequences of behavior
- Assume greater partner negative intent

- Are less able to use reasoning
- Have higher levels of arousal in response to conflict
- Have higher generalized anger/hostility
- Label many forms of negative affect (hurt, jealousy, fear) as anger
- Are more likely to be unemployed
- Are more likely to abuse substances
- Are more likely to have witnessed family violence as a child

More Research on Typologies

Dr. Amy Holtzworth-Munroe (2000b) and her associates at Indiana University generated landmark research in distinguishing male domestic violence offenders, identifying four types. The categories are based on assessment of frequency, severity, and generalization of violence, as well as key personality variables (such as antisocial traits, anger, depression, anxiety, jealousy, and fear of abandonment).

One significant category has been identified as the *generally violent antisocial* (GVA), accounting for approximately 16% in the community sample studied. GVA batterers have early experiences that increase the risk of developing positive attitudes toward violence and negative attitudes toward women while failing to develop social skills in intimate or nonintimate situations. Their relationship violence is simply a part of their general pattern of violent and criminal behavior.

Here are some central identifying characteristics in the GVA category:

- Are generally antisocial and more likely to engage in instrumental violence
- Tend to be violent across situations and across different victims
- Are more generally belligerent
- Are more likely to abuse substances
- Are more likely to have a criminal history
- Are more likely to have been a victim of child abuse
- Are more likely to have witnessed spouse abuse
- Show little remorse
- Are limited in their capacity for empathy and attachment

- Are extremely negative attitudes toward women and conservative views of relationships
- Have a strong tendency to inflict psychological and sexual abuse
- Have a high association historically with deviant peers
- Have attitudes supportive of violence

Items on the *Millon Clinical Multiaxial Inventory (MCMI-III)* that help identify a domestic violence offender as GVA include the following:

- *I got in trouble as a teenager.*
- *I have used illegal drugs.*
- *I have done impulsive things that have gotten me in trouble.*
- *Punishment doesn't stop me from getting into trouble.*

Another category is known as *family-only* (FO), accounting for approximately 36% in the community sample studied. The use of physical aggression emerges as a result of poor partner-specific communication skills, dependence on and preoccupation with the partner, and mild problems with impulsivity.

Here are some central identifying characteristics in the FO category:

- Have little or no significant evidence of psychopathology
- Have mild social skills deficits
- Are moderately dependent and jealous
- Have passive and passive-aggressive style
- Have overcontrolled hostility: tend to suppress emotions and withdraw, later erupting into violence after long periods of unexpressed but seething rage
- Have generally less severe act of abuse
- Are generally remorseful about their actions
- Are the least likely to be violent outside the home
- Are the least psychologically abusive
- Have the most liberal attitudes toward women (compared to other types)

- Have low levels of anger, depression and jealousy, but measure high on "impression management"
- Are the least likely to have been abused as children

This research also generated a mixed category named *low-level anti-social* (LLA), accounting for approximately 33% in the sample studied. This category was identified to include men whose characteristics over-lapped the GVA and FO categories. These domestic violence offenders do not reach the full criteria levels for GVA, but they have enough GVA characteristics that they cannot be appropriately classified in the FO group. This category does not have a set of descriptive criteria inde-pendent of the two categories above.

Finally, a subtype of male domestic violence offenders is best described as *borderline/dysphoric* (BD), accounting for approximately 15% in the sample studied. These emotionally dysphoric men with borderline features, when confronted with relationship conflicts, typi-cally perceive these conflicts as threats of abandonment. Lacking the skills to resolve such conflicts, they impulsively use physical aggression to express their distress and intense anger.

Here are some central identifying characteristics in the BD category:

- Have high scores for psychopathology, impulsivity, and aggression
- Have experienced parental rejection and child abuse
- Are emotionally volatile
- Tend to be violent only within their family
- Are more socially isolated and socially incompetent than other batterers
- Exhibit the highest levels of anger, depression, jealousy, and fear of abandonment
- Find ways of misinterpreting their partners and blaming their partners for their own mood states
- Experience significant depression and feelings of inadequacy
- Were most likely severely abused as children

- Are most likely to react to estrangement with violence
- Are most likely to stalk their partners
- Are most likely to maintain or reestablish a relationship

Items on the *MCMI-III* that help identify a domestic violence offender as BD include the following:

- *I create situations where I then feel hurt or rejected.*
- *I will do something desperate to prevent abandonment.*
- *Being alone frightens me.*
- *Most people think poorly of me.*

Assessment Issues

For counselors and therapists who treat men and couples in a setting that is neither criminal, court-ordered, nor agency-ordered (in other words, the vast majority of mental health professionals), the challenge of properly identifying and intervening in domestic violence issues comes up frequently.

Here's the bad news: Research studies tell us that if no specific questions are asked regarding relationship violence, then it is highly likely that these important (and potentially fatal) issues will not be treated. Surveys at mental health clinics have reported that, during intake sessions, 6% of wives seeking couples therapy spontaneously reported a history of violence, yet 53% were later identified as being on the receiving end of at least some incident of domestic violence (O'Leary, Vivian, & Malone, 1992). Supporting this same phenomenon, Holtzworth-Munroe examined subjects recruited using a variety of methods, including couples seeking marital therapy and couples recruited from newspaper advertisements (Holtzworth-Munroe, Waltz, Jacobson, & Monaco, 1992). Across the studies, up to a third of "maritally nondistressed" (but reportedly nonviolent) couples and half of "maritally distressed" (but reportedly nonviolent) couples reported that husband violence has occurred in their relationship. Therapists who had assessed these couples, and had identified them, had often been treating them as if there were no violence in the relationship.

The clinical lesson to be learned from these data is that counselors and therapists need to specifically investigate the presence of a history of domestic violence in a relationship. The vast majority of domestic violence incidents will not be revealed unless clients are specifically asked—and even then, of course, we rely only on self-report.

There are two user-friendly ways to go about this:

1. Ask directly. If you are interviewing a couple or an individual who is part of a couple, ask questions like the following:

- *During any of your conflicts, has it ever turned physical? Has either of you ever put "hands on" during an argument or conflict?*
- *Has either of you ever felt afraid that the other person might become physically aggressive?*
- *Are you currently worried about this?*

It is better to ask about specific behaviors than about a generic description like *Has there ever been domestic violence in your household?* Plenty of people have been violent or have been victims of violence, but they may be reluctant to label themselves as domestic violence offenders, spouse abusers, or victims. The behavioral information is what we need to know.

2. Use a questionnaire. The most commonly used survey of reporting these behaviors is the Conflict Tactics Scale–Revised (CTS-R) (Straus, Hamby, Boney-McCoy, & Sugarman, 1996). This is a straightforward questionnaire that asks respondents to complete the following task: *Please circle how many times you did each of these things in the past year, and how many times your partner did them in the past year.* In the most current form of the CTS-R, each member of a couple answers 39 questions about themselves and the same questions for their partner. The questions include items like these, which give a range of respectful conflict resolution, psychological aggression, and physical aggression:

- *I showed my partner I cared even though we disagreed.*
- *I insulted or swore at my partner.*

- *I twisted my partner's arm or hair.*
- *I slammed my partner against a wall.*
- *I stomped out of the room or house or yard during a disagreement.*
- *I suggested a compromise to a disagreement.*

The good news about the CTS-R is that it is specific and it gives operational definitions of interpersonal violence. The bad news is that it relies strictly on self-report (and partner report) and it does not assess context or history, does not assess possibility of self-defense, does not assess level of injury, and does not assess level of fear or psychological intimidation. Still—even with these limitations—it is profoundly better to ask and investigate than to not ask at all.

In a forensic setting, more sophisticated assessments need to be conducted. Several have been developed that are worth mentioning here: the SARA: Spousal Assault Risk Appraisal guide (Kropp, Hart, 2000; Kropp, Hart, Webster, & Eaves, 1994); the DAS: Dangerousness Assessment Scale (Campbell, 1995); and the PAS: Propensity for Abusiveness Scale (Dutton, 1995).

One issue for mental health providers to keep in mind when getting information about domestic violence in a relationship is that most states neither require nor allow reporting of this kind of violence without the consent of the client. Unless there is an obvious Tarasoff situation (imminent threat of harm to a specific individual) or if children are exposed to the violence (which often generates a report to Child Protective Services because of the emotional abuse to the child), the information is considered privileged and confidential. One more exception: In many states, if a victim of any kind of relationship violence is 65 or older, even if the offender is a peer or partner, reporting is mandated by elder abuse laws.

Cognitive Distortions

In working with men who have engaged in some form of abusive behavior toward their intimate partners, it is essential to pay especially close attention to the cognitive distortions that so often trigger these behaviors. This is true whether working in a group, individual, or even couples format.

The Perception of Threat

Studies of the reactions of men who have been abusive with their partners show a disturbing and difficult-to-treat pattern (Holtzworth-Munroe & Hutchinson, 1993). Not only do violent men react with defensiveness and hostility in response to aggressive wife behavior—which makes sense, even if the response is abusive—but they also respond with defensiveness and hostility to "distressed" and even "facilitative" statements. In other words, the more abusive men do not discriminate between various types of wife behavior but rather respond negatively to almost anything their wives say.

MGRS studies support some of these conclusions. MGRS assessment measures men's susceptibility to appraise situations that challenge their masculinity ideology as sources of stress. Men with high scores have been found to be especially stressed by a female partner's behavior that they construe as threatening their masculinity ideology and in situations that men construe as masculine gender-relevant (Eisler & Skidmore, 1987).

Attachment Disorders and Distortions

Holtzworth-Munroe's studies on the relationship between attachment styles and domestic violence were also particularly illuminating here. These studies found that rates of insecure attachment were directly correlated with intensity, severity, and frequency of domestic violence (Holtzworth-Munroe, 1997). The more abusive men were more anxious about abandonment (even more prominent than anxiety about feeling controlled). They were more preoccupied with their relationships (past and present). They were more jealous of other men and less trusting of their partners.

To further complicate matters in terms of relationship satisfaction, these men needed more nurturance from their partners—but they also were more avoidant of dependency and experienced more discomfort with closeness in relationships. This is the adult intimate partner manifestation of Bowlby's description of infants arching away angrily while simultaneously seeking proximity when reintroduced to their mothers (Bowlby, 1969).

The group of men in these studies who were identified as nonviolent but maritally distressed were characterized by a lower desire for closeness and intimacy. They were more dismissing of romantic relationships and showed signs of discomfort with closeness and dependency.

In contrast, men who were identified as both nonviolent and not maritally distressed (in other words, reasonably happily married men) were somewhat preoccupied with their partners, needed a lot of nurturance, and desired closeness and dependency. But these needs were reasonable and fundamentally healthy. These men did not experience conflicts or discomfort with closeness. There was no evidence of insecure or anxious attachment. They were desiring of intimacy and comfortable with it: neither dismissing nor fearful.

Central Themes

Regardless of the context of treating men who have acted abusively (court-ordered groups, individual, couples, etc.), there are central themes that guide counselors and therapists in getting through to the men we need to get through to.

The most common and successful programs, in the 21st century, for treating male interpersonal violence are skill-based with a psychological depth-oriented influence. One of the fundamental assumptions of these programs is that abusive behavior as a response to emotional distress is a learned behavior—and learned behaviors can be unlearned. The cognitive-behavioral strategies that are essential to almost all treatment of abusive behavior patterns focus on helping men first become aware of the cognitive triggers and social cues that generate anger, verbal abuse, and physical acting out. In the context of a secure therapeutic relationship, the cognitive distortions are gently but doggedly challenged. The goal is for this man to identify the chain reaction of event, narrative distortion, emotional flooding, and destructive behavioral choice—and the consequences that result. Other issues that inevitably emerge include childhood experiences with violence, recognizing triggers that are based on past experience, identifying alternative ways of handling conflict, learning self-management and self-soothing strategies, implementing time-out methods, and anticipating and eliminating sources of frustration and anger (Wexler, 2006b).

In the process, a man learns that he is responsible for his actions, even when he is in provocative situations that would test any of us.

In trying to reach the men who have patterns of abusive or violent behavior in their intimate partner relationships, any program or intervention should include at least some emphasis on the following themes:

1. *Definitions of abuse:* The client needs to get a very clear picture of the wide range of abusive behaviors, not just the obvious physical and criminal ones. This should include emotional abuse, intimidation and threats, controlling behaviors, isolation and withdrawal, mind games, and so on.

2. *Red flags and self-talk:* Identifying the triggers for abusive behavior, including situations, interpretations and beliefs, physiological states (drugs, alcohol, low blood sugar, fatigue, work and financial stress, etc.), is essential to take control over one's life.

3. *Communication skills:* Men who are abusive usually have a better chance at changing their relationship behaviors when they are equipped with more effective ways to express themselves, problem-solve, make respectful requests, and so on.

4: *Empathy training:* Although the research in this is mixed, practically every man who is dealing with abusive behavior patterns suffers from a deficit in empathy skills (or at least are dysfunctionally "selective" with their empathy). Increased awareness of how their behavior affects the most important people in their lives often has an impact on these men.

5. *Alcohol and drugs:* The correlation between substance abuse and domestic violence is dangerously high, and the more that men in treatment for domestic violence issues recognize and confront these patterns, the better.

6. *Relapse prevention:* Every program emphasizes specific preparation of the man for facing some of the especially provocative situations that have launched the destructive behavior in the past. Counselors and therapists who have worked with addiction programs offer the same preparation (Wexler, 2006b).

Another set of principles to keep in mind is included in the handout called "The Nine Commandments" (Wexler, 2006b). This is a simple list of absolutely central themes that are repeatedly emphasized in group programs for treating domestic violence. This list originated in conjunction with a military study on domestic violence treatment. The original treatment manual included many subjects deemed to be essential for the men in the program to learn about; however, in reviewing audiotapes of group treatment sessions, numerous themes kept appearing that were never written about on any of the 200 pages of the manual. We identified the most crucial of these themes and distilled them into "The Nine Commandments." In treatment centers that use this program, "The Nine Commandments" are included in the group member handouts and poster-size copies of the list are attached to group room walls for constant reference back to these themes.

Even if a man is being treated in another setting, such as individual therapy, these commandments can be applied.

The Nine Commandments

1. We are all 100% responsible for our own behavior.
2. Violence is not an acceptable solution to problems.
3. We do not have control over any other person, but we do have control over ourselves.
4. When communicating with someone else, we need to express our feelings directly rather than blaming or threatening.
5. Increased awareness of self-talk, physical cues, and emotions is essential for progress and improvement.
6. We can always take a time-out before reacting.
7. We can't do anything about the past, but we can change the future.
8. Although there are differences between men and women, our needs and rights are fundamentally alike.
9. Counselors and case managers cannot make people change—they can only set the stage for change to occur.

Rules of Engagement

Although the ultimate goal of any intervention with men who have been abusive with their partners is to provide new interpersonal skills, nothing is more important in getting through to them than establishing a rich therapeutic alliance (although a fear of consequences, like jail, divorce, or limits on access to children, often trumps any therapeutic intervention). Through empathy and respect, and a focus on changing damaging thoughts and behaviors, many men will respond favorably to treatment.

It is often difficult for counselors and therapists to listen dispassionately and compassionately to the stories of the men who have been abusive. We all enter this setting with our own values and judgments—let alone personal experiences—and the process of understanding a man who abuses his partner can provoke difficult emotions.

These men, however, deserve our respect—not, obviously, for the actions they have taken, but rather for the individual stories that have led them to act desperately and destructively. It is helpful to recognize that many of the men in treatment for abusive relationship behavior—like all of us—have become overwhelmed by emotions that they had difficulty handling, and they have lacked the necessary range of skills to handle these emotions in constructive and proactive ways. Although we must always emphasize personal responsibility, it is also essential to recognize our essential similarity and their essential humanity.

The underlying assumption is that when these men become smarter about themselves (more aware of needs, feelings, and motivations) and smarter about options (better skills at self-talk, relaxation, communication, empathy, and problem-solving), they will choose otherwise in the future.

This sequence of communicating empathic understanding and respect for the man's experience, followed by a new perspective or idea, proves valuable in these interventions. Here are some specific issues and challenges that, if handled poorly, will derail the intervention, and if handled successfully, will vastly increase the likelihood of engagement and success (Wexler, 2006b).

Labeling: It is vital to communicate this message: *We treat the man, not the label.* Stay away from labels that sound like put-downs, such as *batterers, perpetrators, abusers,* and so on. They may be true, and they may be the labels in the legal system, but they do nothing but foster shame—and resistance—in this population of men. If this is a group program, we want the men to understand that we could put any man in this group (regardless of what has gone wrong in his relationship patterns) and he would benefit from the approaches used in this treatment model.

Powerlessness and accountability: Although it is obvious that dominance and control are central themes for many male domestic violence perpetrators, it is also important to recognize how powerless many of these men feel. When counselors and therapists can identify this experience of powerlessness, many of these men are much more accessible to what treatment has to offer. They feel less blamed as bad people and more understood as men who have been frustrated or have felt wounded. It is quite possible to communicate this message without absolving men of responsibility for their abusive actions. Consider this message: *We want you to take 100% responsibility for your own behavior, but not necessarily 100% blame for all the problems.*

Shame-free group names: Domestic violence treatment groups should not be called domestic violence treatment groups, at least not as far as the group members are concerned. The names should be neutral, like *Group HAWK* or *Group EAGLE,* or positive, like *Relationship Skills Training* or *The STOP Program.* These men are very sensitive to being and feeling shamed about their behavior, and the shame experience rarely makes them more amenable to change. Instead, it generates defensiveness and resistance.

"Shame-friendly" group environment: The discussion in any treatment setting for men who have acted abusively should not lead to more shaming than they are already experiencing. Challenging men to recognize the ways in which their behavior has been abusive is one thing; communicating disgust is another. There needs to be room for them to discuss their feelings of shame about their behavior without feeling more of it. The goal is to create a "shame-friendly" clinical environment in which shame can be identified and integrated.

Interactive, engaging techniques: In a group treatment program, another important design issue is to make sure that the information that is so vital for men's progress is presented in ways that are engaging and user-friendly. Lectures need to be simple and straightforward. The use of video clips, group exercises, demonstrations and role-plays, and humor all enhance the attention span and receptivity of this audience.

Initial resistance: Frequently—in group, individual, or couples treatment—abusive men enter the treatment setting angry and resistant. They complain about being in treatment, challenge the approaches and the policies, and insist that they will not be talking in these sessions. It is usually best to respectfully listen to their complaints, validate how difficult it is to engage in treatment, respect where they are coming from, and then move on. Power struggles should be avoided whenever possible. Often men who are the most difficult in the early sessions turn out to be the best clients—as long as they have felt respected.

Universal experience: It is valuable for abusive male clients to hear this basic message: "Anybody could benefit from this program." In other words, these men (with the obvious exceptions of psychopaths and true intimate partner terrorists) are not freaks. They are men who—like all of us—have failed sometimes in handling the complexities of intimate partner relationships. Without in any way minimizing the seriousness and tragedy of their offenses, it is still very treatment-friendly to make it clear that the counselors, too, could benefit from going through a program like this, which examines relationship assumptions and relationship behavior.

Structure and Limit-Setting

Respect for men who have committed acts of violence or abuse is essential—but so are clear limits and expectations (Wexler, 2006b).

Women-bashing: "Women-bashing" often occurs in treatment with abusive men. This should be confronted immediately. Group leaders or individual therapists should point out that generalizations about any social group always turn people into categories rather than individuals. It should be emphasized that *it's okay to say that your wife complains a lot, but not to say that all women are complainers* (or worse). Furthermore, men who refer to their wife as "the wife" or "she" or even "my wife" should be consistently asked to refer to her *by name*. In a group program, it can be humanizing to write on the board the names of each of the women discussed in the group as their names come up during each session. The goal is to make the women in these men's lives as real and human as possible.

System-bashing: In any program that includes men who are ordered into treatment for their abusive behavior, there is inevitably "system-bashing": complaining about the unfairness of the court system, Child Protective Services, child custody laws, and so on. These discussions should be short-circuited as quickly as possible. Unlike women-bashing, however, it is rarely effective to confront these complaints. For one thing, the men may be justified in their complaints. For another, it is unproductive to engage in any unnecessary power struggles. The most effective strategy seems to be saying something like this: *You know, you may be right about some of your complaints, but this isn't really the focus of what we are doing here. What we need to talk about here is the things you can do differently in your life.*

Not normalizing violence: One time I was co-leading a domestic violence group with a female co-leader. One of the men described an argument with his wife in which he got so angry that he "felt like picking up a frying pan and smashing her over the head with it." He didn't do it, but he felt like it. My co-leader, in an attempt to relate to the anger component, said, "If my husband ever said something like that to me, I'd feel like picking up a frying pan and hitting him over the head with it, too."

This was a clinical mistake: If a male abusive client reports a violent urge or fantasy when arguing with his partner, it is not appropriate to tell him that you often feel the same way. Even if it is true, this tends to normalize aggressive impulses. The group members get the message that everyone feels like they do, which is not exactly true. Everyone has anger, and perhaps even occasional aggressive urges, but most people do not seriously struggle with whether or not to act on them—as these men have.

In another group, one of the men was angry at the group leader for writing a less than favorable report to his probation officer. He told the group leader: "I feel like punching you in the head right now!" He actually thought he was doing something positive by *verbalizing* his feelings rather than *acting out*. He needed correction on this one: Civilized people might say that they are angry at someone, but they do not report violent fantasies. It is intimidating and inappropriate, even if it is "honest."

Provisional status policy: Men who are in individual or group programs dealing with these issues of abusive and/or violent behavior benefit from getting very specific and clear information about what is expected of them. For example, here is a list of expectations about behavior in a domestic violence group treatment program:

The following are grounds for group members to be placed on Provisional Status in The STOP Program (leading to possible termination). These behaviors are in addition to activity that takes place outside of the group sessions, such as acts of violence, repeated drug or alcohol problems, or failure to attend group:

1. **Consistently** putting down women or minimizing violence
2. **Persistent** disruptive or oppositional behavior in group
3. **Consistent** projection of blame for relationship problems without self-examination
4. **Consistent** lack of participation in group, including failure to complete homework assignments
5. **Consistent** pattern of "telling stories" (bragging or showing off) about controlling, abusive, or violent behavior with little or no signs of remorse
6. **Consistent** pattern of inappropriate messages on clothing (such as t-shirts with sexist messages) (Wexler, 2006b, p. 35).

Special Issues in Working with Men Who Abuse

The following are issues that emerge again and again in working with men who have been abusive with their partners—and strategies for how to approach these issues. Most of these issues apply to all relationships, but they are especially prevalent in relationships that have deteriorated into violence or abuse (Wexler, 2006b).

Feeling "punk'd": Many men who abuse their partners, plagued with excessive MGRS, are obsessed with the possibility of getting "punk'd." Even more than the rest of us, they are likely to view interpersonal situations in an either/or mode based on whether they felt in control or someone else controlled them. This is even true (and, we have learned, often especially true) in their most intimate relationships.

So, when a counselor is helping a man generate a new and more adaptive narrative, leading to a new and more adaptive behavioral response, there is always the possibility that the client will mouth the words but secretly feel "punk'd." We have learned to anticipate this and to ask directly: *Yeah, I know you say you could try this, but don't you think you would end up feeling "punk'd"? Like you'd be saying to yourself, "She found a way to control me and make a fool out me again!"* Sometimes he says no, sometimes yes, but either way, it is extremely valuable to bring this possible obstruction out in the open.

Anger as a secondary emotion: The typical response from angry and abusive men when responding to the classic therapeutic inquiry of *How do you feel?* is *I feel pissed.* Anger is a safe, masculine-friendly emotion. Men who experience more anger, and especially more anger that results in destructive behavior, benefit from conceptualizing anger as a secondary emotion. The primary emotions that trigger anger include frustration, hurt, vulnerability, shame, jealousy, threat, anxiety, powerlessness, hopelessness, helplessness, and so on. These are all emotions that are decidedly not user-friendly for men highly attached to traditional notions of masculinity. Despite the fact that these emotional states are universal and unavoidable, they can make men feel too weak and vulnerable.

When we educate men about this pattern of masking the wide range of primary emotions with the secondary emotion of anger, we open them up to a new world of personal awareness. The line that seems to be helpful for these men is this: *We want you to be powerful—not over others, but over yourself. And the more you know about your true emotions and your true thoughts, the more truly powerful you can become.*

This doesn't always work: Much of the work in helping abusive men involves offering them training and specific strategies for handling tough interpersonal situations more effectively. However, since these situations with intimate partners are so complex, and because their part-ners are not always angelic and following ideal rules of communication themselves, even the best-designed strategies often fail. A valuable message to convey is that learning to handle these situations more maturely offers two benefits: (a) the increased likelihood that things will go better in the relationship and (b) the personal knowledge of knowing you did the right thing.

Don't make a bad situation worse: The stories that abusive men tell about their relationship dramas often involve a partner who (assuming that the story is even 50% accurate) is behaving destructively, unfairly, or abusively herself. And the man enters a state of helplessness and frus-tration because he cannot fix the situation or get her to stop. This often leads to an excessive attempt at control on his part, which sometimes leads him to regrettable actions, divorce, or jail.

At these moments, it is helpful for the man to develop a new mantra: *Don't make a bad situation even worse.* This means that he has to abandon the goal of making the situation all better and set the bar lower: Success means not making it worse. Frustrating and disappointing as this goal is, the reframing of goals here is often enough to keep him out of jail. And he deserves to be congratulated for his success if he can live by this mantra.

The Couples Therapy Controversy

Historically, any use of couples counseling when there are any patterns of domestic violence has been extremely frowned upon. In fact, many states strictly forbid the use or advocacy of any couples counseling for court-ordered domestic violence offenders.

The alarm about couples counseling is primarily based on two fundamental concerns. The first is protection of the victim. The night-mare scenario involves an abuser and victim sitting in a couples session, encouraged to be open and honest. The victim reveals information that is damaging and shaming to the abuser. The abuser keeps his (assuming the abuser is male) cool until they get home. Then he assaults her for humiliating him and airing their dirty laundry in public. In this scenario, the use of couples counseling generates the exact opposite intention of any intervention: It further endangers the victim.

The other concern is more subtle and political. In a classic male abuser/female victim domestic violence situation, the inclusion of the victim in treatment may send the message that she is partly to blame: If *I am part of the solution, I must have been part of the problem.* That's the worst message we can send to a victim (or perpetrator) of domestic violence.

Aldarondo and Mederos offered this set of basic guidelines: "Couples counseling is contra-indicated if the abusive man expresses no remorse, denies his actions, blames the abuse victim or has little commitment to change. Similarly, if the abuse victim shows fear of further violence, assumes responsibility for it, or feels deserving of maltreatment, couples counseling should not be considered" (2008, p. 13).

Advantages of Couples Counseling in Domestic Violence Cases

Despite these very valid concerns, many researchers and therapists are proponents of the value of couples counseling among carefully selected domestic violence cases. Any systems theory therapist would recognize the obvious: When you have both members of a couple in the room, you are more likely to have an impact on the overall system. And when both partners go through the treatment process together, they both learn and practice the skills that increase the likelihood of relationship harmony.

Furthermore, a recent study (Simpson, Atkins, Gathis, & Christensen, 2008) indicated that automatically focusing on the violence is sometimes unnecessary and may even be counterproductive, driving couples out of therapy. This research focused on couples with low levels of physical aggression, excluding partners who had committed severe acts of aggression (like choking, scalding, and forced sex), two or more acts of moderate aggression (like slapping or causing physical pain that lasted more than a day) in the last year, or at least six acts of mild aggression (like pushing or shoving) in the past year.

The authors examined the efficacy of non-aggression-focused behavioral couple therapy for couples with and without a history of mild physical aggression. One hundred thirty-four couples, 45% of whom had experienced low-level aggression in the year prior to therapy, completed up to 26 sessions of couples therapy and 2 years of follow-up assessments.

The study found that when these couples with identifiable but low levels of physical aggression focused on other relationship problems besides the violence, none of the feared escalation in violence took place. Up to 2 years after treatment ended, couples who received therapy directed at the usual issues, like closer emotional attunement and better communication, showed no increase in physical aggression and significantly higher levels of individual and couples satisfaction. In addition, couples maintained very low levels of physical aggression during and after treatment and showed reductions in psychological aggression when relationship and individual functioning improved.

Many couples who engage in mild to moderate physical aggression want to preserve the relationship and end the aggression. I have often, very selectively, chosen to treat couples who reported some patterns of domestic violence (non-court-ordered) because of my concern that it was either this treatment or no treatment at all. If couples are refused treatment because of the perceived risk factors, they may never return or seek help. Furthermore, many couples don't always label such aggression as a problem, so focusing therapy strictly on the violence issues may cause them to feel their therapist isn't listening to their concerns. Or they may leave therapy because they don't want to be labeled as abusers or victims.

Domestic Violence Couples' Treatment Criteria

Counselors and therapists are often restricted from treating couples in which domestic violence is or has been present. However, a national consensus has developed (Aldarondo & Mederos, 2002; Bancroft, Silverman, Jaffe, Baker, & Cunningham, 2004; Baucom, Gordon, Snyder, Atkins, & Christensen, 2006; Bograd & Mederos, 1999; La Taillade, Epstein, & Werlinich, 2006; Vivian & Heyman, 1996) identifying specific screening criteria to guide clinicians on when it might be appropriate and advantageous to offer this counseling option—if this is "allowed."

1. The victim (or victims) must feel safe talking about relationship issues without fear of retaliation or intimidation from the partner. Nothing is more important than this.

2. Both parties desire it. It is essential that partners in this relationship clearly state that they want try this route to deal with their relationship problems.

3. The violence must have some sort of "relationship basis" in which both parties identify ways that they can contribute to a better atmosphere. A guy who comes home drunk and starts beating up on his wife would not qualify. It is important to note that this message must be carefully distinguished from "victim-blaming"; this is simply an acknowledgment that both parties can help this relationship work better.

4. The abuser (or abusers) have engaged in full disclosure to the counselor.

5. The abuser (or abusers) are committed to nonviolence. They both agree that there is no place for violence in their relationship.

6. The abuser (or abusers) has the capacity for empathy.

7. The abuser (or abusers) is accepting of consequences for his or her actions.

8. The victim currently feels safe living with his or her partner and participating in conjoint treatment.

9. The victim currently feels comfortable being honest in the presence of his or her partner.

10. Neither partner currently suffers from any untreated major psychiatric or substance abuse.

11. There is no evidence of a significant pattern of "power and control" or "intimate partner terrorism" issues.

12. There is no evidence of any significant and systematic pattern of psychological abuse.

13. There is no evidence of any serious lethality (use of weapons, sadistic sex, etc.) or bizarre violence.

14. There is no evidence of any stalking or serious obsession with the partner.

If these criteria are met, then—and only then—it might be wise to consider couples counseling for these issues.

Domestic Violence Couples' Treatment Goals
The goals of conjoint treatment in cases in which there is at least some evidence of domestic violence include the following (La Taillade et al., 2006):

1. Educate couples about the patterns of violence that can occur in intimate partner relationships.
2. Increase personal responsibility for the use of violence. Decrease blaming partner.
3. Utilize anger management and conflict resolution skills to offer alternatives to interpersonal violence.
4. Increase positive interactions in couple.
5. Help couple recover from any past trauma and broken trusts due to affairs and patterns of abuse.

Most important of all: Working with couples in which there has been violence requires consistently sending a very clear message about the two layers of work that are taking place. The first invokes the 100% responsibility rule: *We are all 100% responsible for our own actions.* No relationship provocation can make someone go off violently. Just as with infidelity, the person who crossed over that line is fully responsible for his or her behavior. The second layer is the relationship factor: *While we are here, let's do everything possible to bring out the best qualities in this relationship.* Usually, a better relationship eliminates some of the breeding grounds of interpersonal violence and abusive behaviors. Making this clear without victim-blaming is an art.

Psychopathology: Bad Men Behaving Badly
Last, but not least, is a qualifier to this entire chapter: There clearly is such a thing as bad man behaving badly. The greater the level of psychopathy (or, in many cases, substance abuse patterns that generate behaviors that mimic psychopathy), the more unlikely that intervention

in abuse cases will be successful. In the standard interventions (structured groups for domestic violence), some men simply do not benefit. Some who are particularly character disordered not only do not benefit themselves but actually poison the well for the rest of the men who really are open to straightening out these problems—and any of these psychopathic personality patterns completely rule out even the consideration of couples counseling. Fortunately, for those of us in the treatment community, the men who benefit far outweigh the intimate partner terrorists, the psychopathic characters, and the men with antisocial personality disorders who do not benefit. For men with these issues, significant response cost and incarceration are much more the interventions of choice, rather than the sophisticated attempts to reach out, engage, and respect that are so desperately needed for the rest of the men who abuse and have the capacity and motivation to change.

Chapter 9
Treating Men in Groups

Men spend much of their time growing up in groups with other boys or other men. Men play sports in teams, they join gangs, they hang out with buddies. They join fraternities in college and enter military service with intense alliance and bonding with other men. They fish and hunt and go to strip clubs and weekends in Las Vegas in groups with other men. They play music together. They go on church retreats. They play pickup basketball games on Saturday mornings. They play poker on Thursday nights and get together on Sunday afternoons to watch the NFL. Men usually hang with their buddies or colleagues in work environments. And when they are together, men usually have plenty to talk about.

Sometimes this talk is about difficult life experiences, but what men do not typically do in groups is talk much about their feelings or examine their roles as males. And, although men certainly are often extremely loyal to each other, they also typically compete, and they typically keep a mask over their more vulnerable and private inner world.

Men's therapy groups are able to deepen men's experiences and open up possibilities for self-examination. The group experience offers the opportunity for men to genuinely compare notes with their peers in ways that they may never have had the opportunity to do before. Instead of entering a hardened and competitive male world, they enter one that is interpersonally receptive. The men's group, when it's done right, creates a group norm that encourages feelings and vulnerability rather than dampening them. The men in the group nurture each other in a uniquely male way—by what they say, by what they don't say, by how they joke, by their nonverbal responses, and by the behaviors they offer each other.

More than anything else, a good men's group expands the definition of what "real man" behavior is all about. Talking about feelings, speaking respectfully about women, taking personal responsibility for mistakes, not letting circumstances dictate personal responses, and even shedding a few tears all become defined as within the parameters of truly masculine behavior. Just like how it used to take a confident man to wear a pink shirt, it takes a really confident man to shed some tears in a group of men. In this setting, men are asked to give up some of their typical defenses and find the more authentic self beneath the roles. Men support each other in taking on this challenge. And, although there are a lot of ways to go about this, it can be reassuring to men that they don't have to take off their clothes and chant to the beating of drums in the woods to do it.

The range of themes and issues that might emerge from a men's group is vast: "Trust, vulnerability, fear, shame, pride, rage, strength, weakness, the dark shadow self, warrior, father, fathering, male-male relationships, competition, mother, male-female relationships, boundaries, family of origin, friendship, sexuality, tenderness, disappointment, dominance, submissiveness, desire, love, hatred, dreams, pleasure, pain, grief, secrets, will paralysis, obsession, work, and death" (Rabinowitz, 2005, p. 274–275). And that's just the tip of the iceberg.

Types of Groups

Men's groups come in a lot of different shapes and formats. Although, ultimately, the commonalities of the positive group experience transcend the differences in format, it is important to be aware of the different types and some of the issues that may be associated with each.

Forced vs. voluntary: There are probably a lot more men who are in men's groups because some legal authority (a court, probation, Child Protective Services, their work supervisor, etc.) has determined that they have a problem and has required them to attend. And this does not even include the percentage of men who are in groups because their wife or partner has "required" them to attend. When a man comes to a group involuntarily, he needs a little extra room to be resistant and complain about the unfairness of the system that has forced him into this program. But the good news is that, in the vast majority of cases, this passes. Most groups of men ordered into a program look and feel no different, after a while, from groups of men who have chosen the group therapy format for their own healing and personal growth.

Open-ended vs. closed: Another distinction among men's groups is whether or not everyone starts and ends the group together or if it is open-ended. Most men's groups, involuntary or voluntary, are open-ended, which means that the group forms when there are enough men signed up to start a group. Then the group continues and adds group members until the group reaches capacity. The group stays closed until someone leaves and an opening appears. The advantage of a closed group, of course, is that the group starts together and grows together. The group develops a personality, and, if it is a structured psychoeducational group, the group members learn the material in a progressive learning sequence. When the group is open-ended (which is much more typical because of the practical difficulties of always waiting until a full group is assembled before starting), the most prominent advantage is that there are always senior members. These senior group members welcome the new group members and model for them what is expected in the group process, as well as providing compassionate inspiration for men who are apprehensive or downright defensive as they begin the men's group experience. This welcoming committee of male peers is much more powerful than the welcoming committee of one or two group therapists.

Group Leader Characteristics

It is usually preferable to have co-leaders for any type of group. Not only does it offer the men multiple sources of feedback and insight, but it also allows the group leaders to engage in some division of labor. For example, when one group member is dealing with some issues and has the floor, one group leader can focus exclusively on him while the other group leader can keep an eye out for the reactions of other group members. Furthermore, if the group leaders are a male-female team, the men in the group can observe how an effective male-female team works together, including resolving conflict, showing respect, and working collaboratively. There is also the increased possibility of dealing with transference issues on both male and female transference figures. Having two group leaders also allows for the possibility of one of them taking a vacation or getting sick.

However, in practice, many men's groups of all kinds are conducted by a single group leader, usually male, sometimes even female. These often work just fine. Specific issues about women working with men are addressed in Chapter 4.

Another important variable in men's groups involves the qualifications of the group leaders. Many men's groups are therapy groups led by individual mental health professionals or a team of mental health professionals, sometimes a senior-junior combination of a licensed therapists and a therapist in training. Other groups are led by nonprofessionals or, like most 12-step groups, are not formally led by designated group leaders at all.

Process-Oriented vs. Structured/Theme Groups

One more distinction among many of the men's groups of the world is reflected in the structure and purpose of the group. Some men's groups are traditional psychodynamic or humanistic-existential group experiences. These groups involve minimal therapist structuring, few if any group exercises, significant emphasis on affective exploration, consistent attention to the process of the group interaction, and a focus on transference (toward both group and group leaders) phenomena.

Many other men's groups are highly structured and are more likely to be described as psychoeducational. They usually have a specific theme for a group focus (addiction issues, anger and violence issues, parenting and relationship issues, etc.) and include a teaching component in addition to focusing on affect and the group experience. Almost all of the groups in which men are ordered to attend are in this category, and many voluntary ones as well. Many groups, of course, are actually some hybrid of both of these forms, but it is important to recognize these basic distinctions when evaluating a group's effectiveness or when designing a group format.

New Interpersonal Norms: Men Trusting Men

Individual therapy for men has plenty going for it. But the multiple relationships and the multiple stories of other men that normalize private male experiences offer a rare opportunity for many men who otherwise live quite hidden psychological lives. The attractiveness and success of group therapy for men are built on the premise that the group situation is often a better fit for many men, especially those with traditional gender role orientations, than individual psychotherapy (Brooks, 1998).

The trajectory of many men's lives offers a wealth of male bonding opportunities throughout the years of growing up—in school, in sports teams, in gangs or other group affiliations—for better or worse. Young men bond easily in their colleges, their fraternities, their jobs, their military service.

But, not long afterward, men tend to become more socially isolated as they move into a world dominated by a primary attachment to a female partner and ultimately to a home with a wife and kids rather than a dorm room or military unit or shared apartment with roommate buddies. It becomes a lot harder to get away for guy events when job responsibilities, the needs of a significant other, and the needs of kids start to take precedence.

Many men find that the pressures of work and family take most of their energy and time. It is easy to lose touch with one's emotional self by trying to obey the social rules in each aspect of life. In a men's group, it is expected that each man will talk about who he really is, not just his work or social persona. Men learn they are not alone and, in the process, build trust with each other at a personal level.

The men who initially come to group are often emotionally isolated and discouraged, receiving very little positive support from relationships or work (Rabinowitz, 2001). Often they are in the midst of a personal crisis, such as divorce or other significant loss, or they are in a situation they must change in order to avoid family dissolution or incarceration. Some are recovering from addictions to drugs, sex, gambling, or work. A man may begin to feel less alone and find hope from the camaraderie found in the group. In this group environment, men recognize that, despite their individual differences, they share a commonality of social forces and Boy Codes that have shaped them.

It is particularly valuable for men to find ways of turning to other men—not just women—for emotional intimacy and vulnerability. Those of us who are men—and all of us who have worked with men—know of many stories of men who rely exclusively on their female partners to engage in conversations and to grease the wheels of social communication. Many men who are dependent on women for initiating interpersonal conversation and generating a social life find the all-male group challenging. However, this therapy group composed only of men allows a unique brand of male support to emerge.

One of the things that a group allows a man to do is to put together a new and more coherent personal narrative. He tells the group about his current relationship—or his history of failures. He tells the group about his history growing up and some of the key forces that shaped him. The group, and the group leaders, observe him in action: how he expresses himself, how he responds to others, what makes him vulnerable and what makes him defensive. Hearing the stories of other men and engaging in structured discussion about male-specific issues often trigger memories of something his father said or did when he was a boy or how his interactions with siblings helped shape his own views on trust, masculinity, or his sense of self.

Rabinowitz and Cochran quoted a man in a weekly men's therapy group: "I have always gone to women for emotional support of my tender and expressive side. With my male friends, I tended to relate about sports, school, and work and not burden them with the stuff I would tell my mother or girlfriend. I felt like I couldn't be completely real with either women or men. In the men's group, I have found out that most men feel this way. It has been such a feeling of a burden lifted to realize I can be totally myself here; gentle, aggressive, compassionate, wild, or competitive and still be accepted by these guys, who I initially thought were going to judge and reject me" (2002, p. 158).

Appealing to Male Self-Interest

The best way to "hook" a man into a men's group (not just his physical presence, but his full participatory self) is to convince him that there is truly something in this for him. Words are a good start: *Your wife will appreciate you more. You'll get a chance to hear how other guys think. You'll have a safe place to talk about the stuff that's bothering you,* and so on. But words are cheap. Most men only become truly convinced that there is something in this for them when they personally experience it.

Fortunately, in most well-run men's groups, they experience it plenty. Often, the same men who were so resistant to joining or opening up in the group are the ones who find it most difficult to leave. They have never experienced this before and they fear—often with good reason—that they will not have access to this level of conversation and intimacy elsewhere in their lives.

Instead of maintaining rigid patterns of behavior that result in the avoidance of intimacy, addiction, and privately experienced distress, the group encourages warmth, support, and trust so that conflict can be dealt with in a straightforward fashion. Men are free to engage in confrontation because they trust that they will gain personally from the interaction. Affection, rather than being avoided, can be used to show caring among men.

Opportunity to Talk About the Forbidden

Sexual performance is a forbidden subject—especially the fears and narratives attached to declining sexual performance. So are fears about losing important emotional attachments, and fears of death and the losses experienced in the aging process, and profound disappointments about not having accomplished what one once dreamed of. A good men's group allows men the forum to identify and articulate these worries and to have a group of their peers bear witness to the experience.

It is only in a group of men that an individual man can normalize the declining sexual interest of his wife when they have young kids or later when she is menopausal. When normalized, it becomes an issue that plenty of men face rather than a unique and personal assault on one man's masculinity and potential for sexual fulfillment. The voices from a solid and "well-trained" group provide an alternative to the more typical male world of stoicism and competitive masks of masculinity.

Two strategies are particularly helpful in generating a group environment that allows for and elicits the discussion of the forbidden. One is therapist response modeling: When a man in group starts to veer into "forbidden" or vulnerable territory, he and the other groups members are watching carefully to see what happens in the group. The more the group therapist models a response of taking this seriously, the more the group will follow. Taking it seriously is usually communicated by a lowered tone and volume of voice, by offering basic empathic remarks and gently probing for more details, and (at times) offering a personal response to indicate that the listener knows something about what this feels like. If the group members respond superficially by laughing or espousing mere platitudes, the group therapist can best keep the process on track by simply modeling the desired group response, again and again. Only occasionally is it necessary or does it work out well to directly confront group members if they have not responded respectfully.

Another way to elicit meaningful discussion of difficult topics is by the use of videos or other ways to stimulate discussion. The men watch another man going through something difficult, allowing them the comfort zone of some emotional distance but still injecting these issues into the room. This often opens the gate for revealing how they, too, have experienced these issues. We see this in our domestic violence men's groups most dramatically when we play a scene from the movie *The Great Santini* (Carlino, 1979) in which the father is physically assaulting the mother and the four kids restrain him. Inevitably, some men in our group start talking abut what it was like for them as children when they were forced into this horrible position. The barrier to discussing the forbidden breaks down.

Conflicts and Conflict Avoidance in Men's Groups

The male-only experience of a men's therapy group brings with it a unique set of opportunities and issues. While some men's groups may have female co-leaders, in a men's group there are no women to impress (other than a possible female group leader). There is a simple expectation: Check your ego at the door. Job status and income do not count here. Nor does success with women or athletic prowess or physical risk-taking or academic achievement.

Still, despite the stated expectations, there is conflict and competition. It is rarely physical or intimidating, simply because almost all men (even violent men) are socialized better than to act that way in a professional environment.

Men's groups challenge men to constructively deal with interpersonal conflict. Many men have been socialized to avoid conflict through distracting activities, intellectual rationalization, rage, or silence. Heated exchanges sometimes arise in a men's group. Depending on the stage of the group, men will respond to these interpersonal challenges with varying effectiveness. At some key stages when a group is forming or reconstituting with changes in membership, conflict is typically ignored in order to focus on commonality between members. The trust-building and establishment of a safety zone are essential for the group to get anywhere—but no group is really effective unless it allows for the respectful expression of conflict.

My experience of most men's groups is that, rather than being too quick to engage in conflict, most male group members are too likely to engage in conflict avoidance. They subscribe to one of the fundamental precepts of the male code: *I got your back*. When a man complains about his wife in the group, the other men are quick to chime in and encourage him to confront her or dump her. They are much less likely to ask their fellow group member to examine his own behavior or to cut her some slack or to recognize that, just like him, she may be imperfect or insecure. These types of comments are often seen as acts of disloyalty to their brother.

In reality, most men in groups welcome confrontive feedback (as long as it is fundamentally respectful and they get some "love" in the process). A group that takes the leap into mixing constructive negative feedback into the basic support of all group members is a successful group. And the group discovers that getting criticized does not mean getting shamed and does not require sympathetic nervous system responses of either fight or flight.

Once initial trust has been established through mutual sharing and self-disclosure, group members will begin to tire of being "nice" to each other. If allowed to go on for too long, "niceness" will become a group norm that supports safety but no challenge. In order for a men's group to work, it must provide a challenging psychological atmosphere (Brooks, 1998). Group leaders must encourage and model interpersonal confrontation as well as support for the men. Learning to deal with confrontation can help participants acknowledge their own feelings, value interpersonal feedback, and understand the projective nature of many confrontational remarks. These interpersonal skills can be used in relationships in the world outside of the group to facilitate intimacy and connection.

Structure

Although this does not apply to all men, many men entering groups— or, for that matter, any counseling environment—feel unsure of what is expected of them. Many men respond very positively to structure that organizes them and reduces anxiety, which sets the stage for them to participate more fully and more openly in the group experience.

Structure and Expectations

Men entering groups where there is a group expectation of expressing feelings often have no clue about where to start or how to do this right. Offering some specific information about what is expected from them in this group setting is extremely anxiety-reducing and centering. It sets the stage for men to ultimately offer more of what we are genuinely hoping for and more that they can genuinely benefit from.

One of the most valuable contributors to the success of group therapies is the use of appropriate pre-group preparation (Yalom, 1985). This helps foster the alliance necessary for successful group performance. Given what we know regarding men's typical trepidations about entering a group environment like this, it is extremely valuable to properly prepare each participant prior to entering the group. We want to have the new, unsure, and potentially defensive group member form an alliance with the group leader(s) without any competition from the rest of the group. The incoming group member needs to feel assured that whoever is in charge of the group environment will know him and will watch his back. It is also valuable to anticipate the types of concerns that men often have and address them up front, concerns such as:

Will I be forced to express my feelings right off the bat?
Is this just going be a bitch and whine session with a bunch of guys complaining about their wives and their bosses?
I have a professional reputation in the community—what happens if I reveal something that might make me look bad if word gets out?

The group therapist who anticipates these questions and directly brings them up sends a message to the incoming male: *I have done this before and I know some of the things you are probably worried about.*

Structure and Affect

In the course of running men's groups, group leaders are always trying to enrich and expand men's capacity for being and feeling rather than just doing and thinking. But it is always helpful to use what men come in with and play to their strengths. In other words, if a guy is analytical and wants specific goals, the group leaders should speak his language as a way of engaging him and relaxing his defenses.

Men's groups also encourage men to reexplore their family-of-origin roots. But most men in group settings think in quite practical terms and need some genuine and credible rationale for digging into the aversive experiences of the past. I usually frame it like this: *All your issues and experiences from the past are not really relevant for what we are doing here—except when they are directly interfering with the goals you have for the present and the future. Then we have to figure them out; otherwise you are fighting with one hand tied behind your back. When we see how past stuff affects you, we will help you connect the dots: for example, this issue with your father messes you up whenever you hear criticism from you wife. Then it's relevant.*

Left to their own devices and defenses, even in the hands of an experienced group therapist, many men will artfully skirt core emotional issues. The group norm does not automatically generate the depth of emotions that is most valuable—so they need to be "goosed along" with some structure. Specific structured exercises are often very helpful in helping men focus on past issues and feelings.

Some of the exercises that we often find most helpful are the *Put-Downs from Parents* questionnaire, the *Personal Relationship Autobiography*, the *Gut Check* questionnaire, *Masculinity and Sex Homework*, and structured discussions based on selected scenes from films such as *Good Will Hunting, The Break-Up, When a Man Loves a Woman, The Great Santini, Antwone Fisher, Affliction, Parenthood, The Painted Veil, About Schmidt*, and *The Pursuit of Happyness*. For an excellent guide to films that can be used to demonstrate specific clinical points or stimulate important discussions, refer to *Rent Two Films and Let's Talk in the Morning: Using Popular Movies in Psychotherapy* (Hesley & Hesley, 2001).

The *Personal Relationship Autobiography, Gut Check Questionnaire*, and *Masculinity and Sex Homework* appear on the following pages.

Personal Relationship Autobiography

Please answer the following questions about yourself and your history and bring it to group. You should fill out the answers to Week I for next week, Week II for the following week, and so on. Your group leaders will read and return each section to you. You might choose to share parts of it with the group, but that decision will be *completely* up to you. The more honest you can be as you describe yourself and your history, the more you will be able to benefit from this program.

Please attach separate sheets or write on the back if you need more space.

Week I. Basic Family Information

A. What did your parents do for a living?

B. Did you have stepparents?

C. What was the history of your parents' (and/or stepparents') relationships?

D. Where were you in the family (youngest, oldest, etc.)?

E. Briefly describe your father. (Answer the same question for each family member: mother, stepfather, brother, sister, etc.)

F. How you were disciplined and by whom?

Week II. Anger Influences

A. Who influenced you about expressing anger?

B. Who sticks in your mind as a positive or negative model about expression of anger?

C. What did you learn from those influences, positive or negative?

Week III. Life Influences

A. Who were the major people who influenced you, both positively and negatively?

B. Identify several major life events that shaped who you are today in terms of your relationships.

C. Describe key teen and adult romantic relationships that have shaped the way you are today in terms of your relationships.

Week IV. Self Description

A. How would you describe yourself as you are today (particularly in terms of how you relate to your wife or girlfriend)?

Gut Check Questionnaire*

Name _____ Date _____

Answer each of these questions as honestly as you can. None of these answers will be shared with the group without your consent. Use a number from 1 to 10, with 1 being lowest and 10 being highest. When answering questions 4, 5, and 6, remember that the purpose of this is simply to offer some valuable feedback to one of your peers. Most of us have trouble seeing ourselves without honest feedback from others who care about us.

1. How honest am I being in the group? *(Not at all/Completely)*
    _____ (1–10)

2. How much effort am I putting into the group? *(Not at all/Completely)*
    _____ (1–10)

3. How much feedback am I giving to others in the group?
    (None/Very Much) _____ (1–10)

4. Who do I know the most/least in the group?

Most _____ Least _____

5. Who is acknowledging responsibility for his relationship problems most in the group?

Most _____

6. Who is being the most emotionally honest in the group?

Most _____

7. How much am I getting out of the group?

1	2	3	4	5	6	7	8	9	10

Nothing   A little   Pretty Much   A lot   Very Much

*Adapted from Dutton, 1998, pp. 171–172.

Masculinity and Sex Homework[*]

Based on your own life experience, prepare three messages or words of advice you would want to pass on to your son (or what you would suggest a father pass on to his son) about how to handle sex in a meaningful relationship.

1.

2.

3.

[*]from Wexler, 2006b, p. 180.

One thing to keep in mind when using films: Be selective and structured with the clips you select. If you want the group members to watch an entire movie, assign it as homework. The most effective way to use films with the group structure is to pick out a very specific segment from a movie, no more than 7 or 8 minutes, maybe less. The group should get an introduction beforehand of exactly what themes the group leaders are suggesting they focus on. After showing the clip, the group usually benefits most from some more guidance about the key themes, with questions from the group leaders designed to structure the discussion in a way that participants would not always embark upon on their own.

For example, here are the group instructions used in a men's group focused on relationship and domestic violence themes (Wexler, 2006b):

1. Introduce *Good Will Hunting* (Bender & Van Sant, 1997) (begins at 1:30:23 and ends at 1:34:52) about personal shame. In this scene, the main character reveals to his girlfriend his childhood history of abuse and neglect. He expresses it to her in a defensive rage, and it profoundly inhibits him from forming a positive relationship with a good woman who loves him.

2. Introduce the term *shame-o-phobia*. This is a handy way of identifying the profound fear many men have of the possibility of feeling shamed. Shame-o-phobia leads to desperate attempts to avoid possibly shaming situations. It also leads to defensive and aggressive reactions to the experience of shame.

3. Introduce the film: *This movie is about a young man, played by Matt Damon, who has grown up in rough neighborhoods on the streets of South Boston. He has been in and out of foster homes, physically abused, and has run with a real rough crowd. He finally meets a woman who is actually a good match for him, but he is terrified about getting closer to her. Watch what happens in this scene when she invites him to move to California with her. Watch how his fear of being more known by her leads to aggression toward her. This is a classic example of shame-based interpersonal violence.*

4. Play the clip and discuss. Guide the discussion with the following questions:

- *What takes place for Will in this scene that leads him to feel shame?*
- *Can you identify the key words from his girlfriend that seem to trigger his shame reactions (scared, not honest, I want to help you)?*
- *Do you think she is intending to shame him?*
- *How does he react to the experience of shame?*
- *How does the concept of "anticipatory shame" come into play?*
- *Does his behavior qualify as abuse? What is the most hurtful thing he does in this scene?*
- *Can you imagine other ways he could have handled this whole conversation? What self-talk would have been necessary for him to do this?*

Through these exercises and movies, the group can be nudged into addressing issues of father-son relationships, shame, intimacy with women, dealing with loss, narcissistic injuries, etc.

Structure and Behavioral Changes

The other main value, of course, for implementing structure into men's groups is to enhance skill acquisitions and skill development. If a main function of the group experience is to help the men in the group manage their lives better (anger, relationships, addictions, parenting, etc.), then a steady supply of structured behavioral guidelines is almost always valuable. Even in men's groups that are largely process-oriented or psychodynamic, many of the group members ask for and benefit from specific ways to translate these newfound insights into effective behaviors.

General Strategies for Men's Groups

Groups are groups, and many of the same solid principles that govern all good group therapy should of course be applied to men's groups. However, there are some specific issues that tend to be more relevant in order for men's groups to develop more successfully.

Creating Positive Group Norms

Often, male group members will become uncomfortable with the emotionally disturbing discussions that emerge in the group—and they deal with this by laughing or making fun. Sometimes this happens when

216

a group member describes some behavior or attitude toward women. It can get tiring for the group leaders to "lecture" the group about how "this is not a funny subject" or to insist that this obviously resistant behavior be openly interpreted and processed as a sign of resistance. Often, modeling has the most impact. The group leaders should simply maintain a serious tone themselves. The group members usually get the message quickly. Many of these men are surprisingly sensitive to social cues about correct behavior and they don't want to "look bad." A group with an already well-developed core of positive group members and positive group norms generates this on its own.

Humor

Men relate with humor, and the more that group therapists get this phenomenon, the better. Male humor can be affectionate and connecting. It can normalize and soften the blow when some potentially confrontive feedback is being administered. Humor can be used to vividly highlight someone's problem behavior without ridicule or defensiveness. Furthermore, humor offers a break from the emotional intensity of the group experience that men are often overwhelmed by—and, in the spirit of respecting men's defense styles, this should be honored and not just confronted. Humor can also foster the twinship experiences between group leader and group member that relaxes the group member and allows a window of opportunity for the important group messages. If a guy sees that a fellow guy can clown around and get a kick out of something, he tends to relax. He feels like he can be himself. As long as this does not become a predominant defense style that restricts his ability to relate seriously, it should be welcomed.

The Dangers of Men in Groups

The joys and value of a successful men's group are profound. But any therapist running a men's group has to be on the lookout for specific toxic group interaction patterns that are especially "male" in origin and nature.

The competitive, testosterone-driven qualities of men in groups of any sort sometimes threatens to consume the group therapy experience. The men in the room can often find an excuse to compete over anything: success with women, saying something especially meaningful and insightful, income and status, being a badass, sounding smarter or more articulate, getting approval from the group therapists, and so on.

Furthermore, embittered men seek company. And when the most dynamic and articulate men in the room are embittered, they dominate the atmosphere and lure men into their fold who are only marginally embittered. The group norm becomes one of cynicism and victimization, and the greatest status is awarded to the man who can most boldly and articulately dominate with his story.

When this negative attitude takes hold, the group therapist or therapists often find themselves in the crosshairs. Any attempt to confront the negative behavior or to pump some more humanistic air into the room is repelled by the negatively bonded group and is written off as the way naïve therapists think, not reflecting the real world.

When there is only one group member who is being disruptive or obstructionistic, it is usually best to lay out the therapist's concerns clearly and discuss this in the group. Other group members can see that someone is taking charge of the direction of the group, and very often (more often than it might appear based on the negative group atmosphere) other group members also may have valuable feedback for him.

If the therapists are feeling intimidated by a nucleus of group members who are being disruptive, it is often wise to meet privately with problem group members to enlist their alliance with the group goals. Many men who posture in public are much more accessible and reasonable in private. I have often formed a bond with difficult group members by meeting with them personally and appealing to their higher values and better qualities (not to mention their own self-interest, if they are in this group involuntarily).

Regardless of the context, it is essential that any group member whose behavior is interfering with the success of the group hear about it clearly, respectfully, and directly. He needs to get a very clear set of criteria of the kinds of behaviors that have been a problem and the kinds of new behaviors that must replace the old ones for him to continue in the group. In order for him to be held accountable, he must understand what the expectations are.

In the spirit of avoiding shaming men if possible, I am typically in favor of giving him the benefit of the doubt and assuming his "ignorance" rather than his "character disorder": *You may not be aware of this, but . . .* or *I don't think you realize how this comes across, but . . .* There is no point in backing someone into a corner—and inducing a shame-based response—unless absolutely necessary. And I usually find it helpful to employ *pacing and leading* (see Chapter 3) whenever possible. I want him to get the message that his concerns are recognized and respected, even though I am insisting on correcting his behavior.

Last but not least, when it comes to dealing with disruptive group members, group therapists should always remember that they are fully empowered to terminate a group member who is benefiting neither himself nor the group. This does not represent a failure of the program or the group leaders. In fact, when all other therapeutic interventions have been attempted without success, it actually represents a success at taking charge and doing the right thing by this group we care so much about.

Chapter 10

Treating Men of Color

Just as with the issues of women treating men, everything that follow in this chapter should be taken with a grain of salt. In the long run, it is the personal clinical relationship—and the quality of the therapist—that trumps the potential roadblocks when culture, race, or sexual orientation of client and therapist are not a match.

However, even though there are many common themes that characterize all men in therapy, it is essential for all therapists to be both culturally competent and culturally sensitive when treating men of color. This is especially true for any therapist (male or female) who is from the majority culture. Not only is it the therapist's responsibility to be aware (culturally sensitive); it is also the therapist's responsibility to design user-friendly interventions and to create user-friendly environments for minority men (culturally competent).

Cultural Sensitivity

Many of the issues and themes that should guide therapists and counselors regarding men of color are very similar, regardless of the group: Educate yourself about this subculture, be aware of your prejudices and biases, be careful about your preconceptions, be open to learning, and be extra conscious about establishing a shame-free environment.

Diversity Self-Awareness

Before anything else, the primary task for all of us who work with minority culture men (particularly those of us who are majority culture members) is to perform a gut check: What are your own attitudes and experiences with members of this minority culture?

Several authors (Caldwell, White, Brooks, & Good, 2001; Parham, 1999) suggested personal awareness questions for therapists and counselors working with African-American men, and these questions are completely relevant to ask ourselves about working with Latino men, gay men, Asian men, Native American men, and so on.

1. *Am I aware of my own biases and assumptions regarding African-American people?*
2. *What were my first experiences with black males? What are my impressions of African-American masculinity?*
3. *What have I learned from my family, friends, and education about slavery, the civil rights movement, and the black power movement?*
4. *Do I hold images of black males as absent fathers, superstar athletes, entertainers, criminals, or comedians?*
5. *Am I aware of the traditional and recently developed theoretical issues of counseling theory from an Afrocentric perspective?*
6. *What stereotypes of black males do I have?*
7. *What are my fears and attractions to black males?*

I would never trust a therapist who claims that he or she has no prejudices. We all do, and the questions above, applied to anyone from a subculture not our own, help us reveal these prejudices to ourselves. The potential problem for the clinician is not one of prejudice (which is universal), but rather one of unacknowledged and unregulated prejudice.

Reluctance to Seek Help

We know that men, on the whole, face a number of roadblocks regarding seeking counseling services. Male gender role issues and cultural messages contribute to these roadblocks. Minority men, in general, face even more roadblocks.

A variety of research studies have identified the factors that contribute to how and why this is true (Addis & Mahalik, 2003; Good & Wood, 1995; Robertson & Fitzgerald, 1992). First of all, traditional conceptions of masculinity (to which men in minority cultures are often even more strongly attached) are associated with more negative attitudes toward mental health services. In studies comparing men and women of different ethnicities, African-American men endorsed traditional masculinity to the greatest extent (Levant, 2003). African-American adults and cultures, both college students and community adults, endorsed traditional masculinity ideology to a higher degree than their European-American counterparts (although geographical location within the United States affected some of these results as well). Latino adults were midway between African-Americans and European-Americans in their endorsement of traditional masculinity ideology. Among other results, this study indicated that traditional male socialization is associated with normative male alexithymia: Men with the highest scores (more African-American and Latino than European-American) reported lower frequencies of emotional experience (joy, surprise, sadness, disgust, anger, fear, embarrassment, envy, empathy, pride, shame, and guilt).

Research studies confirmed that Latinos, in general, have consistently underutilized mental health services (Rodriguez, 1987) and that they have been inadequately served by mental health systems (Myers, Echemendia, & Trimble, 1991). Latino males are even more likely than men in general to associate the help-seeking aspect of therapy or counseling as humiliating and stigmatizing (Johnson, 1988), and they may strongly associate mental health services as a place reserved for *locos*.

These studies indicate that working-class and lower-income men (again, often even more prevalent in minority cultures) are less likely to seek psychological help than middle-class to upper-middle- class men. Immigrant men have been found to be more reluctant to seek counseling services.

Among minority groups, there is one notable exception to this pattern of reluctance to pursue counseling services: Gay and bisexual men are actually *more* likely than heterosexual men to seek counseling and psychotherapy (Haldeman, 2001).

Assessing Subculture Issues

Unless, for some reason, the client's central issue in seeking therapy has to do with his race or subculture, there is no reason to make his cultural or ethnic identity front and center. Gay boys and men, like African-American, Latino, and Asian-American boys and men, often have relationship problems, suffer from depression and anxiety, get in trouble for substance abuse or aggression, and question the meaning of life without much regard to their cultural identity and the specific social complexity of being gay in a straight world (Haldeman, 2001). And they should be treated for these issues, without assumptions that somehow their minority status makes them fundamentally different. This is identified as an alpha error (Hardy & Laszloffy, 1994): when a therapist assumes incorrectly that race or minority status is central to the presenting problem.

This chapter, however, is designed to help counselors and therapists become more culturally sensitive and culturally competent about the flip side of this: the ways in which membership in this minority club influences or even dominates the experience of this boy or man. Even sensitive clinicians need to be aware of their own biases. The therapist's radar should always be attentive to a number of cultural issues that may define the client's sense of self or affect his ability to openly participate in the counseling process. The therapist cannot afford to be guilty of a beta error (Hardy & Laszloffy, 1994): when race or minority status is central to the presenting problem, but is dismissed as unrelated.

Sensitivity and competence about these issues require the majority of counselors and therapists to keep their eyes and ears open: When dealing with a man of color or a gay man, the therapist must assume his or her client's life is neither so different from—nor so similar to—his or her own.

In assessing subculture issues, there is one immediate question to start with: Is he comfortable with English? Many Latino men or other men come from backgrounds where they learned English as a second, third, or fourth language, and they have learned to function in the English-speaking world. But "functioning" is different from "deeply communicating," and there is nothing more valuable in the therapeutic context than the ability to communicate deeply. Be careful not to confuse limited verbal participation or superficial expression of ideas or feelings with lack of depth or lack of caring; it may simply be that this male client can't go there in English.

Another important issue to be cognizant of is the client's degree of comfort with dominant culture members. In other words, if you are white, and your male client is black, there is a pretty good chance that the client is wary of trusting you. This does not apply to all black men, of course—that would be another naïve assumption. But it would also be naïve to *not* be on the lookout for this. His wariness in group therapy may have more to do with bad experiences with white people in authority than it does with his defensiveness about addressing his alcohol problem or his domestic violence.

Furthermore, any therapist should always listen with the "third ear" for a minority male client's personal experiences with discrimination, disenfranchisement, and hate crimes. Again, this does not necessarily mean that the therapist should insist on addressing these issues if the client does not want to go there or if he reports that these are not relevant to the clinical issues at hand. Trauma is trauma, however. Any therapist who discovers that a female client was sexually abused by her stepfather would definitely spend some time exploring the impact of this and, at least, make it clear that these are the kinds of issues that are safely examined in the therapy setting. The same is true for the trauma of negative experiences because of color, ethnicity, or sexual orientation. There is at least a distinct possibility that these experiences have had a significant impact on the immediate clinical issues at hand. A therapist (*especially* a majority culture therapist treating a minority culture client who is not sure the therapist "gets" it) needs to clearly communicate, with word and deed, that there is validation of these experiences and room to talk about them.

Machismo and Caballerismo

The caricature of masculinity that is implied by the Spanish word *machismo* is, of course, crucial in understanding and engaging Latino men. Machismo is an important concept describing men's behavior in Latino culture, yet it is not well defined.

Most conceptions of machismo focus on a restricted, negative view of hypermasculinity. It represents the stereotypical masculine personification of a Latino man as controlling, sexist, domineering, entitled, and violent. Here is what "Leonardo" has to say on this subject, as quoted in a study of Latino men in group treatment:

> A macho man is always right. If you say, "This is red," he'll say, "No, it's white." Even if it isn't. What he says has to be right, and there's no power on earth that can contradict him. He believes he's the ultimate, he even believes himself. Even if it's a lie. He knows it's a lie, but he'll never say so. . . . It's very difficult for his wife and children to live with him. The wife will probably get in the habit of doing whatever he wants so as not to have problems with him. Because the macho man isn't going to say, "Oh sorry, forgive me," if he's wrong. He would never say that, or accept responsibility for some mistake he's made (Welland & Ribner, 2007, p. 116).

It is even interesting to recognize that notions of traditional masculinity can even come from women in Latino culture. Dr. Alfredo Mirande, professor at the University of California–Riverside, described the expectations many Latinas have regarding male sexual performance and how this reinforces machismo values (Mirande, 2003). He heard Latinas talking about how "real men" should be interested in sex all the time and if they are not, something must be wrong with them: "My sister-in-laws all tell me that they have to fight off my brothers all the time—that's the way men are supposed to be."

Many researchers, however, aim to broaden our understanding of this construct into two subparts, the yin and yang of these cultural beliefs (Arciniega, Anderson, Tovar-Blank, & Tracey, 2008; Falicov, 2000; Mirande, 1997). They identify both traditional machismo and *caballerismo*, which describes a component of manhood with more focus on emotional connectedness. *Caballerismo* represents the positive image of a man as the family provider who respects and cares for his family. It encompasses the role of Latino men as chivalrous, nurturing, and noble. In recent studies of Mexican American men (Arciniega et al., 2008), traditional machismo was related to aggression and antisocial behavior, greater levels of alexithymia, and more wishful thinking as a coping mechanism. *Caballerismo*, in contrast, represents the more positive elements of male gender role. It is positively associated with affiliation, social connectedness, perceiving more value in social relationships, respecting the feelings of others, ethnic identity, and coping strategies via problem-solving. In these studies, traditional machismo was also associated with less education.

The applications of these studies for clinicians are obvious: There are ways to utilize the attachment many Latino men have to their male gender role by emphasizing their commitment more to *caballerismo* than to machismo.

Cultural Competence

Some clinicians feel intimidated by the prospects of treating someone who is markedly different from themselves in race, ethnicity, or sexual orientation. They fear that they will not be able to properly relate and will actually be doing these clients a disservice by attempting to understand issues that they cannot understand.

While there is certainly a time and place for "ethnic matching," this is not the only solution for addressing mental health needs. Sutton advocated the following: "White therapists have to stop buying into the notion that, because they have not lived the African-American male experience, they cannot work effectively with this population. Having biases and discomfort in treating these men does not disqualify a therapist. If therapists are clear about their own growth needs; are conscious throughout the group's evolution of how racism, white male privilege, and old racial fears are manifested; and are willing to become more culturally competent, then the risk of premature termination for African-American men in their groups is minimal" (2006, pp. 145–146).

These same principles, of course, apply to other minority men as well. Majority culture therapists can treat minority culture men and men of color. Biases and discomfort do not doom the therapeutic process, but lack of awareness or the inability to personally address these issues will. If therapists are clear about their own issues, are sensitive to the unique experience of the client, and are willing to become more culturally competent, then the connection and the work can proceed.

This brings us to the issue of cultural competence. It is necessary but not sufficient to be culturally sensitive. It is also necessary to be culturally competent: knowing how to intervene with subculture issues in mind. This empowers the therapist to work with clients different from himself or herself. Caldwell et al. (2001) suggested that mental heath counselors should acknowledge the limits of interpreting minority culture mental health from psychology's traditional Eurocentric world-view. He advocated that interventions and strategies for minority men must be culturally "authentic" (which reflects competence) in order to address the distorted notions that many of us have about minority masculinity issues.

According to some research (Atkinson, Wampold, Lowe, Matthews, & Ahn, 1998), when providing counseling to racial or ethnic minority persons, it is often more important to match client and counselor values than it is to match client and counselor race or ethnicity. Such matching could include the values given to the extended family, the importance of men taking a leadership role in looking out for the welfare of their families, and the importance of maintaining respect across generations.

Let the Client Educate You

If your Latino client has a strong Catholic faith (and you are not religious), ask him about what this means in his life. If your African-American client has grown up in a neighborhood that you have never been to, let him know that you don't know what that was like and ask for his experience. If your client came to this country on an immigrant boat from Vietnam, inquire in detail about how this affected him.

The examples described here are all obvious minority groups, but the same clinical principles apply to any client who belongs to a subculture that is foreign to you: deer hunters, corporate executives, professional gamblers. People will usually forgive your ignorance if you acknowledge it and if you communicate a genuine interest in learning about their world. This is a *mirroring selfobject* experience: The interest you show validates that the details of the client's life are worth being interested in, and thus the client is worthwhile.

Don't Pretend to Be Something That You Are Not

What most minority clients cannot tolerate is faking it. This will alienate clients from the central mission of therapeutic change. Authors who have studied treatment efficacy with African-American men insist that even the most well-intentioned intervention strategy must meet black cultural criteria before it can be deemed appropriate. A counselor who is truly culturally competent must understand but not attempt to unnaturally duplicate black dialect, slang, and mannerisms (Franklin, 2001; Lee, 1999). Unless you are from the 'hood, do not pretend that you know what life is like there. If you don't know much about gay bars, do not pretend that you do. If your client is in a wheelchair, don't talk about how much you understand because you broke your leg skiing when you were a kid. You will look and sound stupid, and your client will lose confidence that you get him and are truly open to getting him.

Recognize the "Trust Gap"

Some of these principles apply to all clients, male or female, but they are especially relevant in bridging the "trust gap" more likely to show up with minority clients. Be cognizant of the mind-set that many minority men have when they are calling you for an appointment or entering your office. They are more likely to be wary of this experience, more likely to worry that they will not be understood or not be given a fair shake, and are less likely to be familiar with how this system works.

Take special care to directly greet the client: Give a firm handshake and make eye contact. Use the art of small talk and chitchat to help put him at ease. Although you want there to be no doubt that there is serious work to be done here, you want to make sure that he feels comfortable and the experience feels "normal." Make sure to express your admiration that he has chosen (or in some cases, has reluctantly agreed to) come in for help.

To help put him at ease, be very clear about the expectations of being in counseling or therapy—especially the exact techniques you will and will *not* be using. Describing confidentiality agreements and informed consent is very important here: The client wants no surprises. Perhaps most important of all, a majority culture therapist (white, straight, male or female) treating a minority culture client must be real and transparent. The client is often highly sensitized to cues that the therapist is putting himself or herself above him, and this perception, if confirmed, will derail the therapy process.

Along these same lines, Lee (1999) has outlined five crucial stages in counseling African-American males (which, again, may be used as a template for the other diverse minority populations we are discussing).

Stage 1: Initial contact/appraisal stage: During the appraisal stage African-American men may feel untrusting of the counselor and the therapeutic process. Personal authenticity by the counselor is crucial. The African-American male client must perceive the counselor is being "for real."

Stage 2: Investigative stage: In this stage, the African-American male client often tries to minimize the status gap—social, economic, professional, or educational distinctions—between himself and the counselor. This is an attempt to generate the "twinship" experience. This stage may require the counselor to step out of the professional role to engage in conversations with the client on a common ground that is not obviously "therapeutic," like talking about sports, family, or current events.

Stage 3: Involvement stage: The key question for the client here is this: *Can I identify with you?* Counselor self-disclosure and the ability to get personal are often the crucial variables in navigating this stage successfully.

Stage 4: Commitment stage: At this stage, the African-American male client makes the crucial assessment: *Can I trust and work with this coun-*

selor or therapist? During the commitment stage the client may make the decision to prematurely terminate counseling. This decision is based on his evaluation of the counselor's openness and genuineness.

Stage 5: Engagement stage: Here, the client makes the decision that the counselor is real and trustworthy. According to Lee, this is the stage in which an authentic working alliance is launched.

Use Familiar Language and Values

If you are working with a Mexican-American male for whom issues of male gender role attachment (a.k.a. machismo) are prominent and seem to be getting in the way of moving forward in his life or in his relationships, then it makes sense to utilize what he already believes in. In other words, it would be foolish and likely to generate defensiveness if you (as a non-Latino) try to convince him of the destructive effects of machismo.

Instead, it is more user-friendly to embrace machismo, but to reframe it. Many Mexicans and other Latinos identify machismo as much with values of honor, integrity, looking out for one's family, and being a leader in one's community and family as they do with the caricature of manhood that machismo has come to represent (more on this later in this chapter). Men who especially identify with feeling powerful cannot be disavowed of this identification, nor should they be. They can, however, learn to reframe power: *A truly powerful man does not allow his temper or selfishness or alcohol to control him. The truly powerful man chooses his own course and values and follows them.*

Similarly, men from minority cultures, particularly African-American and Latino, often have a complicated split in their attitudes toward women. On the one hand, we hear a lot of sexist and derogatory attitudes toward women; on the other, we hear a highly revered and idealized place in their hearts and minds for the women dearest to them, like their mother, grandmother, sister, or aunt. Use this. Instead of automatically confronting derogatory attitudes or generalizations about women, it helps to ask Socratic questions: *When you say that "you can't trust women," are you putting your mother in that same category? How about your grandmother?* Or *If you heard that some guy was treating your sister the way you have been treating your girlfriend, what would you think? What would you do?* These guidelines are not meant to suggest that a clinician should back off from confronting behavior simply because the client is from a different subculture, but it just makes sense to find ways to use language and capitalize on values that are user-friendly to the target audience.

Another indicator of therapist cultural competence involves careful use of language based on cultural awareness. Here's an example of an intervention that backfired (Hardy & Laszloffy, 1994):

In a family therapy session with a black family, a female white family therapist was confronted with a disruption. The 14-year-old son, "Jamar," refused to sit down. The therapist was extremely annoyed by his act of defiance. Although Jamar was participating in the therapy, he adamantly refused her numerous requests to sit down. After he refused her "final request," she said to him: "Listen, *we* don't stand in therapy. Either you sit down or leave and come back when you're ready to sit!" Jamar immediately left the room, with his younger brother a few steps behind him. The family canceled the next session, citing "cultural differences," and requested a referral to an African-American therapist.

The therapist intended no harm and clearly believed that it was her job to maintain certain limits on how the therapy sessions were conducted. It was the "we" word that inadvertently did the damage. "We" implied that this black teenager was a member of the outsiders and was not behaving in the appropriate white way.

Respeto, Personalismo, and *Simpatía*

Researchers on the efficacy of counseling interventions for Latino men (Falicov, 2000; Mirande, 1997; Welland & Ribner, 2007; Welland-Akong, 1999) have identified three primary qualities of therapists that greatly enhance connection, and thus the likelihood that the clients will be open and receptive to the message.

The first quality is *respeto:* being more informal, recognizing the client's experiences, treating his life experience with appreciation and respect. The second quality is known as *personalismo:* the art of chitchat and small talk, making the client feel comfortable, being friendly—and most important, being real and sharing something of yourself. The third quality is *simpatía:* Although no English word quite captures the meaning of this, the closest is probably *empathy*. The experience of *simpatía* is one where the client feels like the counselor really gets him at the deepest level.

Any therapist, with any client, would do well to offer as much of these three qualities as possible. The research and clinical observations with minority men treated by those outside their own culture indicate how especially important these qualities are in getting through to men when others have not.

Clinical Styles with Men of Color

Many researchers and practitioners have identified distinctive patterns in Latino-American culture, and among Latino men in particular, that are valuable to keep in mind when working with men from this background.

Welland-Akong (1999) conducted in-depth interviews of Mexican men in domestic violence treatment groups with the central purpose of analyzing which qualities of this experience worked and which didn't. This research highlighted themes that are especially meaningful among Latino men.

These men responded best to therapists who came across as self-confident, friendly, patient, and open. The teaching styles (in a psychoeducational format) that the men identified as most effective were ones that offered clarity and structure—not authoritarian and not unfocused. The most effective therapists offered a personal touch in their interactions, including liberal self-disclosure. They paid close attention, could be playful and could relate with humor, and were generous with positive reinforcement. The therapists who brought out the most self-disclosure and engagement from the men were described as friendly and empathic—not confrontational or blaming.

I recently treated a Mexican-American man who had run into trouble at his workplace for speaking harshly to staff, making "joking" aggressive comments, and being too physical in "playing around" with employees. He was deeply wounded by the accusations against him. In our first session, I explained to him that I would be recommending psychological testing. He was further injured by this, as if I was accusing him of being a criminal or having a mental health disorder.

He complained bitterly to the owner of his company that I had offended him and almost refused to come back. He was instructed to tell me his concerns, which he did. He said, "How could you think that I would intentionally try and hurt someone on my staff?" I told him I understood how bad that would make him feel. I also went on to explain that that there was a big difference between intentionally trying to hurt someone and accidentally hurting someone.

He nodded and seemed to relax. But the clincher was that I told him that I was learning the same lesson with him. I hadn't intended to hurt him by recommending the psychological testing, but I now realized that I had accidentally done so. We are all capable of this, and he had an opportunity here to learn and adjust, just like I had just learned from him. Now he smiled and tears came into his eyes: "Thank you for understanding me." The turning point was in my self-disclosure and getting real about myself with him. This leveled the playing field and we entered the therapeutic "twinship" experience.

Recognizing the Values of Men of Color

Many researchers and writers have identified a series of ways in which normal good clinical practice can be enhanced by a specific awareness of common patterns and values among men of color (Arcaya, 1996; Casas, Turner, & Ruiz de Esparza, 2001; Mirande, 1997, 2003; Rodriguez, 1987; Welland & Ribner, 2007).

For example, Latinos are generally more formal in their dealings with the world at large than assimilated Americans are. Proper names and titles are used more often, and Latino men often present as more reserved, at least early on, because of the formal relationship with the professional. One Mexican-American man I treated recently had a marriage and family life in deep trouble because of his drinking and aggressive behavior. When I asked him to describe his behavior in detail, he talked about using vulgar language, then looked up at me tentatively and said, "Is it okay if I use a bad word in here?" Plenty of men from other cultures launch much more easily into graphic descriptions without such concern about being impolite.

It is also important to recognize that personal reputation and "face" are highly emphasized among many men of color. Reprimands and conflicts are often communicated through understatement, jokes, subtle sarcasm and teasing, and low-key face-saving comments. Direct confrontation is rarely tolerated in polite Latino society. But, if directly challenged or "dissed," many Latino men will feel especially compelled to save face with aggressive and definitive responses.

Also, in Latino culture there is a strong emphasis on family loyalty and supporting family and group solidarity, especially in the face of external attacks or threats. The sense of family in the Latino community is so strong that academics have coined a term for it: *familismo*.

Religion and spirituality often play a larger role in the daily lives of men of color, particularly Latino men, than they do among majority culture therapists. Here is what "Rogelio" had to say on this subject about his experiences in a men's group for treating domestic violence (Welland & Ribner, 2007):

> I would have liked us to talk about some religion. Because when you're going to make a change you need to hold onto something. You have to have a solid foundation, whatever it is. Whether it's the program or something else. It would be helpful to bring in some religion, to talk about the spiritual side. Our therapist never talked about religion. I felt like he wasn't very open to that, that he wasn't very respectful about that. I think it would be very useful to talk about what we believe as human beings. (p. 227)

Another pervasive attitude that often impacts Latino men more than majority culture or assimilated American men is identified by the Spanish word *fatalismo*, "fatalism," believing that some things are just meant to be. *Fatalismo* refers to a general belief that the course of fate cannot be changed and that life events are beyond one's control. In the health literature, fatalism usually is conceptualized as a set of pessimistic and negative beliefs and attitudes regarding health-seeking behaviors, screening practices, and illness (Abraıdo-Lanza, Viladrich, Florez, Cespedes, Aguirre, & Cruz, 2007). This is often frustrating or difficult for counselors who ascribe to more classic American beliefs about self-determination.

Finally, counselors and therapists should be aware that Latino men often use humor or teasing to communicate their discomfort and to generate some adherence to social norms and rules. This is often very evident in a group counseling setting, where group members sometimes tease a fellow group member as a subtle rebuke to let him know when he has stepped out of line. Up to a reasonable point, the therapist has to be able to appreciate and respect a Latino man's use of humor and some-times affectionately dish it right back—as long as it never crosses the "shame" line as an attack on character or manhood.

Understanding the "Invisibility" Experience

Black men often describe experiences of "personal invisibility" (Rowe, 2007). Their inner lives are often plagued by this sense of not being seen in the culture at large and by a sense of personal talents and abilities being ignored. Black men often complain that no matter what they do, they will never be recognized as a "top gun" or as having talent and competence. Furthermore, most African-American men can recount, some mildly and many very traumatically, their own personal legacy of racial slights and the experience of a steady stream of "micro-aggressions."

This legacy and history of slights and feeling discounted should lead therapists to a heightened awareness of the psychological needs of men of color. It is "especially important to be as knowledgeable of their resourcefulness as resilient persons as we are knowledgeable of their dilemmas as citizens" (Rowe, 2007). Men who are sensitized to invisi-bility and nonvalidation especially need legitimate validation and communication of personal respect. In addition to all the other psycho-logical needs that any man or woman of any color brings to the coun-seling or therapy relationship, black men need to feel recognized and acknowledged.

This narrative about men of color should guide counselors and therapists in several ways. First of all, trust, power, and control are central concerns that must be addressed. These issues often show up as perceived threats to masculinity. Any life situation (in the workplace, on the street, in a marriage, as a parent) that triggers a threat to his masculinity is likely, in the context of these issues, to provoke especially intense emotions in a black male.

Furthermore, any work in a therapeutic context that rests on recognizing, disclosing, and accepting vulnerabilities should be preceded by a focus on strengths first. The fundamental communication strategy of "pacing and leading" (see Chapter 3), in which the therapist systematically communicates respect and understanding for the man's experience prior to saying anything that would sound the least bit challenging or potentially shaming, is especially relevantly here.

One more reminder in working with men of color: Do not assume that any preconceived notion described in this book or that you have come to believe about them is true for any specific man. Listen to his own narrative about his personal problems. Some of these narratives may have major themes related to race, subculture, and the issues stated above, but not all black men, for example, identify primarily as being black. Whether their social world conforms to this or not, some black men think of themselves as being accountants or residents of Chicago or parents or college students first, and African-American much further down the list.

Diversity Language

Many therapists, not steeped in African-American culture, are unfamiliar, uncomfortable, or downright intimidated by some of the language and style of African-American relationships. For example, affirmations are an important part of African-American daily life and interactions. Sutton defined affirmations as "ways that one seeks and gives validation" (1996, p. 133). Among African-Americans, affirmations are expressed as verbal and visual acknowledgments—a practice originating in the "amens" of African-American churches.

Affirmations validate and support, and they enrich the communal experience. In a group therapy situation, African-American men may affirm each other by calling out "Yeah" or "You got that right." They may hand slap or fist bump or vigorously nod. The message from one group member to the other is encouragement. But a group leader unaware or uncomfortable with these expressions might see these as disruptive or acting out. Sometimes, of course, this might be true. But if these culturally normal behaviors are criticized and discouraged in groups, the risk is that African-American men will get the message that their job is to conform, and they will quietly and secretly disengage from the group—or not come back at all.

Many African-American men also operate at a higher volume and intensity of expression that other men in a group setting. They may speak loudly, engage in a little trash talk, or get their point across with satire and verbal jousting. A therapist inexperienced in working with such men may fear that the volume and intensity will create group chaos or even, possibly, violence. A therapist more culturally competent will probably be more familiar and comfortable with these styles—and is less likely to overreact by simply clamping down and banning these styles of expression from group.

Nobody is suggesting that African-American men (or any minority culture men) get a free pass for inappropriate behavior in a treatment environment simply because they are black. But some behaviors that may seem inappropriate to a therapist lacking in cultural sensitivity and competence may be understood and utilized more by other therapists. Since our primary goal is to engage in order to foster change and development, the challenge is to stretch as far as reasonably possible to find creative ways to successfully foster this engagement. Sutton gave majority culture therapists succinct and valuable advice: "Culturally competent group therapists know how to stay out of the way, know what to ignore, and know what to confront and when" (1996, p. 137).

The User-Friendly Diversity Environment
Another central strategy that communicates cultural competence—not

just sensitivity, but competence—involves creating a clinical environment that allows the minority client to feel welcomed and for his needs to be understood. Some of this is symbolic: The magazines in the waiting room should include *Black Enterprise* or *Ebony*, the Spanish-language version of *People* magazine, *Out*, *The Advocate*, and other magazines that will communicate to the nonmajority clients that this office recognizes diversity. It doesn't matter if they read the magazines or not; it only matters that a statement is being made. If Latinos are clients (even if they are fully bilingual), then some of the office signs and instructions should be in Spanish as well as English. This is especially true for information about referrals to other social service agencies, emergency hotlines, victims' services programs, and so on.

Forms, too, should be designed with diversity issues in mind. It doesn't matter if there was no harm intended; cultural competence insists that we be held to a higher standard than "meaning well." If possible, intake forms should be available in non-English versions (most typically, Spanish). The line on the intake sheet that usually asks for "marital status" should be revised to ask for "relationship status," since in most states, there is no option to have a marital status for gay males and lesbians.

Furthermore, any office should be designed with the principle in mind that first impressions run deep. Hotel consultants who study customer service look at the first person the guest encounters: the phone receptionist or the front desk staff. The same principle applies in mental health clinics and offices. The people who have the initial interaction with the client—phone receptionists, front office personnel, intake coordinators—should be carefully trained and monitored for their user-friendly manner in interacting with minority clients. For example, if a client is difficult to understand in English, front office personnel should not communicate irritation or impatience and should be very gracious about steering this client to staff or another agency that can converse in his primary language. Regardless of personal attitudes about gay men who may be flamboyant in dress or attitude, staff should be extremely careful not to transmit a message of disapproval. And if a black man entering an office gets the classic message of fear that black men often receive (like when white women clutch their purse tighter when a black man enters the elevator), things are off to a bad start.

One more issue, perhaps not completely politically correct but still practical and strategic, is often suggested for minority men (Casas et al., 2001). Minority men often are especially uncomfortable entering an environment dominated by women, so a user-friendly clinic or agency would have men represented at all staff levels—from receptionists to service providers. A traditional Latino male, for example, may find entering a counseling center especially intimidating if the majority of key players are women. It can contribute to the belief that counseling is the domain of women run by women to meet women's needs.

Homogenous Groups?

Homogenous men's groups that include only members of a certain subculture or ethnic group are advocated in some circles, but not without some controversy. These subculture-specific groups may not be possible at all sites and many programs may object to this format on theoretical grounds.

The central argument in favor of group homogeneity is that some-times men of various subcultures or minority groups (African-Americans, Mexican-Americans, Filipinos, and certainly gays) feel more comfortable and can be more open in these homogenous groups.

Williams described his rationale for homogenous African-American groups like this: "A racially homogeneous group may provide an excellent environment in which African-American males . . . can feel included, discuss central themes, be resocialized. . . . The homogeneity tends to increase client involvement due to an increased level of trust by group members, greater identification with themes discussed in the group, similar values, and the similarity between the group work environment and natural support networks, traditional communal ways of helping, and traditional socialization forces among African-Americans" (1994, p. 94).

Countertransference and Assumptions About Men of Color

Psychotherapy with the ethnoculturally different patient frequently provides more opportunities for empathic and dynamic stumbling blocks, in what might be termed "ethnocultural disorientation" (Comas-Díaz & Jacobsen, 1991). The first challenge for majority culture counselors or therapists when treating men of color or men who are gay is to recognize one's own biases, assumptions, and prejudices.

For example, any white therapist who claims that he or she does not have any prejudice about black men is almost certainly in denial. Our culture is bombarded with images of black men, sometimes positively (star athletes and entertainers, inspiring political figures) and much more often negatively (criminals, drug dealers, gangsta rappers). The denial of ethnic or cultural differences, identified previously as a beta error, makes the assumption that everybody is basically the same and should be treated the same. This contributes to a negation of countertransferential influences in the therapeutic process.

Second, it is both strategic and respectful (these two qualities very often coincide) for therapists to invite men of color to teach them about their culture: family life, church life, life on the streets, slang and humor, relationship mores, sexual attitudes, and so on. However, oversolicitous therapists sometimes fall prey to the "cultural anthropologist syndrome" (Comas-Díaz & Jacobsen, 1991), becoming *overly* curious about the client's ethnocultural background. This therapist may spend an inordinate amount of time exploring aspects of the patient's culture at the expense of the patient's needs. At first, the client may feel honored and gratified, but these inquiries can also derail the therapeutic process and can even be potentially dangerous. The following is an example in which the therapist dangerously identifies cultural explanations for disturbing behavior rather than actual pathology:

> A Brazilian male patient regaled his Anglo therapist with colorful tales of partying through the night during Carnival and during almost weekly music-making sessions with friends. Substantial time was spent in therapy discussing the cultural meanings of the patient's intense and somewhat erratic interactions with his friends and of various aspects of Brazilian culture and music. However, certain biological aspects of the

patient's experiences, namely hypomanias of a mild bipolar disorder induced by sleep deprivation, were missed. (Comas-Díaz & Jacobsen, 1991, p. 397).

Furthermore, a therapist must walk a fine line when dealing with (or even thinking about) issues of racism and personal responsibility for men of color. One side of the line is cultivating a profound respect for the historical tragedy of being black or brown in America and of dealing with racism; the other side of the line is making sure that nobody gets away with blaming their own problems and behaviors on society or external circumstances. The challenge is to distinguish—and to help the client distinguish—between a man's realistic complaints about racism and his attempts to blame racism for all of his problems in life (Sutton, 1996).

Finally, because of the intense concern most caring professionals have about not being racist, some therapists may fall into the trap of idealizing, in particular, the African-American male experience. Therapists may desperately try to prove to these clients how hip and understanding they are (as in "Hey, bro'" or the classic "Some of my best friends are black"). They may try to overprotect them while refusing to confront them on critical issues in what has been referred to as "oversolicitous caring" (Sutton, 1996). A white therapist who can "talk black" or offer a few fist bumps may be able to connect more effectively, but it is more likely that the client will feel patronized.

In Conclusion

When in doubt, it is almost impossible to go wrong with men from a minority culture not your own as long as you genuinely offer *respeto*, *personalismo*, and *simpatía*. Combine these with pacing and leading and a genuine openness and curiosity about the man's distinct life experience, and the apparent gaps between the therapist's world and the client's world can enrich the therapeutic experience rather than sabotage it.

Chapter 11
Authenticity, Intimacy, and Inspiring "Real Men"

In our clinical work with a male client, we are always looking for a way—any way—to help him deal with his depression, relationship problems, anxiety, aggression, or substance abuse and become more successful on his life path. We focus on his inner conflicts, we recommend medication, we suggest self-help books, we challenge his depressiogenic cognitions. We give homework assignments and bring in other family members.

Sometimes we find that the most powerful treatment path necessitates a journey toward personal authenticity and emotional intimacy. By embarking on this path, he finds that genuine authenticity and genuine intimacy are often absolutely incompatible with his depression and relationship dysfunctions. Get real, get close, and a lot of the other issues fade into the background.

Authenticity breeds the capacity for intimacy. Without the first, the second is almost impossible. And intimacy, in turn, generates authenticity. As Carl Jung once said: "One is always in the dark about one's own personality. One needs others to get to know oneself" (Jung & Hall, 1977, p. 165).

The Authentic Man

The word *authenticity* is rooted in the Greek *authentikos*, and from the French *authentes*, which refers to "one who does things himself." Authenticity represents the internal awareness that a man is his own person, psychologically separated and individuated from his parents, yet still capable of a mature interdependent relationship in the present. The authentic man can see himself clearly, can accept life's limitations without self-pity, and can survive narcissistic injuries.

Accepting Realistic Limitations

The authentic man has successfully navigated a way to find gratification in the opportunities genuinely available to him, rather than spending psychic and emotional energy preoccupied with what could have been or once was. He looks at himself in the mirror and says to himself: "This is who I am." He looks around at his wife and kids and career and church and outdoor barbecues and says to himself: "These are the gratifications available to me."

We are talking here about the man who *used to be* a kid, a party animal, a guy with six-pack abs whom women noticed. At one time, he and his wife couldn't keep their hands off of each other and he was excited about his newborn daughter. He was learning a craft or developing a career and the sky was the limit. Now he is in a long-term marriage (or on his second or third), the supporter of aging parents, an accomplished worker in his field, and playing golf or just going for walks instead of lacrosse or pickup basketball games.

In the movie *Family Man* (Bernstein, Bliss, Davis, & Ratner, 2000), Jack Campbell (Nicolas Cage) is a successful, extremely self-centered, and fundamentally unhappy man who (through the magic of Hollywood) is transported into another life and family that he almost chose at one time in his life but turned down. This family includes a terrific, loving wife, fun and demanding kids, an ordinary job, and no trips to Paris or nameless hot flings in four-star hotel rooms. He goes out shopping with his wife and decides he wants an expensive suit, which his wife appropriately vetoes for budgetary reasons. His wife reminds him that the mall serves the funnel cakes he really likes. He looks around, realizes he can't have the suit, and says, *We'll get a funnel cake. It'll be the highlight of my week.* He is miserable at having to settle for an ordinary life, but he makes a go of it, finding after all that he is quite capable of being fulfilled (more than he ever imagined possible) by more ordinary pleasures.

What is genuinely available to him turns out to be genuinely gratifying, or at least gratifying enough. Men are famous for overlooking the potential gratifications right in front of their faces. Plenty of men who have divorced, who consistently cheat on their wives, or who grumpily settle for a generally miserable relationship have convinced themselves that they really deserve to have something better than what they do have. They withdraw, get critical, and sometimes behave in ways that are directly threatening to the marriage: infidelity, substance abuse, emotional withdrawal, emotional or even physical abuse. And then when their wife or partner gets "bitchy" on them or has even less interest in sex, they blame her for their own increasing unhappiness and low relationship satisfaction.

In this scenario, while plenty of women are certainly not blameless, the tragic feature is that one of the primary pathways out of this dysfunctional system—a man taking responsibility for his emotional distress and taking steps to deal with it without projection of blame—is missing from the equation.

Especially at midlife, the losses of the once youthful body (and of the spouse's body, which can feel like a broken mirror itself), the resignation to a lifetime sentence of "comfortable" love rather than the exhilaration of new love, and the grieving of once unlimited life possibilities often provoke major narcissistic challenges.

Colarusso and Nemiroff describd the authenticity challenge as requiring this: "an acceptance of the self as special but not unique, a part of the mosaic of humanity . . . gradual acceptance of the self as imperfect . . . within the limits imposed by an imperfect, partially gratifying, and sometimes hostile world. Initially a source of narcissistic injury, the recognition of these external and internal limitations gradually becomes a source of pleasure and strength as the self accepts and develops the capacity to act independently within the restrictions imposed by the human condition" (1981, p. 86).

The authentic man accepts these losses and limitations and actively embraces what he has right in front of him and genuinely available. Not every man has all of these things available to him, but most have at least some: an "imperfect but good enough" relationship that holds the promise of the deep love that only emerges over time and history together, children and family connections, competence and mastery in career, friends who have passed the test of time, a deeper sense of spirituality, and the increasing ability to accept with serenity the things that cannot be changed, courage to change the things that should be changed, and the wisdom to distinguish the one from the other.

Surviving the Narcissistic Injury of Authenticity

Authenticity, therefore, means that a man is not bullshitting himself. It is defined by what Colarusso and Nemiroff called "accepting what is real in both the external and inner world, regardless of the narcissistic injury involved" (1981, p. 86).

A hallmark of the mature, authentic self is the ability to appraise the personal past and the personal present with a minimum of denial and distortion. Thus, the tolerance for the narcissistic injury means that a man is able to see himself clearly and take responsibility for his own feelings and behaviors, even if this makes him feel bad, even if it does not conform to his self-image, and even if it makes him look bad to his partner or others.

My client Richard, in his 50s and embroiled in a marriage in which his wife had become increasingly dissatisfied because of his emotional withdrawal and periodic verbal aggression, had agreed to try antidepressant medication a year ago. This helped. Several times, when his behavior seemed to regress and his wife became anxious about a return to the past, she would gingerly ask if he was still taking his meds.

This simple question (as if there is such a thing as a simple question in the complexity of marital politics) triggered a broken mirror experience for Richard. It was as if she were accusing him of being a failure—again— as a husband and family man. It was also as if she declared her role as a controlling mother who had to remind him to brush his teeth because otherwise he would be too incompetent to remember on his own.

The most significant narcissistic injury from her questions was simply the mirroring of himself as a weak and flawed man who was dependent on pills to make him reasonably close to normal. This was profoundly unmasculine. And, in classic broken mirror fashion, he would blow up at her when she would ask this question, in response to the humiliation he experienced.

Missing from Richard's capacity to maturely integrate his wife's anxiety-based question was the ability to see himself clearly *regardless of the narcissistic injury involved.* The reality was that he did need medication to help him stay more emotionally balanced. While we can all relate to the issues that this reality raised for him, still the most mature conclusion is: *So what?* He was faced with the choice of maintaining a false self-image of someone who could handle all this on his own (which history did not support), or he could accept the actual reality that he was resourceful and committed enough to rely on help that was genuinely available to him. We are still working on the latter.

Another client of mine, Daniel, intermittently depressed and moody for years, precipitated a marital crisis when (in a fit of unhappiness and frustration) he picked up an ashtray and threw it at his wife. She needed 14 stitches. Months later, as they were trying to reconstruct this broken marriage, she accused him of rolling his eyes when she asked him to do something around the house for her.

Daniel was outraged: *I was feeling so warm toward her and I was complimenting her and everything. How could she think that I rolled my eyes and that I would do anything that was mean or condescending?*

This is the voice of the narcissistic injury: *How could I? How dare she?* And it interfered with his capacity for authenticity. The authentic man, in this marital encounter, would tell himself this: *Get a clue, man! We know you are capable of aggression—and you are certainly capable of passive-aggressive behavior toward the person you love the most.*

Or the simple version: *Maybe she's right.*

The Authenticity Reward

Many years ago, when my fiancée and I traumatically called off our wedding 3 weeks before the planned event, I plunged into depression. I started my own psychotherapy to make sense of what had happened and to help keep me glued together. Somewhere in the midst of one of my long whiny litanies about how cruel she had been to me, my therapist stopped me short and said to me: *You're the one who was really aggressive to her. You were sneaky about it, but you did plenty of it yourself.* This was not what I was paying the big bucks to hear. I feebly protested, then slunk into feeling ashamed and more depressed, this time for being a fool.

And then, in a matter of hours, I felt a lot better. I knew he was right. Suddenly, with the cloud cover removed, I was able to see myself as a much more flawed person than I had allowed myself to see before. I felt freer, and I felt the depressive and stuck moods just peel away in layers. I still had a lot of work to do, but I wasn't feeling depressed. I took a step forward in the life task of the "gradual acceptance of the self as imperfect" (Colarusso & Nemiroff, 1981, p. 86).

A client of mine in his late 40s came in one day complaining again about the ways his marriage had deteriorated. His wife, whom he was still crazy about, just didn't offer him as much. She was less interested in sex. She didn't glow quite as much when she saw him as she used to. She didn't focus as much on the details in his life because she had more of her own life and because their kids filled her consciousness more. I had met this woman, and she was great. There were no major problems in their relationship, just his nagging feeling of disappointment, rejection, and his increasing irritability.

I decided it was time to lower the boom. I paused dramatically, looked him square in the eye, and said, *You've just got to see this clearly: Your wife is not going to take care of all of these emotional needs now.*

I expected him to be crushed or defensive or angry. He was none of the above. His face brightened and he said to me, *You mean there will come a time when she will?*

I realized that he had zeroed in on my use of the word *now* and had clung to it in a desperate act of denial. I clarified: *Your wife is not going to take care of all of these emotional needs now, or ever. Never.*

He left the session crushed and pouting. He called me that night and left a message telling me how thoroughly depressed my statement had made him. My words, he said, had doomed him to a permanent state of feeling like there was something missing. But when I saw him the next week, he was changed. He told me that he had woken up the next morning feeling so much lighter. He noticed a new wave of affection for his wife. He realized that he felt freer now, free from the expectation that she was supposed to take care of these feelings for him, and free from his disappointment that she didn't. He felt released from these expectations, and as Buddhists know, pain stems from the gap between expectations and reality. When the expectations genuinely change, the opportunity for freedom from pain appears. He was so relieved at not having to be frustrated by his wife again and again, and it allowed him to take in what she genuinely had to offer him. And it was pretty damn good.

Authenticity as the Ultimate Antidepressant

You can always tell when a man is emerging, or beginning to emerge, from a nasty depressive episode. The anhedonia lifts. Simple pleasures become appealing again. Food tastes better. His kids are more interesting. Women look prettier. A project at work feels a little more satisfying as he progresses on it.

Some men I have talked to don't exactly realize this until it is pointed out to them. Developing the appropriate narrative for this shift—or at least consciously noticing it—stimulates the elixir of optimism and hope. Those of us who are witness to a man's depression often have to supply the labels for the experiences that are now taking place.

My client Mickey had spent years living his life under a dark cloud. He was alternately moody, charming, restless, successful, and self-destructive. He was chronically dissatisfied with his marriage and the trappings of domestic life with three kids. He drank. He snorted coke. He secretly (barely secretly, according to his wife, Kathy) partied and had affairs.

Until he was finally, of course, busted. When Kathy found everything out and demanded that he move out, Mickey hit rock bottom. He went to AA. He entered individual and couples therapy. And he began to see how his underlying depression had led to his seeking love in all the wrong places.

I told Kathy everything. I don't have to worry about who I lied to about what. I know I have ruined my marriage vows—I've crossed the line, just like my father did again and again. But now I feel like I'm starting over.

Don't you get it? I had it all! I rocked! I partied hard, put stuff up my nose, screwed around, made a lot of money, and I had a nice family at home. Everything that I wanted I got——and it turned out to destroy me and the people I love the most.

A couple of my buddies got all hyped up about taking a motorcycle trip to Mexico for a long weekend. Lots of drinking and snorting, Mexican whores, biking off-road on the Mexican dunes. I laughed and said I hoped they had a good time. Nothing seemed cool about it—well, maybe, the off-road stuff, but that was it!

But now I feel better with the life I am really turning to. I feel like starting everything over. I didn't know it could feel this good. I don't know how Kathy had it in her to take me back, but I will never forget this.

Mickey told me how liberated he felt to say what needed to be said and reveal himself in ways that elicited his transparent self. He paraphrased Bob Dylan: *I'm invisible now—I've got no secrets to conceal!*

The key line in Mickey's report is *I didn't know it could feel this good.* The anhedonia had lifted. He now found it quite possible to enjoy a "normal" life, with a wife who loved him, kids who loved and needed him, friends who were good for him, work that stimulated and rewarded him. These simpler and more accessible pleasures became "good enough"—and the depression-driven desperate drive for more stimulating and risk-taking experiences faded into the background.

As his wife slowly began trusting him again and warmed to his reborn self, he reported this epiphany: *Being real is sexy!*

The Intimate Man

With authenticity comes the capacity for true intimacy. True intimacy is another invaluable antidepressant.

Men are often crushed under the weight of the losses involved in committing to a loving relationship with a partner, combined with the losses associated with midlife and aging. But the saving grace lies in the enormous rewards of intimacy: "The development of the real-spouse representation greatly facilitates this process by enhancing real intimacy, thus diminishing the narcissistic sting of aging" (Colarusso & Nemiroff, 1981, p. 93).

The losses do generate a narcissistic sting, which often triggers a mad rush to deny, minimize, withdraw, overcompensate, desperately seek reassurance and gratification, and blame others. A man does not have to go that route because the enormous rewards (not only of authenticity but also of the intimacy that only emerges from the "real-spouse representation") can transcend the losses. This hinges on the "appreciation and valuing of long-standing relationships, in contrast to the more youthful gratifications of the body and non-relationship sex" (Colarusso & Nemiroff, 1981, p. 93). Some men, through therapy, spirituality, or just hard knocks, figure this out.

The other blessing of genuine commitment and intimacy to a partner is the enormous, unparalleled opportunity that an intimate relationship provides for personal growth and discovery. Remember Jung's quote: "One is always in the dark about one's own personality. One needs others to get to know oneself" (Jung & Hull, 1977, p. 165).

Emotional Intimacy: Authenticity with His Partner

The authentic man now has the opportunity to reveal his authenticity to a trusted other: a true formula for emotional intimacy.

Author Frank Pittman lamented the allure of infidelity, but he understood the powerful magnetism generated when people choose to reveal themselves to one another: "You become increasingly distant from whomever you lie to, and you become increasingly close to whomever you tell the truth to" (Parker-Pope, 2008).

Intimacy depends on a man's capacity to be authentic with himself—and with his partner. Jungian analyst John Sanford described the personal growth that can be generated when a man finds a genuine way of expressing himself in his relationship with his female partner: "One way for him to get out of his Mother complex is to express himself in relationship. If he fails to do so he remains emotionally a little boy who is afraid of women, who resents them if they don't keep him happy, and who is out of touch with his own masculine strength. . . . (If) a man is to become capable of relationship with a woman he must overcome his fear of her anger and his anxiety about being rejected" (1979, pp. 38–39).

For a man to successfully express his authentic feelings in an intimate relationship, however, he must do it in a "related" fashion (Sanford, 1979). Related anger means that the issues that are brought up are concerned with what is going on between two people. It is an honest expression of genuine feeling. Plenty of men, plagued with a history of normative male alexithymia and deficits in emotional intelligence, think they are expressing themselves when they yell, blame, criticize, or withdraw into a sulky mood. These expressions of feelings are not "related."

Related anger is simple, and it is what is taught in every communication class, couples workshop, and anger management course. He uses "I-statements," as in "It really bothers me when you insist on talking to me at work when I'm really busy. I really need you to respect how hard it is for me to get free sometimes!" No accusations, no character assassinations, no sarcasm, no bull. He is aware of her feelings and her experience when he expresses himself. If he expresses anger in a *related* way, he will tell her just what it is that is upsetting him.

My client Barry had created a relationship mess with his fiancée, Lydia. He had reluctantly agreed to become engaged, even though he had doubts about committing and specific doubts about her. He somehow thought, as many of us do, that the ambivalence would all clear up if they just moved on to the next step of the relationship—just like many couples who decide to have another baby as a "bonding" experience when they are drifting apart. He never quite expressed how reluctant he was to believe that relationships could sort out because he had watched both of his parents fail at multiple relationships and get used by their partners. He never quite expressed how hurt and mistrustful he felt when she had been emotionally attached to another man early in their relationship. And he never quite expressed how irritated he was by what he perceived as her self-centeredness, and how anxious he felt that this would pervade their future family life.

Instead, he acted out his negative feelings. He dragged his feet on the engagement, forcing her to keep pressing him on following through.

He withdrew from her sexually for months. He got picky and critical with her. And eventually he ended up cheating on her and not really knowing how he got there and why.

He felt horribly guilty and ashamed of his behavior and the pain he had caused. Then, finally, as a result of this crisis and the influence of psychotherapy, he summoned up the courage to tell her directly some of the things that had always bothered him. It didn't matter if these worries were fair and rational, as long as he was able to express them in a "related" fashion, without excessive attacks or projection of blame.

Barry realized where he had gone wrong: *I think it might have been really different if I had been able to tell her more of these things when they were happening. But I felt like I didn't even really know what I was thinking and feeling, and it was so much easier to just blame her and push her away.*

Although this new expression from Barry was hard for Lydia to hear (especially in her hurt and rage about his behavior toward her), finally he was being authentic and related. "If a woman cares about a man, she will not reject him if he expresses his anger at her in this way; to the contrary, she will welcome it, for it shows that this relationship is meaningful to him" (Sanford, 1979, p. 39). This relationship was slowly repaired because he finally got real with her, which offered her enough related connection and hope to recover and continue.

Emotional Intimacy: Seeing His Partner Clearly
In the sprit of authenticity, true mature emotional intimacy rests on a genuine appraisal of one's partner. This requires that a man relax his unrealistic standards for his partner. He develops the ability to see her, like himself, not as an idealized partner but as a real person: *She ain't perfect—and neither am I.*

From a self psychology perspective, the transition from a more narcissistic perspective involves a man perceiving his partner as less of a selfobject and more of a "genuine other." In other words, although these two perspectives are never totally separated from one another, her needs, experiences, and behaviors must be viewed much more through the lens of who she really is rather than how she makes *him* feel.

Among other qualities, this capacity for genuine appraisal of the other requires empathy. Empathy is considered to be one of the highest forms of affective development. It is described by different authors as "vicarious introspection" (Basch, 1980) or "mentalization" (Fonagy et al., 2002)—all suggesting that the truest form of empathy requires the capacity and the will to form a mental construct of the experience of the other.

Empathy is often blocked because men become preoccupied with the personal experience that is stimulated by the relationship interaction. If she complains that he is yelling at the kids too much, the broken mirror experience often becomes paramount, blinding him to the needs of his wife and kids. The empathy channels are hijacked. In other situations, like when a woman is simply describing her own pain or anxiety, a man's empathy channels are often blocked because of his fears about vicarious emotional overload: He cannot bear to experience that level of distress. This activates defense mechanisms of disavowing, denying, pushing away, demeaning, or blaming—all of which sabotage empathy.

The genuine empathy experience also requires what Basch (1980) refered to as the "independent center of initiative" (see Chapter 2). The more that a man can de-center and see how his partner's behavior stems from her own needs and personality structure, the more he can be attuned to her without the contamination of how it makes him feel. If a woman doesn't want to have sex with a man, there are a lot of other explanations—based on recognizing her independent center of initiative—besides the narrative that she is trying to humiliate or control him or that she doesn't care about him. Her behaviors may *affect* him, but they are not *about* him. The magical qualities—and magical rewards—of intimacy depend on the ability "to see life through your partner's eyes as well as through your own" (Pittman, 2003, p. xxx).

Intimacy: Behavioral Honesty and Emotional Honesty

An authentic intimate partner relationship almost always requires full behavioral honesty. Maybe there's room for a little deception here and there about eating a cookie when you promised to stay off sweets (or telling your wife that this dress does *not* make her look fat), but not much more. For people to become intimate and to enrich intimacy, they must feel safe. And to feel safe, they must—among other things—trust their partner.

When I ask people if they think they are being truly honest in their relationship, most people claim that they are. Unless they are deliberately withholding important information like infidelity or keeping money in secret accounts, most people of reasonable integrity can genuinely claim that they are honest.

But there are two kinds of honesty in a relationship. Only the first involves facts.

The other kind of honesty is more difficult to quantify. I call this *emotional honesty*. This kind of honesty reflects the capacity, the willingness, and the courage for a man to report his genuine inner world to his partner. It means that, if he is acting cold and she asks him if he's mad, he confirms her reality by acknowledging that "Yeah, I am kind of upset with you for what you said at that party" instead of saying, "No, what are you talking about, I'm just feeling a little tired—is there something wrong with that?"

I do not advocate people in relationships pretending they are in a 24/7 encounter group where they report their feelings all the time. It's boring to live like that, and no successful couple that I know of actually operates in that fashion. But the practice of sharing feelings of competition, hurt, self-doubt, anxiety, jealousy, and excitement are the lifeblood of relationships. If a man does not know his own feelings (denial and repression), or if he knows them but lacks the labeling and language capacity to express them (normative male alexithymia), or if he knows how to express them but is afraid to, he is shortchanging himself and the relationship.

My client Julian spent years feeling run over by his wife. She spent money more extravagantly than he wanted. She insisted on only buying certain foods for the home, even though he wanted some of the "forbidden" ones. He privately grumbled, sometimes bickered, but never really brought up his unhappiness about these patterns in direct and assertive ways. He was not "related" to his wife.

Then one day he found himself in the middle of an affair. And when his wife demanded to know why he was doing this, all he could come up with was that the affair "just helped me feel better." He was not lying about the facts. He was simply not being fully truthful about the inner experiences that generated his behaviors.

With Barry and Lydia (in the example above, Barry dragged his feet about getting married and eventually cheated on her), the damage to the intimacy in the relationship was not only shattered because he had lied about his behavior. Of equal importance is that he had been lying about his feelings for months going on years. He never reported his ambivalence about getting engaged, his doubts about commitment, his worries about her personality. Instead, he just acted them out by dragging his feet, becoming vaguely critical, withdrawing from her sexually, and ultimately cheating on her. When she kept pressing him on what was wrong (prior to the explosion with getting caught cheating on her), he just shrugged it off and made her feel like she was a little crazy or was overreacting.

This is emotional dishonesty. It might be conscious and it might be unconscious, but either way it is emotional dishonesty and corrosive to an intimate relationship.

For a therapist or a partner to confront a man about not being "honest" requires a very clear message about what this means. In the interest of getting through to him, it is important to be careful about making an accusation that will feel like an insult to him.

A great example of this process is evident in the movie *Good Will Hunting*, which has been discussed earlier. Will's girlfriend, Skylar, confronts him about not being honest with her. He explodes with narcissistic injury and narcissistic rage. She's not just talking about specific information he has distorted about his past; even more important, she feels the obstruction of not knowing his truer feelings and fears.

A man may hear the words "I don't believe you" and think that he is being accused of behavioral lying, which outrages any man who considers himself to be an honorable person. When women say "I don't believe you" to their partner, they often mean that he is not being straight about what he is feeling or what his motivations are for the current behavior—why he is withdrawing, moody, getting critical, and so on. Given the broken mirror vulnerability of many men, it is most effective to make this distinction so that there is at least a chance he will hear what the problem is and the effect this is having on his loved one.

I consistently tell men that knowing their own feelings is a sign of authenticity and expressing them opens the door for intimacy. Something's wrong when these are lacking. And I remind them not to tell themselves that they are being honest with their partner just because they are not lying about their actions. Both he and she require more. But here's the good news: It's not that hard for men to get better at this.

Intimacy: Celebrating the Half-Full Glass

The look of love that men rely upon from women is one of the most potent forces in male psychology. Men crave the look. The look serves as a powerful mirror that reflects back to men an image of themselves as being important, valuable, honorable, wanted, smart, or sexy. Rob, the narrator in Nick Hornby's novel *High Fidelity* (1995), complains about his girlfriend:

> I thought there was going to be this sexy woman with a sexy voice and lots of sexy eye makeup whose devotion to me shone from every pore. And there is such a thing as the look of love—Dusty didn't lead us up the garden path entirely—it's just that the look of love isn't what I expected it to be. It's not huge eyes almost bursting with longing situated somewhere in the middle of a double bed with the covers turned down invitingly; it's just as likely to be the look of benevolent indulgence that a mother gives a toddler, or a look of amused exasperation, even a look of pained concern. But the Dusty Springfield look of love? Forget it. As mythical as the exotic underwear (p. 274).

Rob is in the process of becoming authentic, taking more responsibility for his own moods, and thus opening the door for genuine adult nonidealized intimacy. He is discovering that the little looks, in the everyday context of ordinary interpersonal transactions, are plenty. What guy would ever dismiss the thrill of "huge eyes almost bursting with longing?" Very few. But those huge-eyes moments are few and far between in even the most successful relationships (after the honeymoon stage), and men struggle to adjust to appreciating the more ordinary looks of "benevolent indulgence," "amused exasperation," or "pained concern."

The 80/20 rule (see Chapter 5) is especially relevant here. Anybody in a relationship who is getting 80% of what they most need in their intimate partner relationship is blessed, and they should spend as much time as possible expressing gratitude and appreciating their partner. And then they need to take responsibility for dealing with the other 20% without blaming the partner or seeking fulfillment in ways that are destructive or threatening to the relationship.

Our male clients' realistic goal is to become more resilient and flexible about the quantities and qualities they need in order to feel reasonably fulfilled: in other words, to learn to focus on the half-full glass (or 80% full glass) of what they genuinely have rather than on the half-empty glass (or 20% empty glass) of what she was supposed to offer all the time but doesn't, and to be reasonably centered within—and reasonably respectful without—when these needs are not quite fulfilled.

Helping Men Develop Authenticity and Intimacy

Nobody knows exactly how to generate authenticity and intimacy. It's not like coaching a client on communication skills or anger management. But, in addition to hammering away at the themes already discussed, there are a few concepts that have proved to be especially valuable in helping men bring out these qualities in themselves.

Distress Tolerance

Marsha Linehan defined distress tolerance as "learning how to bear pain skillfully" (1993, p. 96). Borrowing from the wisdom of Zen Buddhism, she preaches the development of mindfulness skills, including the nonjudgmental observation of one's present emotional state, however distressing it may be: *I can't do anything for now to change how I feel or to change the situation, so it is better to accept this for now rather than do something to make things worse.*

This capacity is an essential ingredient in emotional intelligence, and a deficiency in this skill is a leading contributor to emotional withdrawal, maladaptive coping strategies (e.g., drugs and alcohol, infidelity), projection of blame, and anger and aggression.

I preach to men the tremendous value in developing their capacity for distress tolerance, and I flag it and celebrate whenever they do it without even realizing it.

My client James described it this way: *I have noticed a real change in myself. Ever since this affair, and everything I have learned about myself, I can listen to my wife better. Sometimes something will set her off. She'll get some worry or some question or suspicion in her head and she's off to the races. And I used to be so defensive. Why? Because I felt terrible about myself, and seeing her so unhappy would just remind me of this.*

But now I can handle the distress better. When she gets into that state, I remind myself that I have really messed with her head and with our marriage. And I have confidence that she, and we, will get through it. So feeling bad is not so terrible, and this allows me to really talk to her and not shut her out.

This is making such a difference!

When James says that *feeling bad is not so terrible*, he is describing his newfound capacity for distress tolerance. Feeling upset or hurt or anxious or alone is not that big a deal. He doesn't have to run. He doesn't have to pretend it's not happening. He doesn't have to defend against it. He doesn't have to counterattack. He is strong enough to tolerate feeling bad—and confident enough to know that it will pass. It is much more likely to pass if he can bear this pain skillfully.

I remember a breakthrough transition in my own marriage when a distress tolerance light finally turned on. My wife and I, in the first few years of our relationship, had some major blowouts: yelling and screaming and not speaking to each other for quite awhile afterward. And I would inevitably panic. This conflict and this rupture felt unbearable, leading me to pressure her to apologize or for me to prematurely and desperately apologize.

Then, during one of those blowouts, I noticed something new: I wasn't panicked any more! I hated the discord and the relationship rupture, but I didn't feel the desperate need to do something right that second to make this horrible feeling go away. I had felt this way enough times—and she and I had always recovered—that I could tolerate it. I could feel awful for a while without doing anything about it. I could actually learn from it, and it was not a level of distress that needed to be avoided at all costs.

A therapist with a male client who is struggling with distress tolerance can remind him, again, and again, of the times when he has been successful at tolerating distress or coping with broken mirrors. There is no better way to cultivate a complex skill like distress tolerance than to capitalize on the way that the client already knows how do it, and how it has paid off in the past.

Necessary Losses

Judith Viorst's book *Necessary Losses* (Viorst, 1986) advanced the concept that all change and growth require losses of some sort. And even though these losses are never attractive or appealing, they are as inevitable as rain. They serve as opportunities for growth. People can either fight them (usually futilely) or learn from them.

His kids not turning out the way he envisioned? Very painful and challenging, but potentially a lesson in overattachment and excessive ego identification. He finds that he sinks into moods and blames others? Very toxic to his most intimate relationships, but offers the opportunity to understand himself better and take more responsibility for his life. He continues to feel self-doubting about his work or how others view him? Very depressing, but offers him the chance to discover that the most important judge of himself is himself.

A male client may not be very receptive to hearing this perspective, because the very nature of depressive moods and narcissistic injuries leads to resistance and defensiveness. But, when the timing and mood are right, with impeccable timing and finesse, it can be very helpful to suggest to him that he can use these difficult times to be a deeper, more knowledgeable, and more compassionate person.

With a man's partner, I often suggest some tactful, respectful ways for her to also frame the distress from this perspective (Wexler, 2006a):

Honey, I know you are really worried about all the pressure you are getting from work, and you are really doubting yourself. Please don't take this the wrong way—but maybe this isn't such a bad thing. You're learning a lot about yourself and you're learning more about how to handle it when things don't go well.

Or

I know that it is really hard for you to see how Luke is having all these problems at school, and you blame yourself a lot. But maybe there's some lesson here for both of us about not getting so attached to how our kids are supposed to be.

Inspiring Real Men

In working with men, the crowning glory is to be an agent in helping them reach their full potential and become true leaders and positive role models.

One image that resonates very well with men is the concept of "relational heroism" (Real, 1998). Terrence Real described it this way: "*Relational heroism* occurs when every muscle and nerve in one's body pulls one toward reenacting one's usual dysfunctional pattern, but through sheer force or discipline or grace, one lifts oneself off the well-worn track toward behaviors that are more vulnerable, more cherishing, more mature. Just as the boyhood trauma that sets up depression occurs not in one dramatic incident, but in transactions repeated thousands of times, so, too, recovery is comprised of countless small victories" (p. 277).

In every important relationship, men are faced with a multitude of opportunities to do it the old way (withdraw, get lazy, feel and act defensive, etc.) or do it a new way (stay connected, place relationship needs as top priority, work on taking disappointments less personally, etc.). The new way is the way of the relational hero, and we are calling upon men to be heroic (a core masculine value) in these contexts.

Another way of bringing out the best qualities in men is by appealing to their sense of legacy: *How do you want to be remembered?* Many men who overreact to disappointments in their kids are often stopped in their tracks by questions like this one: *Do you want to be remembered as the dad who made sure his daughter's room was clean?* And when men are, for reasons of habit or laziness or entitlement or stress or lack of awareness, uninvolved in their family's life, it helps to ask them if they want their kids to grow up expecting that men are kind of limited in how much they participate in family activities and the personal concerns of family members.

One more message that appeals to many men to inspire them in bringing out their most noble and manly qualities is the *sanctification* of relationships (Mahoney, Pargament, Murray-Swank, & Murray-Swank, 2003; Pargament & Mahoney, 2005). This has nothing to do (or nothing necessarily to do) with religious affiliation or religious ceremony. The sanctification experience simply applies when people perceive an object, an experience, or a relationship as having spiritual character and significance by attributing qualities to it that are typically associated with divine entities: attributes of transcendence, ultimate value, and purpose and timelessness.

People can perceive virtually any aspect of their lives as having divine character and significance. In our daily lives, sacred matters are often interwoven into the fabric of life experience—and these experiences take on a special character. The ordinary becomes extraordinary.

When men sanctify their relationships in this way, when they see the connection with partner and children as a sacred mission that is more important than anything else and will have repercussions for generations to come, good things happen (Mahoney et al., 2003). They are more protective of the relationship. They have increased global marital satisfaction. They engage in more collaborative problem-solving, have less marital conflict, and withdraw less frequently. They have lower levels of verbal aggression to their children and more consistent parenting behavior because they realize that there is so much at stake.

Tips for Good Men

The following guidelines are designed to remind men (and those of us who work with men) of what is most important:

1. Think of the changes that you are being called upon to make as actions of "real men" and "relational heroes." Think about this in men's language like "taking charge," "becoming powerful," and being "captain of your own ship."

2. Take personal responsibility. You are not a victim of a bad childhood, life stress, or a nagging girlfriend. Real men don't make excuses.

3. Learn to tolerate distress. Feeling bad is not necessarily a cause for escape, avoidance, or immediate corrective action. Real men can handle negative affect by talking and thinking—and only then taking possible smart actions.

4. Be very careful how you describe the events in your relationships. Take responsibility for your moods. Just because you feel injured or self-doubting does not necessarily mean that your partner has *tried* to make you feel that way.

5. Even when you have done something destructive in a relationship, you are still a "good man behaving badly" or a "good man acting cluelessly." Build the good man part while you analyze and correct the behaving badly part.

6. Pay attention to your possibly excessive attachment to the "look of love."

7. Keep a running list of times when you are tempted to act badly in a relationship, but instead find a different way. These can serve as nuggets of hope and models to guide you in the future.

8. Do whatever you can to let the other key people in your relationships (partners and children) know that you believe in them and appreciate what they are going through, even if you do not always like their actions.

9. Be a responsible leader and bystander. Don't laugh and implicitly approve of other men who mistreat women or children.

10. Think of your kids all the time. Act in ways that you want them to model throughout their lives.

11. Take a chance. When you sense that the woman in your life needs emotional support or needs to hear more about you, talk to her. Admit if you feel helpless or don't know what to say or do.

12. Take care of your side of the street, even when you believe that she or he or they are not taking care of hers or his or theirs.

13. Take a chance. Try talking to other men about some of your feelings—not just your incessant complaints, but your actual fears, self-doubts, worries, and so on. Tell them about things you have done or said in your relationships that you regret.

14. I know this is not easy, but try learning how to validate yourself, instead of needing a woman to validate you. Or try to find other ways to take in this validation that neither lead you to withdraw emotionally from her nor threaten your primary relationship. In other words, remember that it is healthy to need, unhealthy to need excessively, and essential to do nothing that is fundamentally disrespectful to someone you love and need.

References

Abraido-Lanza, A. F., Viladrich, A., Florez, K. R., Cespedes, A., Aguirre, A. N., & Cruz, A. A. D. L. (2007, Winter). Commentary: Fatalismo reconsidered: A cautionary note for health-related research and practice with Latino populations. *Ethnicity and Disease*, 153–158.

Addis, M. E., & Mahalik, J. R. (2003). Men, masculinity, and the contexts of help seeking. *American Psychologist, 58*(1), 5–14.

Aldarondo, E., & Mederos, F. (Eds.), (2002). *Programs for men who batter: Intervention and prevention strategies in a diverse society.* Kingston, NJ: Civic Research Institute.

Aldarondo, E., & Mederos, F. (2008). Common practitioners' concerns about abusive men. Retrieved on 01 Oct. 2008 from *http://www.melissainstitute.org/documents/abusivemen.pdf*

American Psychiatric Association, 2000. *Diagnostic and Statistical Manual of Mental Disorders DSM-IV-TR (Text Revision).* Washington, D.C.: American Psychiatric Association.

Antill, J. K. (1983). Sex role complementarily versus similarity in married couples. *Journal of Personality and Social Psychology, 45*, 145–155.

Antonucci, T. C., & Akiyama, H. (1987). An examination of sex differences in social support among older men and women. *Sex Roles, 17*(11), 737.

Arcaya, J. M. (1996). The Hispanic male in group psychotherapy. In M. P. Andronico (Ed.), *Men in groups: Insights, interventions, and psychoeducational work* (pp. 151–161). Washington, DC: American Psychological Association.

Arciniega, M. G., Anderson, T. C., Tovar-Blank, Z. G., & Tracey, T. J. G. (2008). Toward a fuller conception of machismo: Development of a traditional machismo and caballerismo scale. *Journal of Counseling, 55*(1), 19–33.

Atkinson, D. R., Wampold, B. E., Lowe, S. M., Matthews, L., & Ahn, H. N. (1998). Asian American preferences for counselor characteristics: Application of the Bradley-Terry-Luce model to paired comparison data. *The Counseling Psychologist, 24*(2), 230–258.

Bancroft, L., Silverman, J. G., Jaffe, P. G., Baker, L. L., & Cunningham, A. J. (2004). Assessing abusers' risks to children. In P. G. Jaffe, L. L. Baker, & A. J. Cunningham (Eds.), *Protecting children from domestic violence: Strategies for community intervention* (pp. 101–119). New York: Guilford Press.

Basch, M. F. (1980). *Doing psychotherapy.* New York: Basic Books.

Baucom, D. H., Gordon, K. C., Snyder, D. K., Atkins, D. C., & Christensen, A. (2006). Treating affair couples: Clinical considerations and initial findings. *Journal of Cognitive Psychotherapy, 20*(4), 375–392.

Bender, L. (Producer), & Van Sant, G. (Director). (1997). *Good Will Hunting* [Motion picture]. United States: Miramax Home Entertainment.

Bepko, C., & Johnson, T. (2000). Gay and lesbian couples in therapy: Perspectives for the contemporary family therapist. *Journal of Marital and Family Therapy, 26,* 409–419.

Bergman, S. J. (1995). Men's psychological development: A relational perspective. In R. F. Levant & W. S. Pollack (Eds.), *A new psychology of men* (pp. 68–90). New York: Basic Books.

Berko, E. H. (1994). *Shyness, gender-role orientation, physical self-esteem, and gender role conflict.* Albany: State University of New York.

Bernstein, A., Bliss, T., & Davis, A. Z., (Producers), & Ratner, B. (Director), (2000). *The family man.* [Motion picture]. United States.

Bograd, M., & Mederos, F. (1999). Battering and couples therapy: Universal screening and selection of treatment modality. *Journal of Marital and Family Therapy, 25*(3), 291–312.

Bowlby, J. (1969). *Attachment and loss: Vol. 1. Attachment.* New York: Basic Books.

Bowlby, J. (1973). *Attachment and loss: Vol. 2. Separation.* New York: Basic Books.

Boyd, K. L. (1994). *The relationship between self-disclosure, intimacy, and satisfaction in African-American and European-American heterosexual relationships.* Unpublished doctoral/thesis, Old Dominion University, Norfolk, VA.

Breiding, M. J. (2004). Observed hostility and observed dominance as mediators of the relationship between husbands' gender role conflict and wives' outcomes. *Journal of Counseling Psychology, 51,* 429–436.

References

Brody, L. R., & Hall, J. A. (1993). Gender and emotion. In M. Lewis & J. M. Haviland (Eds.), *Handbook of emotions* (pp. 338–349). New York: Guilford Press.

Brooks, G. R. (1996). *A new psychotherapy for traditional men.* San Francisco: Jossey-Bass.

Brooks, G. R. (1998). Group therapy for traditional men. In R. F. Levant & W. S. Pollack (Eds.), *New psychotherapy for men* (pp. 83–96). New York: Wiley.

Brooks, G. R., & Good, G. E. (2001). *The new handbook of psychotherapy and counseling with men: A comprehensive guide to settings, problems, and treatment approaches.* San Francisco: Jossey-Bass.

Brooks, G. R., & Good, G. E. (2005). *The new handbook of psychotherapy and counseling with men: A comprehensive guide to settings, problems, and treatment approaches, revised edition.* San Francisco: Jossey-Bass.

Brooks, G. R., & Silverstein, L. (1995). Understanding the dark side of masculinity: An interactive systems model. In R. L. Levant & W. S. Pollack (Eds.), *A new psychology of men* (pp. 280–333). New York: Basic Books.

Bruch, M. A., Berko, E. H., & Haase, R. F. (1998). Shyness, masculine ideology, physical attractiveness, and emotional inexpressiveness: Testing a mediational model of men's interpersonal competence. *Journal of Counseling Psychology, 45*(1), 84–97.

Buck, R. (1977). Nonverbal communication of affect in preschool children: Relationships with personality and skin conductance. *Journal of Personality and Social Psychology, 35*(4), 225–236.

Burda, P. C., Vaux, A. C., & Schill, T. (1984). Social support resources: Variation across sex and sex role. *Personality and Social Psychology Bulletin, 10,* 119–126.

Caldwell, L. D., White, J. L., Brooks, G. R., & Good, G. E. (2001). African-centered therapeutic and counseling interventions for African American males. In G. E. Good & G. R. Brooks (Eds.), *The new handbook of psychotherapy and counseling with men* (pp. 737–753). San Francisco: Jossey-Bass.

Campbell, J. C. (1995). Prediction of homicide of and by battered women. In J. C. Campbell (Ed.), *Assessing dangerousness: Violence by sexual offenders, batterers, and child abusers* (pp. 96–113). Thousand Oaks, CA: Sage.

Campbell, J. L., & Snow, B. M. (1992). Gender role conflict and family environment as predictors of men's marital satisfaction. *Journal of Family Psychology, 6*(1), 84–87.

Casas, J. M., Turner, J. A., & Ruiz de Esparza, C. A. (2001). Machismo revisited in a time of crisis. In G. R. Brooks & G. E. Goode (Eds.), *The new handbook of psychotherapy and counseling with men* (pp. 754–779). San Francisco: Jossey-Bass.

Clements, K., Holtzworth-Munroe, A., Schweinle, W., & Ickes, W. (2007). Empathic accuracy of intimate partners in violent versus nonviolent relationships. *Personal Relationships, 14*(3), 369–388.

Cochran, S. V. (2001). Assessing and treating depression in men. In G. R. Brooks & G. E. Goode (Eds.), *The new handbook of psychotherapy and counseling with men* (pp. 229–245). San Francisco: Jossey-Bass.

Cochran, S. V., & Rabinowitz, F. E. (1996). Men, loss, and psychotherapy. *Psychotherapy: Theory, research and practice, 33*(4), 593.

Cochran, S. V., & Rabinowitz, F. E. (2000). *Men and depression: Clinical and empirical perspectives.* San Diego, CA: Academic Press.

Colarusso, C. A., & Nemiroff, R. (1981). *Adult development: A new dimension in psychodynamic theory and practice.* New York: Plenum Press.

Comas-Díaz, L., & Jacobsen, F. (1991). Ethnocultural transference and countertransference in the therapeutic dyad. *American Journal of Orthopsychiatry, 61*(3), 392–402.

Conroy, P. (1976). *The great Santini.* New York: Bantam Books.

Cournoyer, R. J., & Mahalik, J. R. (1995). Cross-sectional study of gender role conflict examining college-aged and middle-aged men. *Journal of Counseling Psychology, 42*(1), 11–19.

Cox, A. J. (2006). *Boys of few words: Raising our sons to communicate and connect.* New York: Guilford Press.

Cutrona, C. E. (1996). *Social support in couples: Marriage as a resource in times of stress.* New York: Sage.

David, D. S., & Brannon, R. (1976). *The forty-nine percent majority: The male sex role.* Reading, MA: Addison-Wesley.

Davidson, L. (1979). Preventive attitudes toward midlife crisis. *The American Journal of Psychoanalysis, 39*(2), 165–173.

Diamond, J. (1997). *Male menopause.* Naperville, IL: Sourcebooks.

Diamond, J. (2004). *The irritable male syndrome: Managing the 4 key causes of depression and aggression.* Emmaus, PA: Rodale Books.

Dobash, R. E., & Dobash, R. P. (1979). *Violence against wives.* New York: Free Press.

Dunn, J., Bretherton, I., & Munn, P. (1987). Conversations about feeling states between mothers and their young children. *Developmental Psychology, 23*(1), 132–139.

References

Dutton, D. G. (1995). A scale for measuring the propensity for abusiveness. *Journal of Family Violence, 10,* 203–221.

Dutton, D. G. (1998). *The abusive personality: Violence and control in intimate relationships.* New York: Guilford Press.

Dutton, D. G., & Nicholls, T. L. (2005). The gender paradigm in domestic violence research and theory: Part 1-The conflict of theory and data. *Aggression and Violent Behavior, 10*(6), 680–714.

Dweck, C. S. (2007). *Mindset: The new psychology of success.* New York: Ballantine Books.

Eisler, R., & Skidmore, J. R. (1987). Masculine gender role stress: Scale development and component factors in the appraisal of stressful situations. *Behavior Modification, 11*(2), 123.

Eisler, R. M. (1995). The relationship between masculine gender role stress and men's health risk: The validation of a construct. In R. F. Levant & W. S. Pollack (Eds.), *A new psychology of men* (pp. 207–225). New York: Basic Books.

Engel, L. B., & Ferguson, T. (1990). *Imaginary crimes: Why we punish ourselves and how to stop.* New York: Houghton Mifflin.

Englar-Carlson, M., & Shepard, D. S. (2005). Engaging men in couples counseling: Strategies for overcoming ambivalence and inexpressiveness. *The Family Journal, 13*(4), 383–391.

Epstein, M. (2005). Bald is to male as fat is to female (and other strange secrets of the male ego). *O, The Oprah Magazine, 6*(6), 216.

Erickson, M. H., & Rossi, E. L. (1979). *Hypnotherapy: An exploratory casebook.* New York: Irvington Publishers, Inc.

Falicov, C. (2000). *Latino families in therapy: A guide to multicultural practice.* New York: Guilford Press.

Farrell, W. T. (1987). *Why men are the way they are.* New York: McGraw-Hill.

Finn, J. (1986). The relationship between sex role attitudes and attitudes supporting marital violence. *Sex Roles, 14*(5), 235.

Fivush, R. (1989). Exploring sex differences in the emotional content of mother-child conversations about the past. *Sex Roles, 20*(11), 675–691.

Fogel, B., & Stone, A. (1992). Practical pathophysiology in neuropsychiatry: A clinical approach to depression and impulsive behavior in neurological patients. In S. C. Yudofsky & R. E. Hales (Eds.), *The American psychiatric textbook of neuropsychiatry* (pp. 329–344). Washington, DC: American Psychiatric Press.

Fonagy, P., Gergely, G., Jurist, E. L., & Target, M. (2002). *Affect regulation, mentalization, and the development of self.* New York: Other Press.

Franchina, J. J., Eisler, R. M., & Moore, T. M. (2001). Masculine gender role stress and intimate abuse: Effects of masculine gender relevance of dating situations and female threat on men's attributions and affective responses. *Psychology of Men and Masculinity, 2*(1), 34–41.

Franklin, A. J. (2001). Treating anger in African-American men. In R. F. Levant & W. S. Pollack (Eds.), *New psychotherapy for men* (pp. 239–258). New York: Wiley.

Gilligan, S. G. (1984). *Therapeutic trances: The cooperation principle in Ericksonian hypnotherapy.* New York: Brunner/Mazel Publishers.

Gittes, H. & Besman, M. (Producers), & Payne, A. (Director). (2002). *About Schmidt* [Motion picture]. United States: New Line Home Entertainment.

Gjerde, P., Block, J., & Block, J. H. (1988). Depressive symptoms and personality during late adolescence: gender differences in the externalization-internalization of symptom expression. *Journal of Abnormal Psychology, 97*(4), 475–486.

Gleason, J. B., Grief, E. B., & Thorne, B. (1983). Men's speech to young children. In C. Kramare & N. Henley (Eds.), *Language, gender and society* (pp. 140–150). London: Newbury House.

Goldberg, H. (1976). *The hazards of being male: Surviving the myth of masculine privilege.* New York: Nash.

Goleman, D. (1995). *Emotional intelligence: Why it can matter more than IQ.* New York: Bantam Books.

Goleman, D. (1998). *Working with emotional intelligence.* New York: Bantam Books.

Good, G. E., Dell, D., & Mintz, L. (1989). The male role and gender role conflict: Relationships to help-seeking. *Journal of Counseling Psychology, 68,* 295–300.

Good, G. E., & Mintz, L. B. (1990). Gender role conflict and depression in college men: Evidence for compounded risk. *Journal of Counseling and Development, 69*(1), 17–21.

Good, G. E., & Sherrod, N. B. (2001). Men's problems and effective treatments: Theory and empirical support. In G. R. Brooks & G. E. Good (Eds.), *The New Handbook of Psychotherapy and Counseling with Men: A Comprehensive Guide to Settings, Problems, and Treatment Approaches* (Vol. 1, pp. 22–40). San Francisco: Jossey-Bass.

References

Good, G. E., & Wood, P. K. (1995). Male gender role conflict, depression, and help seeking: Do college men face double jeopardy? *Journal of Counseling and Development, 74*(1), 70–75.

Gottman, J., & Levenson, R. (2008). 12-year study of gay & lesbian couples. Retrieved 14 Aug., 2008 from *http://www.gottman.com/research/projects/gaylesbian/*

Gottman, J. M. (1994). *Why marriages succeed or fail.* New York: Simon & Schuster.

Gottman, J. M. (1999). *The marriage clinic.* New York: Norton.

Gottman, J. M. (2000). *The seven principles for making marriage work: A practical guide from the country's foremost relationship expert.* New York: Three Rivers Press.

Gottman, J. M., Levenson, R. W., Gross, J., Frederickson, B. L., McCoy, K., Rosenthal, L., et al. (2003). Correlates of gay and lesbian couples' relationship satisfaction and relationship dissolution. *Journal of Homosexuality, 45*(1), 23–43.

Gottman, J. M., Levenson, R. W., Swanson, C., Swanson, K., Tyson, R., & Yoshimoto, D. (2003). Observing gay, lesbian and heterosexual couples' relationships: Mathematical modeling of conflict interaction. *Journal of Homosexuality, 45*(1), 65–91.

Greene, R. (1998). *The explosive child: A new approach for understanding and parenting easily frustrated, "chronically inflexible" children.* New York: Harper-Collins.

Haldeman, D. C. (2005). Psychotherapy with gay and bisexual men. In G. R. Brooks & G. E. Good (Eds.), *The new handbook of psychotherapy and counseling with men: A comprehensive guide to settings, problems, and treatment approaches* (Rev. ed.) (pp. 796–815). New York: Jossey-Boss.

Hales, D., & Hales, R. (2004, June 20). Too tough to seek help? *Parade Magazine,* p. xxx.

Hardy, K. V., & Laszloffy, T. A. (1994). Deconstructing race in family therapy. *Journal of Feminist Family Therapy, 5*(3/4), 5–33.

Hart, A. D. (2001). *Unmasking male depression.* Nashville, TN: Thomas Nelson.

Hartl, T. L., Zeiss, R. A., Marino, C. M., Zeiss, A. M., Regev, L. G., & Leontis, C. (2007). Clients' sexually inappropriate behaviors directed toward clinicians: Conceptualization and management. *Professional Psychology: Research and Practice, 38*(6), 674–681.

Healy, M. (2005, October 17). Depression's machismo mask. Special Men's Health Section. *Los Angeles Times,* Oct. 17, 2005.

Hesley, J. W., & Hesley, J. G. (2001). *Rent two films and let's talk in the morning: Using popular movies in psychotherapy.* New York: Wiley.

Holmes, J. (2001). *Search for the secure base: Attachment theory and psychotherapy.* London: Routledge.

Holtzworth-Munroe, A. (1997). Violent versus nonviolent husbands: Differences in attachment patterns, dependency, and jealousy. *Journal of Family Psychology, 11*(3), 314.

Holtzworth-Munroe, A. (2000). Social information processing skills deficits in maritally violent men: Summary of a research program. In J. P. Vincent & E. N. Jouriles (Eds.), *Domestic Violence: Guidelines for Research-informed Practice* (pp. 13–36). London: Jessica Kingsley.

Holtzworth-Munroe, A. (2000). Testing the Holtzworth-Munroe and Stuart (1994) batterer typology. *Journal of Consulting and Clinical Psychology, 68*(6), 1000–1019.

Holtzworth-Munroe, A., & Hutchinson, G. (1993). Attributing negative intent to wife behavior: The attributions of maritally violent versus nonviolent men. *Journal of Abnormal Psychology, 102*(2), 206.

Holtzworth-Munroe, A., Waltz, J., Jacobson, N. S., & Monaco, V. (1992). Recruiting nonviolent men as control subjects for research on marital violence: How easily can it be done? *Violence and Victims, 7*(1), 79–88.

Hornby, N. (1995). *High fidelity.* New York: Riverhead Books.

Horne, A. M., & Kiselica, M. S. (1999). *Handbook of counseling boys and adolescent males: A practitioner's guide.* Thousand Oaks, CA: Sage Publications.

Husaini, B. A., Moore, S. T., & Cain, V. A. (1994). Psychiatric symptoms and help-seeking behavior among the elderly: An analysis of racial and gender differences. *Journal of Gerontological Social Work, 21,* 177–195.

Ickes, W. (1985). Sex-role influences on compatibility in relationships. In W. Ickes (Ed.), *Compatible and incompatible relationships* (pp. 187–208). New York: Springer.

Ickes, W. (1997). *Empathic accuracy.* New York: Guilford Press.

Isenhart, C. E. (2001). Treating substance abuse in men. In G. R. Brooks & G. E. Good (Eds.), *The new handbook of psychotherapy and counseling with men.* San Francisco: Jossey-Bass.

Johnson, M. E. (1988). Influences of gender and sex-role oreintation on help-seeking attitudes. *Journal of Psychology, 122*(3), 237–241.

Johnson, M. P. (1995). Patriarchal terrorism and common couple violence: Two forms of violence against women. *Journal of Marriage and the Family, 57*(2), 283–294.

References

Johnson, M. P. (1999). *Two types of violence against women in the American family: Identifying patriarchal terrorism and common couple violence*. Paper presented at the Annual Meetings of the National Council on Family Relations.

Johnson, M. P., & Ferraro, K. J. (2000). Research on domestic violence in the 1990s: Making distinctions. *Journal of Marriage and the Family, 62*(4), 948–963.

Johnson, M. P., & Leone, J. M. (2005). The differential effects of intimate terrorism and situational couple violence: Findings from the National Violence Against Women Survey. *Journal of Family Issues, 26*(3), 322–349.

Johnson, N. G. (2005). Women helping men: Strengths of and barriers to women therapists working with men clients. In G. R. Brooks & G. E. Good (Eds.), *The new handbook of psychotherapy and counseling with men: A comprehensive guide to settings, problems, and treatment approaches* (Rev. ed.) (pp. 291–307). New York: Jossey-Bass.

Jones, D. C. (1991). Friendship satisfaction and gender: An examination of sex differences in contributors to friendship satisfaction. *Journal of Social and Personal Relationships, 8*(2), 167–185.

Jung, C. G., & Hull, R. F. C. (1977). *C.G. Jung speaking*. Princeton, NJ: Princeton University Press.

Kazan, E. (Director). (1954). *On the waterfront* [Motion picture]. United States: Horizon Pictures.

Kivel, P. (1999). *Men's work: How to stop the violence that tears our lives apart*. (DVD). Center City, MN: Hazelden.

Kohut, H. (1984). *How does analysis cure?* Chicago: University of Chicago Press.

Kropp, P. R., & Hart, S. D. (2000). The Spousal Assault Risk Assessment (SARA) guide: Reliability and validity in adult male offenders. *Law and Human Behavior, 24*(1), 101–118.

Kropp, P. R., Hart, S. D., Webster, C. D., & Eaves, D. (1994). *Manual of the Spousal Assault Risk Assessment Guide* (2nd ed.). Vancouver, British Columbia, Canada: British Columbia Institute on Family Violence.

Krystal, H. (1988). *Integration and self-healing: Affect, trauma, alexithymia*. Hillsdale, NJ: Analytic Press.

Kurdek, L. A. (1998). Relationship outcomes and their predictors: Longitudinal evidence from heterosexual married, gay cohabiting, and lesbian cohabiting couples. *Journal of Marriage and the Family, 60*, 553–568.

Kurdek, L. A., & Schmitt, J. P. (1986). Interaction of sex role self-concept with relationship quality and relationship beliefs in married, heterosexual cohabiting, gay, and lesbian couples. *Journal of Personality and Social Psychology, 51*(2), 365–370.

Lambert, M. J., Barley, D. E., & Norcross, J. C. (2002). Research summary on the therapeutic relationship and psychotherapy outcome. In Anonymous (Ed.), *Psychotherapy relationships that work: Therapist contributions and responsiveness to patients* (pp. 17–32). New York: Oxford University Press.

Lamke, L. K. (1989). Marital adjustment among rural couples: The role of expressiveness. *Sex Roles, 21*(9–10), 579.

Lash, S. J., Eisler, R. M., & Southard, D. R. (1995). Sex differences in cardiovascular reactivity as a function of the appraised gender relevance of the stressor. *Behavioral Medicine, 21*(2), 86–94.

Lash, S. J., Gillespie, B. L., Eisler, R. M., & Southard, D. R. (1991). Sex differences in cardiovascular reactivity: Effects of the gender relevance of the stressor. *Health Psychology, 10*(6), 392–398.

La Taillade, J. J., Epstein, N. B., & Werlinich, C. A. (2006). Conjoint treatment of intimate partner violence: A cognitive-behavioral approach. *Journal of Cognitive Psychotherapy, 20*, 393–410.

Lee, C. C. (1999). Counseling African American men. In L. E. Davis (Ed.), *Working with African American males: A guide to practice* (pp. 39–53). Thousand Oaks CA: Sage.

Levant, R. F., Good, G. E., Cook, S. W., O'Neil, J. M., Smalley, K. B., Owen, K., et al. (2006). The normative male alexithymia scale: Measurement of a gender-linked syndrome. *Psychology of Men & Masculinity, 7*(4), 212–224.

Levant, R. F. (2007). Why study men and boys? Retrieved June 12, 2007 from *http://www.drronaldlevant.com/whystudy.html*

Levant, R. F., Good, G. E., Cook, S. W., O'Neil, J. M., Smalley, K. B., Owen, K., et al. (2006). The Normative Male Alexithymia scale: Measurement of a gender-linked syndrome. *Psychology of Men and Masculinity, 7*(4), 212–224.

Levant, R. F., Hirsch, L. S., Celentano, E., & Cozza, T. M. (1992). The male role: An investigation of contemporary norms. *Journal of Mental Health Counseling, 14*(3), 325–337.

Levant, R. F., & Pollack, W. S. (1995). Toward the reconstruction of masculinity. In R. F. Levant & W. S. Pollack (Eds.), *A new psychology of men* (pp. 229–251). New York: Basic Books.

Levant, R. F., & Pollack, W. S. (1998). Desperately seeking language: Understanding, assessing, and treating normative male alexithymia. In R. F.

Levant & W. S. Pollack (Eds.), *New psychotherapy for men* (pp. 35–56). Hoboken, NJ: Wiley.

Levant, R. F., Richmond, K., Majors, R. G., Inclan, J. E., Rossello, J. M., Heesacker, M., et al. (2003). A multicultural investigation of masculinity ideology and alexithymia. *Psychology of Men and Masculinity, 4*(2), 91–99.

Levant, R. F., Wu, R., & Fischer, J. (1996). Masculinity ideology: A comparison between U.S. and Chinese young men and women. *Journal of Gender, Culture, and Health, 1*(3), 207–220.

Levinson, D. (1978). *The seasons of a man's life.* New York: Knopf.

Levit, D. B. (1991). Gender differences in ego defenses in adolescence: Sex roles as one way to understand the differences. *Journal of Personality and Social Psychology, 61*(6), 992–999.

Linehan, M. (1993). *Skills training manual for treating borderline personality disorder.* New York: Guilford Press.

Lisak, D. (2001). Male survivors of trauma. In G. R. Brooks & G. E. Good (Eds.), *The new handbook of psychotherapy and counseling with men: A comprehensive guide to settings, problems, and treatment approaches* (pp. 147–158). San Francisco: Jossey-Bass.

Lisak, D., Brooks, G. R., & Good, G. E. (2001). Homicide, violence, and male aggression. In G. R. Brooks & G. E. Good (Eds.), *The new handbook of psychotherapy and counseling with men: A comprehensive guide to settings, problems, and treatment approaches* (pp. 278–292). San Francisco: Jossey-Bass.

Ludlow, L. H., & Mahalik, J. R. (2001). Congruence between a theoretical continuum of masculinity and the Rasch Model: Examining the Conformity to Masculine Norms Inventory. *Journal of Applied Measurement, 2*(3), 205–226.

Mahalik, J. R. (2000). Gender role conflict in men as a predictor of self-ratings of behavior on the Interpersonal Circle. *Journal of Social and Clinical Psychology, 19*(2), 276–292.

Mahoney, A., Pargament, K. I., Murray-Swank, A., & Murray-Swank, N. (2003). Religion and the sanctification of family relationships. *Review of Religious Research, 44*(3), 220–236.

Malatesta, C. Z., Culver, C., Tesman, J. R., & Shepard, B. (1989). The development of emotion expression during the first two years of life. *Monographs of the Society for Research in Child Development, 54*(1), 1–104.

Mandela, N. (1994). *Long walk to freedom: The autobiography of Nelson Mandela.* New York: Little, Brown.

McCarey, L. (Director). (1933). *Duck soup* [Motion picture]. United States: Paramount Productions.

McFall, R. M. (1982). A review and reformulation of the concept of social skills. *Behavioral Assessment, 4*(1), 1–33.

McGraw, S. L. (2001). *Masculinity ideologies, men's relationship behavior, and relationship satisfaction in heterosexual couple relationships.* Berkeley/Alameda, CA: California School of Professional Psychology.

McPherson, D. (2005, February 14). *Solutions to gender-based violence.* Paper presented at the 5th Annual Men's Leadership Forum, San Diego, CA.

Meichenbaum, D. (2001a). *Trauma and violence in intimate relationships: A life-span cognitive–behavioral treatment approach.* San Diego, CA: Relationship Training Institute.

Meichenbaum, D. (2001b). *Treatment of individuals with anger-control problems and aggressive behaviors: A clinical handbook.* Clearwater, FL: Institute Press.

Metz, H., & Lowinger, R. (1995). Epidemiology and inferences regarding the etiology of late life suicide. In G. J. Kennedy (Ed.), *Suicide and depression in late life* (pp. 3–22). New York: Wiley.

Miller, L. C., Berg, J. H., & Archer, R. L. (1983). Openers: Individuals who elicit intimate self-disclosure. *Journal of Personality and Social Psychology, 44*(6), 1234–1244.

Mirande, A. (1997). *Hombres y machos: Masculinity and Latino culture.* Boulder, CO: Westview Press.

Mirande, A. (2003, May). *Latino issues and domestic violence.* Paper presented at the Domestic Violence 2000 Conference (sponsored by the Relationship Training Institute), San Diego, CA.

Mosciki, E. K. (1997). Identification of suicide risk factors using epidemiological studies. *Psychiatric Clinics of North America, 20*(3), 499–517.

Mosley, W. (2004). *The man in my basement: A novel.* New York: Little, Brown.

Myers, H. F., Echemendia, R. J., & Trimble, J. E. (1991). The need for training ethnic minority psycholgists. In H. Myers, P. Wohlford, L. P. Guzman, & R. Echemendia (Eds.), *Ethnic minority perspectives on clinical training and services in psychology* (pp. 3–11). Washington, DC: American Psychological Association.

Nelsen, J., & Lott, L. (1994). *Positive Discipline for Teenagers.* Rocklin CA: Prima Publishing.

Nolen-Hoeksema, S. (1990). *Sex differences in depression.* Palo Alto, CA: Stanford University Press.

Nolen-Hoeksma, S. (1992). Sex differences in control of depression. In D. M. Wegner & J. W. Pennebaker (Eds.), *Handbook of mental control* (pp. 239–257). Englewood Cliffs, NJ: Prentice Hall.

Noyes, B. (2007). *A qualitative examination of men's therapy decision-making processes and therapy experiences.* University of Utah, Salt Lake City.

O'Leary, K. D., Vivian, D., & Malone, J. (1992). Assessment of physical aggression against women in marriage: The need for multimodal assessment. *Behavioral Assessment, 14*(1), 5–14.

Oliver, J. M., Reed, C. K. S., Katz, B. M., & Haugh, J. A. (1999). Students' self-reports of help-seeking: The impact of psychological problems, stress, and demographic variables on utilization of formal and informal support. *Social Behavior and Personality, 27*(2), 109–128.

O'Neil, J. M. (2008). Summarizing 25 years of research on men's gender role conflict using the Gender Role Conflict scale: New research paradigms and clinical implications. *The Counseling Psychologist, 36*(3), 358–445.

O'Neil, J. M., Good, G. E., & Holmes, S. (1995). Fifteen years of theory and research on men's gender role conflict: New paradigms for empirical research. In R. F. Levant & W. S. Pollack (Eds.), *A new psychology of men* (pp. 164–206). New York: Basic Books.

Pargament, K. I., & Mahoney, A. (2005). Sacred matters: Sanctification as a vital topic for the psychology of religion. *International Journal for the Psychology of Religion, 15*(3), 179–198.

Parham, T. A. (1999). Invisibility syndrome in African descent people: Understanding cultural manifestations of the struggle for self-affirmation. *The Counseling Psychologist, 27*(6), 794 –801.

Parker, J. D. A., Taylor, G. J., & Bagby, R. M. (2001). The relationship between emotional intelligence and alexithymia. *Personality and Individual Differences, 30*(1), 107–115.

Parker-Pope, T. (2008, October 28). Either infidelity is on the rise or honesty is, studies find. *The New York Times.*

Philpot, C. L. (2001). Family therapy for men. In G. R. Brooks & G. E. Good (Eds.), *The new handbook of psychotherapy and counseling with men: A comprehensive guide to settings, problems, and treatment approaches* (pp. 622–636). San Francisco, CA: Jossey-Bass.

Pittman, F. (2003, November 8). *Couples and commitment: Treating the crisis of infidelity.* Conference. San Diego, CA.

Pleck, J. H. (1980). Men's power with women, other men and society. In J. H. Pleck & E. H. Pleck (Eds.), *The American man* (pp. 417–433). Englewood Cliffs, NJ: Prentice Hall.

Pleck, J. H. (1983). *The myth of masculinity.* Cambridge, MA: MIT Press.

Pleck, J. H., Sonenstein, F. L., & Ku, L. C. (1993). Masculinity ideology:

Its impact on adolescent males' heterosexual relationships. *Journal of Social Issues, 49*(3), 11–29.

Pollack, W. S. (1995). *Treating the fallen hero: Empathic psychoanalytic psychotherapy designed for men*. Paper presented at the American Psychological Association Annual Convention, Toronto, Ontario, Canada.

Pollack, W. S. (1998). Mourning, melancholia, and masculinity: Recognizing and treating depression in men. In W. S. Pollack & R. F. Levant (Eds.), *New psychotherapy for men* (pp. 147–166). New York: Wiley.

Pollack, W. S. (1998b). *Real boys: Rescuing our sons from the myths of boyhood*. New York: Random House.

Pollack, W. S. (2001). "Masked men": New psychoanalytically oriented treatment models for adult and young adult men. In G. R. Brooks & G. E. Good (Eds.), *The new handbook of psychotherapy and counseling with men: A comprehensive guide to settings, problems, and treatment approaches* (pp. 527–543). San Francisco: Jossey-Bass.

Potts, M. K., Burnan, M. A., & Wells, K. B. (1991). Gender differences in depression detection: A comparison of clinician diagnosis and standardized assessment. *Psychological Assessment, 3*(4), 609–615.

Prince, J. E., & Arias, I. (1994). The role of perceived control and the desirability of control among abusive and nonabusive husbands. *American Journal of Family Therapy, 22*(2), 126.

Rabinowitz, F. E. (2001). Group therapy for men. In G. R. Brooks & G. E. Good (Eds.), *The new handbook of psychotherapy and counseling with men: A comprehensive guide to settings, problems, and treatment approaches* (pp. 603–621). San Francisco: Jossey-Bass.

Rabinowitz, F. E. (2005). Group therapy for men. In G. R. Brooks & G. E. Good (Eds.), *The new handbook of psychotherapy and counseling with men: A comprehensive guide to settings, problems, and treatment approaches* (pp. 264–277). San Francisco: Jossey-Bass.

Rabinowitz, F. E. (2006). Crossing the no cry zone: Doing psychotherapy with men. Retrieved 14 January 2007 from *http://www.continuingedcourses. net/active/courses/course026.php*

Rabinowitz, F. E., & Cochran, S. V. (1994). *Man alive: A primer of men's issues*. Pacific Grove, CA: Brooks/Cole.

Rabinowitz, F. E., & Cochran, S. V. (2002). *Deepening psychotherapy with men*. Washington, DC: American Psychological Association.

Ragle, J. D. (1993). *Gender role behavior of male psychotherapy patients*. University of Texas - Austin, Austin, TX.

References

Real, T. (1998). *I don't want to talk about it: Overcoming the secret legacy of male depression.* New York: Scribner.

Robertson, J. M., & Fitzgerald, L. F. (1992). Overcoming the masculine mystique: Preferences for alternative forms of assistance among men who avoid counseling. *Journal of Counseling Psychology, 39*(2), 240–246.

Rochlen, A. B., & Mahalik, J. R. (2004). Women's perceptions of male partners' gender role conflict as predictors of psychological well-being and relationship satisfaction. *Psychology of Men and Masculinity, 5*(2), 147–157.

Rodriguez, O. (1987a). *Hispanics and human services: Help-seeking in the inner city* (Monograph No. 14). New York: Fordham University, Hispanic Resaerch Center.

Rodriguez, O. (1987b). *Hispanics and human services: Help-seeking in the inner city* (Monograph No. 14). New York: Fordham University, Hispanic Research Center.

Rowe, D. (2007). *African-American issues and domestic violence. Paper presented at the The STOP Program Conference* (sponsored by the Relationship Training Institute), San Diego, CA.

Rybarczyk, B. (1994). Diversity among American men: The impact of aging, ethnicity and race. In C. T. Kilmartin (Ed.), *The masculine self* (pp. 113–131). New York: Macmillan.

Salovey, P., & Mayer, J. D. (1990). Emotional intelligence. *Imagination, Cognition and Personality, 9*(3), 185–211.

Sanford, J. A. (1979). *The invisible partners: How the male and female in each of us affects our relationships.* New York: Paulist Press.

Sanford, J. A., & Lough, G. (1988). *What men are like.* New York: Paulist Press.

Sapadin, L. A. (1988). Friendship and gender: Perspectives of professional men and women. *Journal of Social and Personal Relationships, 5*(4), 387–403.

Saunders, D. G. (1993). Husbands who assault. In N. Hilton (Ed.), *Legal responses to wife assault.* Newbury Park, CA: Sage Publications, p.556.

Saurer, M. K., & Eisler, R. M. (1990). The role of masculine gender role stress in expressivity and social support network factors. *Sex Roles, 23*(5), 261–271.

Scher, M. (1990). Effect of gender role incongruities on men's experience as clients in psychotherapy. *Psychotherapy, 27*, 322–326.

Scott, R. P. (2001). *The relationship between family structure and male gender role development.* Athens: University of Georgia Press.

Seligman, M. E. P. (1998). *Learned optimism.* New York: Pocket Books.

Shapiro, S. (1995). *Talking with patients: A self psychological view of creative intuition and analytic discipline.* Northvale, NJ: Jason Aronson.

Sharpe, M. J., & Heppner, P. P. (1991). Gender role, gender-role conflict, and psychological well-being in men. *Journal of Counseling Psychology, 38*(3), 323–330.

Sharpe, M. J., Heppner, P. P., & Dixon, W. A. (1995). Gender role conflict, instrumentality, expressiveness, and well-being in adult men. *Sex Roles, 33*(1), 1–18.

Siavelis, R. L., & Lamke, L. K. (1992). Instrumentalness and expressiveness: Predictors of heterosexual relationship satisfaction. *Sex Roles, 26*(3), 149–159.

Sifneos, P. E. (1987). *Short-term dynamic psychotherapy: Evaluation and technique (Topics in General Psychiatry).* New York: Plenum Medical Book Co./Plenum Press.

Sifneos, P. E. (1991). Affect, emotional conflict, and deficit: An overview. *Psychotherapy and Psychosomatics, 56*(3), 116–122.

Simpson, L. E., Atkins, D. C., Gattis, K. S., & Christensen, A. (2008). Low-level relationship aggression and couple therapy outcomes. *Journal of Family Psychology, 22*(1), 102–111.

Sonkin, D. J., & Dutton, D. (2003). Treating assaultive men from an attachment perspective. *Journal of Aggression, Maltreatment and Trauma, 7*(1), 105–133.

Stark, E., & Flitcraft, A. (1996). *Women at Risk: Domestic Violence and Women's Health.* London: Sage Publications.

Stets, J. E. (1988). *Domestic violence and control.* New York: Springer.

Stock, B. (2007). The five competencies of emotional intelligence. Byron Stock & Associates LLC. Retrieved 21 February 2007 from *http://www.byron-stock.com/ei/eicompetencies.html*

Stosny, S. (1995). *Treating attachment abuse: A compassionate approach.* New York: Springer.

Stosny, S. (2001). The compassion workshop for partner and child abusers. In E. Aldarondo & F. Mederos (Eds.), *Batterer intervention programs: A handbook for clinicians, practitioners, and advocates.* Kingston, NJ: Civic Research Institute.

Straus, M. (2006, July/August 2006). Hungry for connection. *Psychotherapy Networker, 30*(4), 59–74.

Straus, M. A., Hamby, S. L., Boney-McCoy, S. U. E., & Sugarman, D. B. (1996). The revised Conflict Tactics Scales (CTS2): Development and preliminary psychometric data. *Journal of Family Issues, 17*(3), 283–316.

References

Straus, M. A., Steinmetz, S., & Gelles, R. J. (1980). *Behind closed doors: Violence in American Families.* New York: Doubleday.

Straus, M. A., & Smith, C. (1990). Family patterns and primary prevention of family violence. In M. A. Straus & R. J. Gelles (Eds.), *Physical violence in American families: Risk factors and adaptations to violence in 8,145 families* (pp. 507–526). Brunswick, NJ: Transaction Press.

Sutton, A. (1996). African American men in group therapy. In M. P. Adronico (Ed.), *Men in groups: Insights, interventions, and psychoeducational work* (pp. 131–149). Washington, DC: American Psychological Association.

Sweet, H. B. (2002). *Engaging men as a female therapist: Jennifer Melfi meets Tony Soprano.* Paper presented at the American Psychological Association Annual Conference, Chicago.

Sweet, H. B. (2006). Finding the person behind the persona: Engaging men as a female therapist. In M. Englar-Carlson & M. A. Stevens (Eds.), *In the room with men: Casebook of therapeutic change* (pp. 69–90). Washington, DC: American Psychological Association.

Taffel, R. (2001). *The second family.* New York: St. Martin's Press.

Tannen, D. (1990). *You just don't understand: Women and men in conversation.* New York: William Morris.

Vass, J. J., & Gold, S. R. (1995). Effects of feedback on emotion in hyper-masculine males. *Violence and Victims, 10*(3), 217–226.

Vessey, J. T., & Howard, K. I. (1993). Who seeks psychotherapy? *Psychotherapy: Theory, Research, Practice, Training, 30*(4), 546–553.

Viorst, J. (1986). *Necessary losses: The loves, illusions, dependencies and impossible expectations that all of us have to give up in order to grow.* New York: Simon & Schuster.

Vivian, D., & Heyman, R. E. (1996). Is there a place for conjoint treatment of couple violence? *In Session: Psychotherapy in Practice, 2*(3), 25–48.

Weiss, J., & Sampson, H. (1986). *The psychoanalytic process: Theory, clinical observations, and empirical research.* New York: Guilford Press.

Welland, C., & Ribner, N. (2007). *Healing from violence: Latino men's journey to a new masculinity.* New York: Springer.

Welland-Akong, C. G. (1999). *A qualitative analysis of cultural treatment components for Mexican male perpetrators of partner abuse.* San Diego: California School of Professional Psychology–San Diego.

Wexler, D. B. (2006a). *Is he depressed or what: What to do when the man you love is irritable, moody, and withdrawn.* Oakland, CA: New Harbinger.

Wexler, D. B. (2006b). *STOP domestic violence: Innovative skills, techniques, options, and plans for better relationships.* New York: Norton.

White, M. T., & Weiner, M. B. (1986). *The theory and practice of self psychology.* Philadelphia: Brunner/Mazel.

Williams, O. J. (1994). Group work with African American men who batter: Toward more ethnically sensitive practice. *Journal of Comparative Family Studies, 25*(1), 91.

Winokur, G. (1997). All roads lead to depression: Clinically homogeneous, etiologically heterogeneous. *Journal of Affective Disorders, 45*(1), 97–108.

Wohlgemuth, E., & Betz, N. E. (1991). Gender as a moderator of the relationships of stress and social support to physical health in college students. *Journal of Counseling Psychology, 38*(3), 367–374.

Wong, Y. J., & Rochlen, A. B. (2005). Demystifying men's emotional behavior: New directions and Implications for counseling and research. *Psychology of Men & Masculinity, 6*(1), 62–72.

Yalom, I. D. (1985). *The theory and practice of group psychotherapy* (3rd ed.). New York: Basic Books.

Yllo, K., & Bograd, M. (1988). *Feminist perspectives on wife abuse.* Newbury Park, CA: Sage.

Zillmann, D. (1979). *Hostility and aggression.* Hillsdale, NJ: Erlbaum.

Index

Index

Index

Index